A MOST
PECULIAR BOOK

# A MOST PECULIAR BOOK

*The Inherent Strangeness of the Bible*

Kristin Swenson

OXFORD
UNIVERSITY PRESS

### OXFORD
UNIVERSITY PRESS

Oxford University Press is a department of the University of Oxford. It furthers the University's objective of excellence in research, scholarship, and education by publishing worldwide. Oxford is a registered trade mark of Oxford University Press in the UK and certain other countries.

Published in the United States of America by Oxford University Press
198 Madison Avenue, New York, NY 10016, United States of America.

Library of Congress Cataloging-in-Publication Data
Names: Swenson, Kristin M., author.
Title: A most peculiar book : the inherent strangeness of the Bible /
Kristin Swenson.
Description: New York, NY, United States of America :
Oxford University Press, 2021. | Includes index.
Identifiers: LCCN 2020015469 (print) | LCCN 2020015470 (ebook) |
ISBN 9780190651732 (hardback) | ISBN 9780190651756 (epub)
Subjects: LCSH: Bible—Appreciation. | Bible—Criticism, interpretation, etc.
Classification: LCC BS538 .S94 2021 (print) |
LCC BS538 (ebook) | DDC 220.6—dc23
LC record available at https://lccn.loc.gov/2020015469
LC ebook record available at https://lccn.loc.gov/2020015470

3 5 7 9 8 6 4 2

Printed by LSC Communications, United States of America

*For Leland and Lowell*

# CONTENTS

# ACKNOWLEDGMENTS

This book has been a long time coming. If I'm honest about it, I suppose it began back when, as a churchgoing kid, I started stumbling and fumbling past the Bible's internal contradictions and bewildering passages. At first, I thought it was just me, some failure on my part to see the seamless whole and consistent peace-and-loveliness that I'd assumed must be true of God's Word, the Good Book, Holy Scripture, and all that.

I'm grateful to my parents always, Cec and Dick, and to those senior members of my family and early faith community who demonstrated both respect and even love for the Bible while at the same time honoring the kind of questioning inquiry that inevitably arises when one reads that most peculiar book. I'm lucky to have landed among them. St. Olaf College, where I majored in both biology and religion, elegantly synthesizes rigorous study in the hard sciences with a vibrant, dynamically lived Christianity. I'm grateful for the education and encouragement I received there, not least their emphasis on orienting one's learning to be of service to others, including the nonhuman with whom we share this glorious planet.

The matter of learning—both the ongoing business of gaining information and the self-struggle of making sense of things with compassion and responsibility—always depends on the wisdom of others. I am grateful to those who have graced my life and learning with the fruits of their own work. This includes not only the scholars of centuries past that I've had the privilege to study and learn from but also those family—my sisters and their families, in-laws, cousins, aunts, uncles, grandparents – and friends too many to name, who have generously shared with me their own knowledge and candor about the Bible. Our conversations informed this project.

This book really began to take the shape you see today thanks to OUP editor Theo Calderara, whose interest, expressed years ago, in our doing a book together led to conversations about just what that book might be. Here it is. Well, with inevitable shortcomings and probable failings, all of which are most definitely my own.

Along the way, I've had continued support from Virginia Commonwealth University, where I learned more than I can say from wonderful students and colleagues and earned tenure, only shortly thereafter to leave. Mark Wood of the School of World Studies and others there have graciously extended my affiliation, which has helped my research and writing tremendously. Virginia Humanities supported this project with fellowships that grant faculty association at the University of Virginia and the opportunity to share (read: "try out") some of this book's material with a marvelously curious and intelligent community. I'm grateful to UVA's excellent libraries and community of religious studies faculty and writers, including especially Martien Halvorson-Taylor, for help and counsel in developing this book.

To my "lit salon" of Richmond writers and the "Cville women writers" who have heard fits and bits of this project along its way and encouraged at every step, thank you. Thanks also to my *Writer's Story* podcast cohost, Meredith Cole, whose companionship and good humor have eased the effort a book such as this requires.

My agent, Joanne Wyckoff, has been a wonderful advocate. And I'm grateful to the anonymous readers who commented first on the proposal and again after I'd drafted the book. Their remarks and ideas, corrections too, make this book better. Thanks also to Oxford University Press's amazing book-making team, including Asish Krishna, Brent Matheny, Judith Hoover, Rick Delaney, and Leslie Johnson.

Finally, thanks in full always to my husband, Craig, whose confidence in the value of my work never seems to shake. Thank you, thank you for being partner to me in this whole life-making endeavor of creativity and compromise. You're right. Most of the time.

# INTRODUCTION

## *An Arranged Marriage*

I have a confession to make. But I'm worried that what you, an intelligent and discerning reader, will hear is not exactly what I mean. Then you'll close this book and put it right back on the shelf. Yet what I want to tell you—and the fact that it feels like a confession—is what drives this entire project. So, here it is:

I love the Bible.

That statement gives me the willies. It's something millions of Americans would nod right along with because it sounds so simple to understand. But my love for the Bible is not a tacit acceptance of everything in it as lessons or truths for immediate application. Not hardly. This is not a love for facile public display. It's not of the swept-off-my-feet, love-at-first-sight variety, but rather more like the complicated love that might develop after decades in a marriage. An arranged marriage. I grew up with the Bible in an open-minded, garden-variety Protestant congregation. And I've come to love the Bible for all sorts of reasons, including some of the same reasons that can make it problematic and exasperating, even for reasons that make me disagree with it.

Look closely. Besides texts of lofty wisdom, inspiration, comfort, and guidance, the Bible contains bewildering archaisms, inconsistencies, questionable ethics, and a herky-jerky narrative style. Yet those features barely get a passing glance these days. Some believers simply explain them away, while nonbelievers use them as a reason to dismiss the Bible entirely. This book looks squarely at what's so weird, difficult, and disconcerting both about and in the Bible, and in the process shows how those qualities can actually enrich one's relationship, religious or not, to the text. I am not trying to convert anybody to anything except to learning. I'm committed to providing information, digging into the text and its background, and sharing questions of my own that might resonate with you. Those questions are both what make me love the Bible and what make that love so complicated.

For starters, the Bible is a cacophonous gathering of disparate voices. Not only are there different books within The Book, but they come from a range of places, from the Dead Sea to Rome, Egypt to Antioch, from tiny towns and huge metropolises, rural hillsides and palace halls, prisons and podiums, and from a wider-still range of times—spanning as much as 1,500 years. The Bible covers subjects so vast that it begins with creation itself. The people responsible for putting down those words, the people responsible for passing them along, for collecting and canonizing what we have, and the people who have translated original ancient texts for modern readers come from and reflect a dizzying range of times and places, all of which influence the way we read what we now call the Bible.

And yet, despite all of that, this collection of texts is said to be "the word of God." Think about that. *The* singular, one expression, *of God*. A person could spend a lifetime unpacking only that. Many have.

Which brings us to another of the Bible's compelling qualities: it champions no single, simple portrait of God. That is one of the things I love most about it. Though we may wish to define a "biblical God," the better to predict and manage, the Bible refuses to lay out a systematic theology. Even the popular generalization that the God of the Old Testament is vengeful while the New Testament God is forgiving doesn't hold up to scrutiny.[1] God as presented in the Bible is simply far more complicated than these reductive efforts can sustain.

Within only the first couple of its pages, the Bible portrays God as both a cosmically distant creator of no single gender (Genesis 1) *and* a guy walking around an orchard, chatting with people (Genesis 2). Read further, and you find a God who regrets, delights, mourns, angers, protects, punishes, soothes, and demands. God is an intimate lover and a remote king, likened to a mother bird and a cuckolded husband. The depictions are nearly endless. And that's just the Hebrew Bible. If you include the New Testament in your Bible (i.e., if you're Christian), then you get yet another variation on God as coming to earth as a poor Jewish man in Palestine, and at least four variations on that (thanks to the Gospels). In the Bible, God is responsible for both good and evil but is also categorically opposed to evil. In other words, biblical images of God defy any and every limitation, which (while exasperating) feels right. According to the Bible, God is far too big to be just one thing.

It should come as no surprise, then, even if you have never read the Bible, to find that it is full of holes. From the very beginning, the story leaves us modern readers scratching our heads. For example, where did the supposedly first children—two boys—get their wives? The Bible doesn't say. Those responsible for delivering the Bible that we have apparently didn't always care about the kinds of things that we, who expect a story to proceed with a certain narrative logic, get hung up on.

Just how many times does a patriarch pass his wife off as his sister? How could approximately two and a half million people, with all their animals, collectively leave Egypt to wander in the Sinai Desert for forty years?[2] We are told that they drew water from a rock and that food miraculously appeared, but practically speaking, that's a whole lot of people with dependent animals in a barren space for a very long time. Then there's the man swallowed by a fish and vomited up three days later to resume his God-given activity, which is not even the most unbelievable part of that story. How is it that, for a while, Israel's most respected leader was a woman? And where did she go? The Bible is blasé about life spans of hundreds of years and a talking donkey and why an earthly king would have heard of, much less worried about, some poor Jewish infant. What happened to Jesus between birth and age thirty? And what did the apostles' wives and children do while they were on the road? These are simply not matters that the text is all that concerned about.

The Bible's silences invite readers to set aside their assumptions and engage in further study with intelligence, imagination, and curiosity. This book aims to help in that endeavor.

Which leads to yet another reason for why I love the Bible: as an object of study, it's inexhaustible. Sure, it's really big and the stories and poems and laws and all provide rich ground for interpretation, sermonizing, and such. But learning *about* the Bible is equally inexhaustible—and vitally important. From understanding the historical, social, economic, and theological contexts out of which these texts emerged to examining how the literary shape of the texts informs their meanings today, the Bible is the ultimate subject for interdisciplinary scholarship. Those who study the Bible for a living draw on the sciences (social and hard), literary arts, philosophy, history, philology, theology, and more.

Finally, the Bible invites—nay, *demands*—interaction, even argument. And I don't simply mean argument about what the Bible says or means (though that's inevitable) but argument with the text itself. For the qualities I have cited—its disparate voices and images of God, its fissures and cracks and the endless ways and things to learn about it—the Bible defies the simplistic treatment of so-called literalism. (I say "so-called" because what exactly does it mean to "read the Bible literally," especially if what one is reading is itself a translation from the Hebrew, Aramaic, and Greek?) The Bible's diversity of perspectives and tone, not to say those texts in blatant disagreement with each other, actually models conversation, dialogue, and debate. It could issue no bolder invitation to engagement, no more compelling demand to bring the best of one's faculties to bear on any interpretation of it.

Take the book in your hands as an opportunity to step outside assumptions about dogma, traditional interpretations, and received opinion. Read it as if in conversation, and argue just as much as you like, as much as you can stand. Much of what we think about the Bible is actually received ideas and assumptions, passed along through other sources, themselves interpretations: holiday traditions, music and art, pop culture, children's stories. You'll be surprised how many things "the Bible says" don't actually appear anywhere in the Bible. I want to return us to the text itself, in all its oddness—to show how strange is some of what's familiar and to make the engagement inviting again.

Some of what you find here may be old hat; some of it might be new but easily digested; and some of it might make you a little (or more than a little) uncomfortable. I hope you'll wrestle with that discomfort and in the process discover a richer way to think about the Good Book, maybe even about thinking itself. I hope that you'll feel empowered to engage biblical texts with nuance and deepened appreciation, and also with the confidence to be not merely a blank slate on which it writes the old stuff but an agent in the conversation, to "gird up your loins" and be a partner with the text in the business of its meaning-making.

A brief aside: There are many more head-scratching oddities, absurdities, and exasperating lacunae in the Bible than could possibly fit in this modest book. What I've tried to do is show and discuss some of the most popular or glaring and in the process offer ways for readers to deal with others. For good or ill, wittingly or not, what I offer here is inevitably informed by my circumstances: my scholarship has focused on the Hebrew Bible or Old Testament—a collection I've discovered to be far richer in the kinds of things we're hungry for (love, forgiveness, compassion, and beauty, for example) than many readers assume. And my personal religious history is Protestant Christian. Consequently, readers may want more New

Testament discussion than they'll find here (and more attention to texts of the Apocrypha, canonical to Christians of other stripes). Add that the Hebrew Bible is a lot longer than the New Testament, and you'll find that I've included more references from that collection than from the New Testament. I fear that may feed, ironically, into a presumption that this book actually seeks to dispel: the simplistic (and anti-Semitic) notion that contrasts a "bad" Old Testament (Judaism) with a "good" New Testament (Christianity). At any rate, my choices of biblical texts for inclusion, much less my discussions of them, will not satisfy everyone. I hope that readers' interest in the subject will lead them to further learning. A final caveat: because I've tried to include especially familiar figures and stories, readers will find references to some of them in more than one chapter, reflecting different issues and concerns.

If you're someone who's comfortable simply saying that you love the Bible, then this book is for you. If you're someone who could never in a million years imagine saying that you love the Bible, then this book is for you too. If you're somewhere in the middle, well, there's a lot of good reading out there. I'm happy to issue recommendations. Kidding! I hope you'll all stay with me on this strange journey.

In that spirit, here we go.

# PART I

## A Book Like No Other

# Chapter 1

# A Problematic Book

The title of this chapter may already have you questioning my judgment. "Problematic"? The Bible? That lovely leather-bound tome your grandparents gave you, your name embossed in gold on the cover?

Problematic indeed. In this case, I don't mean "problematic" in the way the term is sometimes used today, to mean racist or sexist or homophobic—though there is plenty of that too. I mean "problematic" in a more fundamental way, a way that makes reading the Bible vastly more complicated than it might seem. Just off the top of my head, I can think of seven (a good biblical number) ways that the Bible is deeply problematic, even before considering its contents.

But these "problems" are really opportunities. Recognizing and naming them enables us more deeply to understand and appreciate the Bible's richness. Take the Bible's moniker, for starters. That alone is deliciously problematic in at least a couple of ways.

## 1.1 The Bible is not a single book

We use "the Bible" as a title, as though its author (or publisher) gave it that label—a name to identify the volume, just like any other volume on our bookshelves. And since those other books on our shelves generally have authors, we might add, "by God," for good measure, but more on that problem later.

Yet the Bible has little in common with, say, a biography of Theodore Roosevelt or the Harry Potter series. After all, the term "the Bible" comes from the Greek *ta biblia*, which means "the books." Note the plural. The Good Book is actually a collection of many books. (How many? It depends.) A cursory glance at its contents will confirm this. The major sections don't all look alike. You'll find narrative here, poetry there, lists over yonder. And once you delve into its contents, you swiftly discover wildly different tones and perspectives. Downright contradictions. Is the Bible an anthology? Kind of, if by anthology we allow for multiple editors and communities of curators working over a span of centuries.

One cannot expect, then, to read through the Bible, cover to cover, and encounter the kind of neat dramatic structure that, since before Aristotle, has defined a single story. Yes, people talk about the Bible as "the greatest story ever told," but that's taking some serious liberties with the text as a whole. While its editors have arranged its contents to very roughly suggest a particular historical and theological trajectory, it simply doesn't have a clear narrative course in which every literary element drives with a single purpose and direction toward a conclusion. There is no neat progression all the way through, from beginning to end.

This plurality brings me to another way the term "the Bible" can be misleading. Namely, the "the" part.

## 1.2 There isn't only one Bible

This fact makes it difficult to talk about the "whole" Bible or about the Bible "as a whole." There isn't only one version of the collection. And I don't mean different translations. I mean that what constitutes "the Bible" isn't exactly the same for everyone.

In general, Jews have one Bible, Protestant Christians have another, and Orthodox Christians and Roman Catholics have yet another—the biggest of them all. These Bibles are related, and there is a great deal of overlap. But they are not the same. The process of deciding which texts got into which Bible and which didn't is called "canonization."

Against tremendous odds, ancient Jews collected over the course of centuries the books that form the Hebrew Bible.[1] The acronym "Tanakh," another name for the Bible, reflects its collective nature. It refers to the Hebrew Bible's three parts: Torah (the first five books), Nevi'im (meaning "prophets," which refers not only to books with prophets' names as their titles but also to the historical books of Joshua, Judges, Samuel, and Kings), and Kethuvim (meaning "writings," which includes everything else).

The collection that composes the Jewish Hebrew Bible developed over centuries in roughly that chronological order: Torah, Prophets, and Writings. Although some books in the Writings section are as late as the second century BCE (Before the Common Era, or what used to be known as Before Christ), their setting qualifies as coming from before the ancient rabbis had determined that the divine inspiration of prophecy had ceased (in the fourth century BCE). Despite this criterion, the Hebrew Bible, or Tanakh, wasn't finalized until after the Christian New Testament was well on its way.

Those Hebrew Bible books not only form the entirety of the Bible as Jews conceive it but also represent the bulk of both varieties of Christian Bibles. But Christian Bibles put the books in a different order than they appear in the Jews' Tanakh in order to prioritize how Christians thought about those books in light of Jesus.[2] Some people call the Hebrew Bible the Old Testament. The New Testament, which is the second major part of Christian Bibles, has to do with Jesus. And Jesus was Jewish. This is not incidental or a matter of political correctness. It goes to the heart of the matter.

The evolution of Christianity had everything to do with Jesus's Judaism. It had everything to do with the Hebrew Bible. Jesus taught from "the law and the prophets" (the Hebrew Bible of his time). And over the centuries that the New Testament took shape

Jesus's followers would interpret him in light of the existing Hebrew Bible/Old Testament (predominantly in translation, Greek or Aramaic). There would be no Christianity without the Hebrew Bible/Old Testament.

Interpretation and reinterpretation are at the heart of the Bible and the act of reading it. This was true then, and it is still today. The community that formed around Jesus continued a long tradition of rethinking and reinterpreting their sacred texts, in this case in light of what they understood and concluded about Jesus.

Now, about those Christian Bibles. The Roman Catholic and Orthodox Bible is the biggest of all. Consider: for a long time (since about the fourth century CE) it was *the* Christian Bible. The pared-down version found in Protestant churches came into being only with the Reformation. Among the whole complex array of issues that drove Martin Luther and others to defy the leaders of the Catholic Church, none was more important than the doctrine of *sola scriptura*: scripture alone. The phrase may not sound like a rallying cry, but it does announce a major preoccupation of the time. The reformers' goal was to, well, *reform* the church, which, in the estimation of many, had gotten a bit too full of itself. Luther came along and insisted on going back to the Bible.

That meant returning to a "pure" Old Testament: the Hebrew Hebrew Bible, not the Greek Hebrew Bible.[3] You see, before the Jews had finalized their particular collection of books of the Bible, the Hebrew in which most of its texts were written had to be translated into Greek, since many Jews, including the Jews of Jesus's time and place, no longer spoke Hebrew. A collection of Greek manuscripts, bigger than what would become the Hebrew Bible, began to circulate. This collection of authoritative books is called the Septuagint, or LXX.[4] The name reflects the legend that seventy scholarly translators independently arrived at seventy exactly identical, word-for-word translations, hence "Septuagint" (from the Latin for "seventy"). That collection endured within what would become the Christian Orthodox and Roman Catholic traditions. Protestant

Bibles sometimes package together those texts, "extra" to their Bibles in a group called the Apocrypha. Sometimes identified as Deuterocanonical (a "secondary canon"), Protestants consider them to be important and useful but not bearing the same authority as the other, primary books.

Talk of canonization—the process of establishing an endorsed collection—necessarily brings up another, related problem with the Bible.

## 1.3 The texts themselves were composed over a long period of time

The actual composition of the texts that constitute these Bibles is even messier than the process of canonization just outlined. In brief, many of the texts that would become part of the Bible didn't even start out as texts but rather as songs or stories orally communicated, or even as rituals. Over the span of centuries, even millennia— as long ago as 1800 BCE—these ancient records were constantly changing. The community that preserved the texts edited and also added to them until finally, beginning in the last centuries before the Common Era and stretching into the first few centuries CE, some texts assumed greater authority and importance than others, and our Bibles were born. Still, the earliest Bibles were a mass of individual scrolls. Binding them as pages into a book (called a "codex") marks yet another stage of development. (And don't get me started on chapter-verse divisions; they didn't appear as such until the sixteenth century.)

We obviously don't know everything about the time before the Bible took its present shape. Indeed, the process was likely quite messy as only organic and enduring things can be. But we do know that the texts themselves evolved over a long period of time. We can identify some of the momentous events that affected their development.

Two historical crises had especially profound effects: the two times the temple in Jerusalem was destroyed, first by the Babylonians in the sixth century BCE and then by the Romans in 70 CE. That these would affect the composition and collection of texts makes a lot of sense. A religion dependent on a geographical location or physical object is vulnerable to political vicissitudes. Take those things away—temple and throne, say—and the religion will fail. A religion based on stories, even if those are recorded in a physical book, is much harder to destroy. Books travel; temples cannot. Stories cannot be razed or defeated in military battle. So it was that Jews became a people of the Book. Christianity naturally followed its mother tradition.

Given this centuries-long process, it's easy to see how those books that came to be considered biblical, the ones that passed into canonization, were those that the community at large referred to, revered, or otherwise kept alive because they were of significant value to them vis-à-vis their present experiences and beliefs. In the early days, that even included reworking the texts themselves in light of the effects of history and changes in belief. If this sounds democratic, it is (to a point). Canonization was probably less the product of a one-time sit-down with the religion's powerbrokers than it was a gradual sorting by ordinary, *if pious and learned*, folks. Other texts fell by the wayside—some important, valuable even, but for whatever reason not quite up to sacred snuff.

Early, significant initiatives for editing included great national defeats—for example, the Assyrian conquest of the northern kingdom of Israel at the end of the eighth century BCE and the Babylonian exile (first half of the sixth century BCE), when most scholars think that what are now the Bible's first five books began to take their current shape. Both blows launched major rewritings of some of the existing biblical history books. The reason: reality-shattering crises.

When Nebuchadnezzar's Babylonians conquered Judah in 587 BCE, it called into question two foundational points of theology: that

God had chosen the temple in Jerusalem as the site where God in all God's holiness would be especially present to God's people (as God's "house," if you will) and that God would make sure that someone from David's genetic line would always rule as monarch over God's chosen people.[5]

Apparently the Babylonians missed that memo and brought devastation on the temple and the nation, destroying the former and dismantling the latter. No more temple, no more king. Adding insult to injury, they removed the elite—Judah's best educated, the scribes, artisanal craftsmen, and leaders of every stripe—and took them to Babylon, the better to enrich Babylonian culture while also diminishing the chances that the kingdom of Judah would rise again.

You can imagine the effect—the destruction, of course, but also the questions that decent and conscientious Judahites had: How could God have let this happen? Where was God when this was happening? Was God kidnapped or God's holiness compromised when the Babylonians stormed the temple? For that matter, didn't the defeat of Judah as a nation prove that the Babylonian god(s) were more powerful than Yahweh? Other questions also inevitably arose, such as Did God lie about David's line always being on the throne?

Following the ancient worldview that when peoples or nations went to war, so did their particular gods, the logical conclusion was that when a people were defeated, so was their god. Some people simply accepted that the Babylonians and their god were more powerful. They assimilated to this new and admittedly not altogether awful circumstance of living in wealthy, cosmopolitan Babylon. But a critical mass of highly educated exiled Judahites did not accept this worldview and would not give up on their god. Rather, they focused on collecting and preserving the stories and traditions that made them distinct as people of Yahweh. In the process, they revisited and revised what they'd received to make sense out of what had happened.

Two important developments ensued. One was that the people didn't prioritize temple building as much as they had earlier and instead turned to stories and texts and whatever traditions could travel. Another was that they changed and added to the texts and traditions they'd inherited in order to make sense of what had happened.

Many scholars believe that the first chapter of Genesis, describing the creation of the world in seven days, was written in this period—that it was important to say that the God of the exiles was not only the god of Judahites but was the creator of the entire universe, and that God made the universe to be sensible and orderly, even "good." It is also from this period that we get a famous story from the prophet Ezekiel, who had been taken into exile in Babylon. Though he is far from Jerusalem, Ezekiel tells of seeing a flying chariot on which was something that looked like a supernatural man and what could be the throne of God. Being a priest, he's careful to qualify, not saying outright that he saw God but rather that it appeared to be the likeness of the glory of Yahweh.[6] Caveats notwithstanding, this is a powerful theological statement if ever there was one. Yahweh was not kidnapped or otherwise destroyed in his temple, Ezekiel is saying, nor had God abandoned Judahites to their captors. God had elected to leave the Jerusalem temple before its destruction and would be present to God's people wherever they were—even behind enemy lines.

Another effect that the exile had on received traditions was that the stories had to be edited to meet present circumstances. Unless one adopted the reasoning that God had lied or was otherwise unreliable—impotent or careless or nonsensically capricious—then God must have actually intended for the destruction of the temple to happen. God must have let the Babylonians defeat Judah, the reasoning went, at least for anyone unwilling to throw God under the bus.

Unfortunately, if it wasn't God's fault or failing, it fell on the Judahites to accept the blame themselves: they must have done something that was so incredibly horrible that it would justify such terrible punishment by God at the hands of the Babylonians. That's the line of thinking we've inherited in a good bit of the Good Book. And it has contributed to the anti-Semitism that Jews have faced for millennia since. Their own efforts to exonerate God have led, in part, to centuries of abuse because "it says in the Bible" that they failed God over and over again. Such passages (and there are many, whole books even) are driven by a desire to get God off the hook in the face of a calamity and destruction that defied pretty much every other explanation. In short, Judahites chose to blame themselves rather than abandon their faith in God.

The Jews didn't get a nation again for centuries, though they did gain considerable independence about fifty years after Nebuchadnezzar and his hordes had devastated Judah. That independence enabled the canonization process to continue. After Cyrus II, aka "Cyrus the Great," emerged from what would be called Persia and conquered Babylonia in 539 BCE, he gave the peoples who had been taken into exile permission (and resources) to return to their native lands and to reestablish their own systems of worship. For our purposes, you could say he commissioned the repopulation of Judah and the rebuilding of the temple (though both were slow to happen).

Again we can see how the Bible's development over time is reflected in the texts. Cyrus is called "messiah" in the Bible, and he actually gets the final word in (the Jewish ordering of) the Hebrew Bible.[7] Yup, a gentile king's is the last voice we hear, there at the end of Chronicles. And what he says is Return. Rebuild. Some have considered it a mandate ever since.

The second temple's destruction by the Romans in 70 CE had an equally catalyzing effect on the Bible's development. In this case, it not only spurred ancient rabbis to finalize the Hebrew Bible, but it also informed the theology and writings of a fringe Jewish group: the followers of an itinerant preacher named Jesus.

It took a long time to rebuild the temple in Jerusalem. It took even longer for Jews to regain an independent state with their own monarch. To a few Jews, Jesus represented the longed-for hope of a king from David's line—a *mashiach*, or "messiah." After all, the nature of that hope had changed over the centuries since the Babylonians destroyed Judah and its throne. The term "messiah" was no longer associated only with those anointed as priests and kings but came to be identified with the idea of a cosmic savior. Paul did much to further the terms of such an idea, while the Gospels, which told varying stories of Jesus's life, death, and resurrection, also reckoned with the kind of apocalyptic expectations that came with persecution and the (second) temple's destruction.

The rich and long historical development of biblical texts reminds us of another problematic aspect of the Bible.

## 1.4 The Bible has a lot of different authors and editors, most of whom are anonymous

Over the millennia of the Bible's existence, close readers noticed duplications and contradictions in the text but were reluctant to call attention to them. Only within the past 150 years or so (which is extremely recent when it comes to a text like the Bible) have people owned up to the multivocal nature of the Bible and appreciated that on its own terms.

For example, almost everyone is familiar with the creation story in Genesis 1, the one that begins (in many translations) "In the beginning." But that is not the only creation story in Genesis. In fact, the very next chapter begins a whole separate, and rather different, account of creation. Situated as they are, the text invites us to read them together. But it's important to recognize Genesis 1 as one kind of creation story, with its own image of God, elegant literary style, and concerns about the world, and Genesis 2–3 as another creation story, with its own quite different image of God, gritty style, and concerns about the world. That they appear next to each other in one, larger whole is surely no accident and invites yet another level of reading. But we do the texts a disservice to read them only as a seamless whole composed by a single author's pen.

In many but not all cases, it doesn't even make sense to talk about a single author. Rather, most of the ancient stories, poems, and even laws are likely the products of something more like a group effort, passed down and altered over time, than of a given individual recording his or her thoughts and experiences. In that case, the editors should be considered at least as creatively involved in the texts as any author.

Appreciating diverse authorship frees us to see how the Bible can contain narratives arguing that suffering is a punishment for wickedness and narratives such as the book of Job, which is an extended meditation on the suffering of a decidedly innocent person. It makes sense that we'd have stories about the adult Jesus going to Jerusalem only for the Passover of his assassination (Matthew, Mark, and Luke) and also of his going back and forth from Jerusalem several times over the period of his ministry before that fateful journey (John). Recognizing that these texts were written by diverse authors working in different times allows us to see that texts forbidding and commanding divorce each have their place. (More on that later.)

But this matter of having different authors, of editors revising over the centuries, and of us knowing almost nothing about any of these individual persons is strange to our modern sensibilities. We get hung up on our particular expectations about authorship in ways that complicate how we read and understand the text at hand.

For example, we could be excused for thinking that the book of Isaiah was written by or at least is the record of things that a particular prophet by that name said and did. Yet while we can be quite confident that there really was a historical prophet by the name of Isaiah who lived in Jerusalem in the decades around 700 BCE, we can also be confident that a lot of what's in that book didn't come from him. Take the text's explicit reference to Cyrus the Great, despite the fact that Cyrus lived about 150 years later than Isaiah.

We don't know exactly who wrote the four Gospels. Their names are the product of tradition, not based on the signatures of men named Matthew, Mark, Luke, and John. But we do know that the Gospels weren't composed in a vacuum. Scholars agree that Mark is the earliest (ca. 70 CE) and that both Matthew and Luke had Mark's gospel on hand when composing their own. (A cursory glance at these three reveals parallels that none shares with the fourth gospel, John's. Hence they're referred to as synoptic, "seeing-with.") John's gospel betrays discord between Jewish sects as it attacks the inherited privilege of the temple's religious authorities (simply "the Jews" in that gospel, with unfortunate, anti-Semitic effect) and is very different from the others in style, tone, and narrative.

Then there's the matter of Paul. Paul's letters are the earliest texts in the New Testament, although the Gospels appear first in the books' canonical order. Paul had a huge influence on the development of Christianity, and one way that manifests is in the proliferation of books attributed to him. Scholars have taken to arranging "Paul's" books into three categories: those for which Paul is definitely the author (e.g., 1 Corinthians and Romans); those that are definitely not Paul's (e.g., Hebrews); and the "disputed" letters (e.g., Ephesians), for which scholarship is inconclusive on whether or not they come from Paul.

Or consider the book of Daniel. It has a guy's name for its title, but while Daniel is indeed the speaker in the book's second half, in the first chapters he's a character in stories someone else tells. The tones, the styles, even the languages in which it's written (differ within this single book. Some is in Aramaic, some in Hebrew. The Septuagint's version of the book contains additional material, and while the stories suggest that a man named Daniel became an important figure in the Babylonian court, the only extrabiblical reference we have to a historical person named Daniel is to a Ugaritic king who lived a thousand years earlier.

What's more, although we read a lot in Daniel about the Babylonian king Nebuchadnezzar, biblical scholars have determined, based on a lot of different kinds of evidence, that the book of Daniel was not written during the time of Nebuchadnezzar but much, much later. Because what the author of Daniel wanted to say about the tyrannical foreign ruler of his time, Antiochus IV, would have cost him his head, better to blame it on Nebuchadnezzar, who had been dead for centuries, and call it historical fiction, should the Greek authorities come looking for him.

In other words, while the history *in* Daniel is of the Babylonian exile, the history *behind* Daniel, or much of it, was a period of Greek oppression some centuries later. As for the history *of* the Bible, Daniel just squeaked by, admitted under the wire. Composed and/or finalized some two hundred years before the birth of Jesus, Daniel (whoever wrote it) may be the latest book admitted into the Jewish canon.

You can see, then, that unlike with modern books, when dealing with the Bible there are a few histories to take into consideration. It's helpful to think of three kinds: the history *in* the Bible, the history *of* the Bible, and the history *behind* the Bible.

We have been dealing, so far, mainly with the history of the Bible—the development of this collection of writings over time. The history in the Bible (the history the Bible tells) rarely conforms to the standards we expect of a history today. The Bible tells its history from the perspective of faith, which allows for supernatural actors such as God, for one thing. It also prioritizes including some things rather than others, and it interprets events through the lens of faith. In other words, to expect these texts to give us an objective, disinterested reporting of facts exactly as they happened is again to do the texts a disservice.

Which brings us to the history *behind* the Bible. Of that, we can say one thing for sure.

## 1.5 Even the latest of the Bible's texts comes from a very long time ago

In other words, the worlds out of which the texts come—practical, cultural, religious, and so on—are very different from our own, which makes the Bible problematic yet again. We simply cannot presume to lift from it perspectives, ideas, and assumptions that immediately align with modern ones. By "the history *behind* the Bible" I mean the cultural and social contexts out of which the stories, laws, poems, genealogies, and so forth come. (As the example of Daniel illustrates, that may not be the same point in time and space that a passage with history in it tells.)

The history *behind* the Bible is where we get to play Indiana Jones. This is the realm of archaeologists, anthropologists, and, less sexy but no less important, linguists. It is the quest for clues that might reveal the historical context of any given bit of text.

Such research into the history behind the Bible has yielded valuable and sometimes provocative insights. For example, we know that, despite what the biblical story says, Jericho was already a heap of ruins by the time Joshua and company might have come along. And we know that there was a scribe named Baruch with his own personal signature who might have written stuff down for the prophet Jeremiah. There's no reason to doubt that Jesus grew up in Galilee, just as the Bible says, and there's no reason to doubt that during the particularly chaotic Passover season he died in Jerusalem on a cross like many other Roman criminals. The site of Jesus's birth, on the other hand, remains a mystery: was he really born in Bethlehem, or is the story only told that way to conform to a prophecy in Micah? To date, there is no conclusive evidence one way or the other (the other candidate being Nazareth). As for a resurrection, that, even Christians note, is a function of faith.

There is the story of the slew of demons named Legion, whom Jesus cast out of a man and into the bodies of pigs, who ran off to drown themselves in the sea. Yet the place where this allegedly happened, called Gerasa, was about forty miles from the nearest body of water. Either those are some extremely athletic pigs, or the story is doing something else. For one thing, "Gerasa" sounds suspiciously similar to a Hebrew verb (based on the consonants *g-r-sh*) meaning "to drive out," or "to cast out" (er, exorcise?). Research suggests that Mark may have written less a concrete report than a bit of a revenge fantasy, picked up by Matthew and Luke.[8] Legion may have referred instead to the Roman 10th Legion, which participated in the siege of the Galilean city of Gamla/Gamala in 67 CE. Among their insignia is the boar.[9]

The history *behind* the Bible is not merely cool information and cocktail party trivia; it is crucial to understanding the text. For example, think for a moment about where the Bible was formed—or to start, where it wasn't. Not a peaceful, temperate, and fertile island, and not a sparsely populated, barely survivable tundra. It grew up at a lively crossroads of the ancient world's great superpowers—broadly Egypt and the modern Middle East—populated by diverse peoples struggling either to hang on to power and wealth or simply to make ends meet in a climate whose kindnesses were rather capriciously meted out. Is it any wonder there's so much battling involved, with God and the gods being no exception? The peoples at the center of biblical narratives are people confronted over and over by others; that is, there's a lot of concern about how to deal with people different from their own, for good and for ill. One thing all these societies shared throughout the centuries of the Bible's development is a patriarchal social structure. That explains a lot. Managing women's independence (and sexuality) is a central biblical concern.

Appreciating that the world out of which the Bible came is very different from ours requires that we do some thinking of our own when considering the application of texts for use today. For example, consider the mandate God gives to *adam* in Genesis 1 to "be fruitful and multiply" and to "have dominion" over the earth and everything in it. Remember that whatever else we might *not* know about its ancient context, we *do* know that the earth was far less populated then than it is now. We know that the people who lived then didn't have combustion engines or electricity. What's more, the image of God in that text—an image in which *adam* is simultaneously both male and female—was a creating God who facilitated a "good" world. The human being, then, made in the image of God, is expected to be and do the same. In other words, s/he is to exercise such "dominion" as to preserve the prolific, fruitful, "good" world that God ushered into being.

Appreciating the difference in our historical context, to be fruitful and to have dominion in our context today could be interpreted as a mandate to exercise restraint in human reproduction and to exercise care and conservation of the nonhuman natural world, the seeming opposite of a literal application.

You may have picked up on my using the italicized *adam* to reflect that it's a foreign word (Hebrew) rather than our familiar English name Adam. That points to another, crucially problematic aspect of the Bible.

## 1.6 The Bible was written in languages that are utterly unfamiliar to most readers today

Some time ago, I happened to sit next to a gregarious man on a cross-country flight to the West Coast. When he asked where I was headed, I explained that I was on my way to a conference, an academic gathering of Bible scholars. He perked right up, launching into what he believed King James really meant when he wrote Genesis.

The experience served to remind me that as much as whiling away many a long hour in many a dusty library corner poring over ancient scholarship on even more ancient texts could seem a colossal waste of time, that text remains influential today in ways that are sometimes inverse to people's understanding of it. Such study is vitally important. It's too easy to imagine that the Bible was composed in whatever language a person is reading it in, not least because of how frequently people appeal to what "the Bible says" by citing what they've read in their language. We get into all sorts of trouble on account of this.

The Bible was actually composed in varieties of ancient Hebrew, a smattering of Aramaic, and the colloquial Greek of its time (if your Bible includes the New Testament). With the exception of Aramaic, these are languages that linguists rather unfeelingly call "dead." They do have living relations, which can help, but in the manner of living things, they've evolved. What's more, the Hebrew spoken and written in Israel today is actually the product of an intentional effort to resurrect the Hebrew of the Bible for modern purposes.[10]

As anyone who has learned even a wee bit of another language can tell you, there is seldom a one-to-one correspondence between languages that allows a perfect translation from one into another. Any and every translation requires interpretation.

The English poet and critic John Dryden identified three kinds of translation: "metaphrase," what we call word-for-word; "para- phrase," which works more on the level of sense, sentence by sen- tence; and "imitation," which strives to match the "feel" of the original.[11] When it comes to the Bible, an argument could be made (and has been) that one should keep it weird. The text should be a little alien, reminding us that what we're reading wasn't written in modern English and isn't actually modern at all.

To find the best translation, to work woodenly, word-for-word, may be a necessary start, though to call this translating is stretching the word a bit. It's more like laying out the tools, assembling the ingredients; it requires that you include all possibilities for consider- ation on any given word. Translators use what are called "trots," es- sentially annotated texts. In a trot, above a line of the original runs information such as a word's part of speech and range of definitions. For example, corresponding to the Hebrew *ruach*, one might read "noun, fem. sing.; spirit, breath, wind." Once you've assembled all this info, you can start making decisions, start interpreting. It gets complicated fast.

I failed my first doctoral comprehensive exam in biblical Hebrew because, my advisor said, although it was clear that I could read and translate from ancient Hebrew (I should have suspected I was in for a long haul when he said that—silly me, assuming that that's what the exam was supposed to show), I needed to make it sound "more like modern English." Also, in my heart-pounding anxiety, I had misread which verse numbers of text the exam required me to translate. I had overshot and done too much. Decades later, this still smarts. The point, though, which I've also never forgotten, is that translation is much more than approximating word, phrase, or sentence equivalents. For most purposes, it must make the same natural kind of sense in the target language as it does in the original.

What exactly the target language should sound like is the translator's judgment call. Who's going to be reading it matters. Sure, accuracy is key. But what exactly does that mean? This is where Dryden's categories can help. A translator makes choices to prioritize one approach over another. Is it most important to get as close as possible to literal word-for-word meaning? Is it more important to communicate the general, larger idea of the thing? Or should one go for tone and feeling over literal accuracy? Different genres of literature may lead a single translator to prioritize differently. Poetry may call for seeking a tone in the target language that the translator believes is most important in the source text, while a legal text might call for a more so-called literal approach.

Don't get me wrong: not everything goes, and it's important for a translator to be transparent about his or her choices, given the opportunity. The discussion of a translation—why this and not that— can be wonderfully revealing. After all, most any given text is far richer in possible meaning than any single translation can deliver. Take, for example, the following, a passage from the Hebrew book of Micah, chapter 6. It's a favorite among the faithful for its seemingly tidy condensation of religious obligation. To compare only two, the

New Revised Standard Version (NRSV), the translation I frequently use in this book, renders the passage this way:

> He has told you, oh mortal, what is good;
> and what does the Lᴏʀᴅ require of you
> but to do justice, and to love kindness,
> and to walk humbly with your God?

The Jewish Publication Society's (JPS) Tanakh translation reads:

> He has told you O man, what is good,
> and what the Lᴏʀᴅ requires of you:
> Only to do justice
> And to love goodness,
> And to walk modestly with your God.

A few things to note: though this is poetry, there are no line breaks in the original Hebrew. The JPS Tanakh breaks the text into five lines versus the NRSV's four. It also notes an alternative reading for the NRSV's "to walk humbly with your God" as "It is prudent to serve your God." Syntactically, it has another line, a phrase that appears in verse 9 and yields an odd construction, different in different ancient versions: the JPS translates "then will your name achieve wisdom" and adds a note saying that some versions of the Hebrew text are different and could be translated to read "And it is worthwhile to revere his Name." In the NRSV, this phrase is not the first but the second line of verse 9 and is translated as "(It is sound wisdom to fear your name)," parentheses included.

But back to the beginning. Behind "mortal" and "man" is *adam*, that common, not necessarily gender-specific noun meaning "human being," "humankind," or "man." Oh, and there's no punctuation in the "original" Hebrew. Sometimes Hebrew indicates a question with a particular prefix, but only sometimes. Most often a translator has to figure out whether to make a question or a statement.

Hebrew also has a few ways of saying "only." In this case, it's a function of deciding how to work with a very common and versatile conjunction, hence the variation between these translations: "but" versus "only." What a relief that the Hebrew behind "justice" in both cases really is as close to our English "justice" as a word might be. On the other hand, the word translated "kindness" and "goodness" is one rich with possibility. This is the word, *chesed*, that has yielded that wonderfully old-fashioned and biblically specific "lovingkindness." The New International Version (NIV) translates it as "mercy," which has yet other layers of (partially judicial) meaning.

And then there's love. Both translations use "love," which would seem straightforward, except that "love" in the ancient Near East did not necessarily connote the warm, emotive experience we moderns romantically embrace. For one thing, it appears frequently as the object of a command in treaties between unequal parties. The inferior was to "love" the superior. Failing to do that (expressed by concrete behavior having nothing to do with one's feelings) had dire consequences.

In the Bible, "love" can be (and is) commanded, with the same tenor of a charge to fulfill an obligation as, say, showing up on time for work. "You shall love the LORD your God," Deuteronomy famously commands, at least in English. I recently attended the talk of a colleague, Martien Halvorson-Taylor, who is engaged in research on the biblical Song of Songs in which the word for "love" appears many, many more times than in any other book of the Hebrew Bible. She showed that outside of that book, the word is indeed used in this commanding way, off-putting to those of us who think of love as an emotional thing, not something a person can demand of another.[12]

In the biblical world, a person could get into a mess of trouble carrying such notions around. Love, in many cases, is the severe duty an inferior owes his or her superior. The term is used in ancient treaties between two kings or nations, with the lesser (vassal) required to "love" the greater (suzerain). Being a treaty, fulfilling the obligation to love brought some benefit to each party—usually protection for the lesser by the more powerful party, if only the promise by the greater not to smash the lesser.

In the next line, both translations use the word "walk," which is perfectly fine for the Hebrew, but it doesn't cover the range of sense that in this context is so worth exploring. The super common *halak* can mean "to go," "to come," "to move about," and by extension more figuratively the manner in which one lives. And what of our English "humbly" and "modestly"? The Hebrew *tsana* is rare, with a couple of other occurrences suggesting "lowly," so this is a best guess.

Finally, isn't it intriguing to read "your God"? Unlike English, Hebrew doesn't distinguish between capital and lowercase and letters. And it does distinguish in the second person forms between singular and plural (masculine and feminine too). There's a "you" referring to one person and a "you" referring to more than one. (Actually, the English of the American South does arguably distinguish. Hence "y'all.") Here, the "you" is quite decidedly singular. That "god" should be qualified at all raises the question: Does this suppose other gods to whom other peoples should be beholden, or at least with whom they should "walk"? And it suggests that it might actually be wrong for one person to go about with another person's god.

That the text refers to its god specifically, as (what appears in English as) the LORD (all caps), argues for distinguishing between gods. But you wouldn't appreciate that without knowing that behind the English convention LORD is the Hebrew Tetragrammaton, the four-letter name for God that tradition forbids speaking aloud. Its appearance in the Hebrew Bible, spelled out in that scene in which Moses asks the voice from the burning bush who he should say sent him on his liberating errand, suggests that it's the particular moniker by which this particular god would be known to God's people. In other words, it's personal.

The vagaries of translation, especially when it comes to the Bible, together with the other issues I've noted, lead to yet another reason the Bible is problematic.

## 1.7 Most of its readers today "believe in" it

Given all of the above, the fact that millions of readers express their fidelity to the Bible by using this phrase—that they "believe in" it—demands a whole heap of nuance. What does it mean to "believe," and what exactly is the "it"?

I don't mean to be dismissive or snarky in saying that one of the ways the Bible is problematic is that most of its readers "believe in" it. I certainly don't mean to suggest that I think believing in the Bible is wrongheaded, just that such a statement is insufficient to explain the complex ways that a person might accept the Bible as authoritative. To say that one believes in the Bible can itself be misleading.

I am arguably one such reader, one who can claim to "believe in" the Bible. But by that I don't mean that I accept whatever it says as literally true—historically, theologically, or culturally. Nor do I think that one should apply everything one reads in it. I mean that I accept it as an authoritative text within my religious tradition and as in some way holy and sacred. So I treat it in the same ways I treat any authority: with suspicion and no small amount of questioning and argument. And I treat it as something holy and sacred—to be respected for its very existence, as a source or at least a reflection of mystery. In other words, I aim to engage the text with both heart and head, appreciating the dynamic nature of such a relationship.

If I'm veering into the dangerously esoteric here, suffice it to say, one of the ways that the Bible is problematic is that *in the face of all its oddities*, many readers seem to think that in order to live up to their religious responsibility as Jews or Christians, they must set aside other learning (in the sciences, say, or history or geography), universal human ethics (such as the inherent equality of persons, the rightness of exercising kindness and goodwill), and simple common sense (that a text composed millennia ago wouldn't originally refer to a modern individual, that one person's idolatry may be another's orthodoxy, and that actual human beings were involved in composing the Word of God). It is deeply problematic to assume that to be a good religious person one must take the Bible not only to mean exactly what one reads it to say (in the translation one happens to be using) but also that it is prescriptive as such, without any space for interpretation, much less protest.

"Belief" in that case is not an engagement with the text at all but a simplistic application of it to how one feels, thinks, and acts.

To really, genuinely "believe in" the Bible surely begins with saying yes to its invitation for a relationship. Taking it seriously means considering what the Bible is, how it comes to us, and what it contains. It means recognizing its oddities and engaging with them. The Bible includes texts that disagree with each other. Why? Couldn't God make up God's mind? Or maybe God recognizes that different contexts demand different approaches. Maybe God is playfully if directly requiring us to think for ourselves on the subject at hand. The notion that to question the Bible is to disrespect or otherwise belittle it is not just intellectual malpractice; it is cheap faith. The Bible demands that we investigate it, interrogate it, learn *about* it. To do anything less is to fail to take the text seriously.[13]

One more thing on the topic of belief and the Bible. We tend to divide reading into two approaches: the Bible-as-literature and the Bible-as-scripture. The simplest distinction is that to read the Bible as literature is to approach this compilation of texts from a secular perspective, without the overlay of theological principles or expectations derived from religious orthodoxy. To approach it as scripture is to come with all those religious trappings recognizing that it is a sacred text but claiming that it is sacred *to you*.

As always, the simplest definition doesn't cover the matter. Jews and Christians—for whom the Bible is Scripture, that is, religiously authoritative—benefit from reading the Bible, thinking about it, analyzing and critiquing it as literature. To do so does not require they abandon their faith or belief in the Bible as God's Word. It might, however, mean rethinking assumptions about how God speaks. More peculiar is the flip-side truth: people who do not accept the Bible as authoritative can nevertheless read it as Scripture, and I don't mean only by recognizing that it's sacred and/ or treating it with the respect of a text that is authoritative for some people. I mean that a so-called secular, maybe atheist reader might discover passages or qualities that stimulate his or her own sense of the holy, a sense of truth and beauty. That doesn't mean that he or she will convert to Judaism or Christianity. Such a reader may well be profoundly committed to another religion, or to none. But the Bible endures and invites continual engagement, and there is something in it for everyone—something if not holy, then at least intriguing, even meaningful.

# Chapter 2

# But in the Original . . .

Whenever there's a disagreement about the Bible, an appeal to "what it says in the original" usually isn't far behind. Indeed, going back to an original can resolve disagreements, shed light on interpretations, peel away accretions of interpretation, and lend credibility to one reading over another. When it comes to the Bible, "going back to the original" usually means referring to the ancient Hebrew and Greek texts, since those are, respectively, the languages of the Old Testament or Hebrew Bible and of the New Testament, from which our translations come.[1]

The trouble is, we don't actually have an original Bible.

We simply don't have a single Bible that old or that otherwise stands as The One that gave rise to them all. Our earliest versions come from hundreds of years after the Bible's contents (both Jewish and Christian versions) were finalized. There is no authoritative *ur*-text that we can consult for the final word. For readers accustomed to appealing to the Bible as the definitive Word of God, this information can land like a heavy blow—disorienting at best, debilitating at worst. For me, it was not unlike learning that the players on professional sports teams don't actually come from the place they're playing for. What, the Minnesota Vikings don't all come from Minnesota? But worse. After all, if there's no original Bible, how can we confidently know what to believe?

Just because we have no original Bible doesn't mean that we shouldn't seek out and read the earliest available texts. It's challenging but not impossible. That is, many a biblical scholar earns her bread and butter by learning the ancient languages of early manuscripts and then examining, comparing, and investigating the earliest possible versions that we *do* have, canonical or not. So all is not lost. But, as with all things biblical, it's hardly simple or straightforward. For one thing, not only did the people responsible for the Bible treat authorship in a rather fast-and-loose manner—ascribing names to books that those people didn't actually write and leaving anonymous most everything else—but also, over time, whole cadres of people had their fingers on the texts, trimming a bit here, adding a piece there, tweaking in light of new experiences and information. And different versions could be in circulation at the same time, making it difficult to nail down just which Bible a given person may have been appealing to.

***

In 1947, a Bedouin herder discovered, in a cave near the Dead Sea, tall clay jars containing scrolls that archaeologists dated to the first century CE. When the scrolls were found to contain biblical material, the world went nuts. Indeed, among the scrolls are fragments, at least, of every biblical book except Esther, and some nonbiblical books, too. Here, finally, some people concluded, lay fragments of an original Bible. Surely, since some scrolls date to the first century CE, we would find firsthand accounts of the great preacher from Galilee whose revolutionary message and miraculous resurrection so altered the shape of human history. They were soon disappointed. When archaeologists reported that Jesus isn't mentioned in these scrolls, some people concluded that the archaeologists must be lying, that there's no way a community contemporary with Jesus's and concerned about the messiah(s) wouldn't have written about him. But that ancient community didn't.

What's more, the texts show that the Bible hadn't yet taken its modern shape. Rather than offering an original Bible, the Dead Sea scrolls show how complicated such a notion is. The scrolls instead reveal an organic, dynamic process of collection, transmission, and canonization. Consider its fragments from the book of Jeremiah. The Dead Sea Scrolls shows that that book had not yet reached its final form, that variations were still circulating in the first century CE. Those variations are reflected in differences between the Eastern Orthodox Christian Bible and the Jewish and Western Christian Bibles.

The Roman Catholic and Eastern Orthodox traditions follow the Septuagint translation of a Hebrew version that has been lost over time. That version is quite a bit shorter and orders texts differently than the version that appears in the Jewish and Western Christian canons. Both versions appear among the Dead Sea Scrolls.

Remember that the Septuagint is a Greek translation of Hebrew biblical texts. Generated in the third century BCE, it allowed Greek-speaking Jews to read the scriptures (not yet technically a canonical "Bible") in their customary language. The authoritative Hebrew collection behind Jewish and Western Christian canons is called the Masoretic Text, thanks to the Masoretes, scrupulous Jewish scribes and scholars who over centuries copied and transmitted biblical texts along with detailed notes for reading. Though Hebrew through and through (with the exception of a smattering of Aramaic), the Masoretic Text dates to a time centuries later than the Septuagint, though much of its contents go further back. While the Masoretic Text may reflect earlier traditions than the Septuagint in some cases, many scholars believe that the Hebrew behind the Septuagint's Jeremiah is older than the Hebrew behind the Masoretic Text.

The Masoretic Text was itself an effort to keep the Bible accessible in new and changing times. The earliest Hebrew versions were written without vowels. As biblical Hebrew became more and more antiquated, Jewish scholars added vowels to the text to aid the Jews of their time in reading and understanding. Although they began this work around 500 CE, the earliest Masoretic Hebrew Bibles that we have date to the tenth century CE. Most modern translators, Jewish and Christian, appeal to Masoretic versions for authority.

Other ancient versions that scholars consult to determine the oldest or most authoritative Old Testament, when versions differ, include translations into Aramaic (called the Targums or Targumim, dating from 100 BCE to 600 CE) and Syriac (the Peshitta, dating to the second century CE). Incidentally, a Syrian Christian, Tatian, translated a New Testament that wove the disparate Gospels into one consistent narrative, called the Diatessaron. That version held sway among Syrian Christians until the fifth century CE, when a few powerful bishops urged Christians to keep separate the Gospels as we're accustomed to seeing them in the New Testament.

***

The earliest extrabiblical references to the Gospels don't name the texts at all but assume a certain familiarity with them.[2] It's possible that readers simply knew who the authors were, so it wasn't necessary to call them out by name. Or maybe the authors intentionally chose anonymity in the hopes that the message would be more widely disseminated, that it would be accepted more universally on account of its generic authorship.

As time went on, and the end of the world didn't come, as many early Christians had expected it would, church leaders began to choose which writings would be considered scripture and which wouldn't. These Gospels, which retained authority within the early Christian community, needed apostolic attribution—something that would link them to someone who knew Jesus or someone who knew someone who knew Jesus. Without such apostolic authority, they would carry much less weight. These early anonymous yet authoritative books, books with some claim to apostolic authority and in wide circulation among early Christians, needed authors, and they needed them now.

The earliest reference to the biblical Gospels by the names they now bear appears in the second-century Irenaeus's *Against Heresies* (ca. 180–185 CE), which is a text that is exactly what the title suggests. Irenaeus makes a case for four Gospels, which he names

Matthew, Mark, Luke, and John.[3] In keeping with earlier rumors that Matthew, a Jew, had done some writing, and observing that the first Gospel has a strong Hebrew Bible and Jewish orientation, it came to be known as the Gospel of Matthew. Early rumors also held that Peter's accounts of Jesus had been written by a follower of Peter, so the second (and earliest) Gospel came to be attributed to Mark, believed to be an indispensable companion of Peter's.[4] Luke, also responsible for Acts, is called Luke because he claims to have been a companion of Paul's and he was a gentile. (Acts tells of Christianity's success in the gentile world.) As for John, that Gospel refers to a "beloved disciple" in such a way that early readers understood it to be the work of that disciple. The pool narrows quickly, since early Christianity identified three super-disciples: Peter, James, and John. Peter is named in the fourth Gospel and is therefore unlikely to be its author. James was killed in the movement's early days. That left John, son of Zebedee, to whom the fourth Gospel was attributed.

That said, we still don't know who "Matthew," "Mark," "Luke," and "John" were. These are Gospels, the first four books of the New Testament, books that tell the story of the life, works, death, and resurrection of Jesus with an eye to sharing "good news." We're accustomed to refer to each Gospel as though Matthew, Mark, Luke, and John are their actual authors. They are not. That is, the Gospels were not written by the individuals so named but circulated anonymously before being attributed to people with clout.[5]

It may be surprising in our time of self-publishing, when nearly everyone who puts words to a page self-identifies as a published author, but a couple of thousand years ago people frequently wrote anonymously or otherwise attributed their writing to someone famous. In that context, the anonymity of the Gospels' authors was perfectly normal.

If you read each with this in mind, you'll notice that none of the Gospels names its writer, none of them is written in the first person, and none of them includes the kind of personal details we would expect from a person writing with a transparent connection to the people or happenings he or she is writing about. Rather these Gospel writers, following the Hebrew Bible's historical trajectory (in each Gospel, Jesus is interpreted in light of the Old Testament as a continuation of God's relationship and fulfillment of promise to Israel), chose the same anonymity as the authors of Joshua, Judges, Samuel, and Kings—the Hebrew Bible's historical books. They stood in a long biblical tradition of anonymous authorship.

***

Paul stands in contrast to this and poses a different set of problems. Since the New Testament's focus is on Jesus and his teachings, it's remarkable that the bulk of the New Testament actually comes from or is attributed to someone who never met Jesus. Take a second to appreciate that: Jesus, the heart of the whole New Testament, didn't write anything that we have, and Paul, who is responsible for most of what we do have, never met Jesus in person. What's more, the earliest writing in the New Testament is Paul's. Mark, the earliest gospel, dates to 70 CE; Paul's first letter to the Thessalonians dates to a time twenty or more years earlier.

Paul's defense of his call to ministry, that he received the call "before [he] was born," isn't unique.[6] It presumes familiarity with the Hebrew Bible, specifically the defenses of prophets Jeremiah and "Deutero-Isaiah."[7] And Paul was nothing if not a studious Jew. "Formed in the womb" is part of the literary formula of a prophet's defense in justifying that role (namely, that the man didn't, indeed couldn't have chosen to become God's prophet; God elected him, and so his words are true). In Paul's case, he claims to have had a close-encounters experience that catapulted him into the category of those who'd met Jesus (i.e., having apostolic authority), but Paul never met him. Yet the writings associated with Paul dominate the New Testament in bulk and influence.

Paul did sign his name, so to speak, to these epistles (letters) to developing congregations. But others also used Paul's name or reputation. I write "attributed to" and "associated with" because scholars have shown that some of the writings that came to be associated with Paul (e.g., Hebrews) were penned not by Paul but by anonymous authors who used Paul's name in order to give greater credibility to what they had to say.

The historical span between authorship and canonization of New Testament books is a good millennium shorter than for the books of the Hebrew Bible, allowing less time for changes in transmission. Nevertheless, even the texts that scholars agree do come from Paul may have undergone editing by later hands.[8]

\*\*\*

It wasn't until the fourth century CE that the initiative to develop an authoritative biblical canon really took hold. Before then, different Christian communities appealed to different gospels, letters, narratives, and apocalyptic writings. Indeed, for a good century or more after Jesus's death, the gospel genre alone spun off many faith-based stories, such as *The Gospel of Philip* and *The Infancy Gospel of Thomas*. While it's intriguing to imagine one moment in history when a committee of Christians determined what should be in the Bible and what should not, the reality is probably much more organic and messy. There was the general rule that a text should have apostolic authority, of course, but also some texts simply rose to the top more often than others. Religious communities appealed to some books more than to others for theological as well as historical reasons. These were more likely, then, to be adopted for the Bible.

This doesn't necessarily mean that the chosen texts represented every concern of their time or place, of course. After all, then as now the interests of some members of any given community had more sway than others. What's more, cultural assumptions and worldview informed the decision-making process. For example, we know that these were patriarchal communities; the status of women was inferior to that of men. So of course texts that got the most attention were texts that assumed, if not supported, that worldview.

Consider also that for a long time, the order of biblical books wasn't fixed because which were the canonical texts was still undetermined and because the Bible wasn't a book. Rather, the collection of texts that became the Bible to Jews and Christians circulated as independent documents in the form of scrolls. In other words, the physical form of the text affected the arrangement of the collection. It wasn't until the first century CE that the text as pages stitched together began to replace texts kept on discrete rolls. As scrolls, the texts might be arranged and rearranged, but an individual scroll could get only so big before it became unwieldy. As a codex (in pages such as hard-copy books today), their order was fixed and the size virtually unlimited.

The division of texts into chapter and verse came later still. Our means of locating a text within the Bible by book, with verses (the tiny numbers) as subdivisions of chapters (bigger numbers) as subdivisions of books (so named), is a relatively recent development. It's a pretty slick system for efficiently finding a particular text (e.g., Exodus 3:14 directs readers swiftly to the book of Exodus, chapter 3, verse 14), though sometimes the numbers vary a little between versions or in where they suggest breaks, and the books may have names reflecting an ancient variant (e.g., Ecclesiastes is the Latin transliteration of the Greek translation of the Hebrew Qoheleth).

It has become a sign of knowing your Bible to be able to cite chapter and verse. But in doing so, it's easy to forget that those divisions are not original to any ancient version. Rather, they're the product of an intentional effort launched in the case of Christian Bibles in the thirteenth century, when biblical books were divided into the chapters that we have now. Individual verses such as we see today didn't come along until the sixteenth century.

As for the titles of books, they too are not original but came along later, as the product of the need to identify. So they're not always the same across Bibles. For example, the Hebrew title of the book of Numbers is Bemidbar, meaning "In the wilderness/desert," since the book takes place there; Leviticus is Vayikra, meaning "And he called," which is the first word of that book in Hebrew. We talked about the Gospels' titles earlier, how they came to be assigned to people by the titles' names. Most scholars think Acts was originally volume 2 of Luke-Acts.

The earliest complete New Testament that we have was discovered at a monastery at the base of what some think to be Mount Sinai. Called the Codex Sinaiticus, it's not simply the Bible that we have today but also includes the Epistle of Barnabas and the *Shepherd of Hermas* (neither of which was ultimately included in the Christian canon) and only about half of the Old Testament. The Codex Vaticanus also appears to date to the fourth century CE. It contains much of the Septuagint and New Testament, except for part of Hebrews, some of Paul's letters, and Revelation. So neither is an original Bible.

That's where the work of academics toiling in dusty library basements becomes so important. Comparing all of these ancient witnesses to biblical texts before they were the Bible involves a process called textual criticism, and it's not for the faint of heart. Today's translations of the Old Testament or Hebrew Bible are based for the most part on the Masoretic Text, with consideration of other ancient translations and versions such as the Dead Sea Scrolls. Today's translations of the New Testament are mostly based on the latest edition of the United Bible Society's Greek New Testament, now in its fifth edition, which is informed by the rigorous textual criticism of the Nestle-Aland Novum Testamentum Graece, currently in its twenty-eighth edition. The quest to determine the best, most original text continues as scholars work with the more than five thousand extant ancient manuscript copies of New Testament texts and incorporate new methods for determining the most authoritative versions.

\*\*\*

This is all to say that the Bible's development was far more dynamic than we're inclined to think, given modern assumptions about the transmission of important texts. Speaking of an original may be misleading in the first place. The result of the Bible's developmental process is a collection that shows its seams, the wrestling and rethinking of people involved in its transmission.

Given all of this, what could it possibly mean to speak of the Bible as the "word of God"? Considering that we don't have one original and indisputable Bible but rather a collection that evolved over a long period of time for which our evidence is copies of copies, not all of which agree with one another, how can a person "believe in" it, much less live by it?

Rather than despair at the lack of an original Bible to which the faithful might appeal for a straightforward and definitive Word of God, I submit that the facts of the Bible's development, the admission that we have fragments of copies sometimes with competing claims or inscrutable passages, invites us to reconsider the most basic ways that we read it. Rather than treating the Bible as a transparent rulebook, history lesson, or theological treatise, the sheer fact of the Bible's messiness with its millennia of manipulation invites us to read more as participants in meaning-making than consumers of absolutist declarations. Maybe the "word of God" is more an ongoing conversation than absolute declarations. Maybe as long as people keep engaging with the text, God keeps speaking.

# PART II

## Beings Odd and Otherwise

# Chapter 3

# God

"Gosh," we're taught to say, instead of "God." Or "Golly" or "Jeez." The impulse comes from prohibitions against blaspheming the name of God, "taking the name of the LORD in vain," or otherwise misusing it.[1] In the ancient world out of which the biblical texts came, people would invoke deities as witnesses to binding promises. The divine name was a powerful thing. To use it in a false oath was a grave offense.[2] But just what *is* that name, biblically speaking? There isn't only one. For that matter, what does "the name" mean, anyway?

The very first character, the first person to take action at the very beginning of the Bible—book 1, chapter 1, verse 1—is, you got it, God. The Bible's very first verb indicates, by its particular form, that its subject is singular. So far so good. But the word that follows, the word that names the subject, *elohim* in transliteration, is a plural form: "gods." In Hebrew grammar a noun's ending shows whether it is singular or plural. Those endings are also gender specific.[3] The *-im* on the end of *elohim* tells us that it's a masculine plural noun from the singular *eloah*. In Hebrew as well as cognate languages such as Ugaritic, *el* is a generic word meaning "god." So with this grammatically plural form, we begin with a theological conundrum that you'd never appreciate if you didn't know this little bit about the Hebrew behind our translations.

The word *elohim* appears elsewhere in the Bible to refer quite clearly and explicitly to other gods; that is, it functions in a traditional sort of way with the translation "gods." But here in Genesis chapter 1, the verb, which also contains the number and gender of its subject, indicates that the word should be read as singular. What's more, the context and tone of the chapter would seem to support such a reading: "God," not "gods." In other words, we have good reason to assert that *elohim* in the Hebrew Bible can function as another name for God and that "God" is indeed a fine translation for it.

Still, why the plural? *El* by itself, in the singular, is also a divine name. It is a name of the (Canaanite) Ugaritic high god, who incidentally is described as an old man with a long white beard who sits on a throne in the clouds. In the Bible, God is variously called El Something-or-Other. We read that Abraham spoke of *el olam*, "the everlasting God."[4] Moses refers to *el elyon*, "the Most High."[5]

And we read of *el shaddai* (especially popular in the book of Job), an *el*-construct that translators don't quite know what to do with. One possibility, leaning on cognate languages, is "the one (in charge) of deities." Other possibilities have to do with hills or breasts. "The one of breasts," as in a nurturing or even female God? Maybe. Fertility and specifically female fertility figurines were common in the places and times from which these texts come. Whatever the case, that's the Hebrew, *el shaddai*, behind what's frequently rendered in English as "God Almighty."

While *el* names that specify a quality of God are common, one especially stands out. In only one case does a person take the initiative and presume to name God (with impunity, I might add). Remarkably, that person is a woman, not even Hebrew, and a slave at that. Hagar was an Egyptian slave of Abraham and Sarah, compelled to bear them the child Sarah could not herself conceive. When pregnant, Hagar became intolerable to Sarah, who behaved so hurtfully toward her that she ran away.[6] In the wilderness, an angel confronts Hagar and gives her the kind of future-telling promise otherwise reserved for the Hebrew patriarchs: that Hagar would have many descendants ("a great nation," in chapter 12). And she should name her son Ishma-el, "God hears." After that, Hagar "named the LORD who spoke to her, 'You are El-roi'; for she said, 'Have I really seen

God and remained alive after seeing him?' "[7] The Hebrew *roi* here has to do with seeing, whether it's "the one seeing" or "God who sees."

So there are all these perfectly serviceable *el* names for God in the Bible. Why the plural Elohim to launch the whole collection of texts? With this beginning, we run smack into the fact, like it or not, that there's going to be more to God both in this story and throughout the Bible than a monotone, singular, consistently recognizable (read: predictable) deity. Elohim continues throughout the Bible to be a very common moniker for the seemingly singular God at the heart of the faith of the people responsible for the texts.

Elohim is not the only plural moniker for a (singular) biblical deity. So is Adonai, typically translated "my lord." The noun *adon* or *adoni*, to which a first-person possessive singular ("my") suffix is appended, is plural. In other words, a grammatically correct translation of the Hebrew *adonai* is "my lords."

That story in Genesis chapter 1, the creation of the world in seven days, gives us a couple of other intriguing bits of information about God. Consider the peculiar creation-of-human-beings passage. For one thing, there's God saying, "Let us . . . in our image," further teasing out the possibility that the name Elohim does indeed suggest plurality. Quick side note: some modern Christian readers assume that this is a reference to the Trinity. But that would require reading into an ancient text (five hundred years or so before the Common Era) a theological position that arose seven hundred years or so later. A Christian might *choose to interpret* Genesis 1's plural Elohim to be a reference to the Christian Trinity, but the text as it comes to us predates any such perspective.

So what's with God referring to God's self in this first chapter as plural, as an "us" ("Let us make *adam* in our image")? Scholars familiar with the finer points of the Bible's greater ancient Near Eastern context observe that the idea of a "divine council"—a gathering of the gods—was common among ancient Israel's neighbors and is probably what is going on in the text. Indeed, several biblical texts assume the same worldview: the commandment "Thou shalt have no other gods before me" suggests the existence of others, for example. But the clearest example is probably Psalm 82, which begins, "God [*Elohim*] has taken his place in the divine council" and goes on to portray God excoriating the other deities for failing in their divine task—meting out justice on behalf of the most vulnerable persons—and declaring that despite their divinity they shall "die like mortals."[8]

So in Genesis chapter 1, maybe God speaks as chairman of the board of deities.

But there's another level of intrigue to the matter of the plural God: note how the creation of humans in the image of God unfolds. While it begins with God's declared intention to create humans "in our image," plural, it concludes with "in his image," masculine singular. What transpires in between is God's creation of *adam*, referred to in the episode as "them." The fluid plural-singular nature of God anticipates the singular-plural nature of humans in the story.

After all, the grammatically singular form *adam* is, in this telling, plural—both male and female. While *adam* is often translated "man," it is equally appropriate to translate it as "human being" or "humankind." The word *adam* can indeed be the guy Adam that you might guess from its transliteration, or the gender-specific "man." But the word also refers collectively to human beings, regardless of gender. The context of this passage indicates that the latter is to be preferred. After all, it says that *adam* is male and female.

What's more, somehow this combo male-female *adam* is made in the image of this sort of plural God, which complicates assumptions that God is strictly "he." Right here at the very beginning of the Bible, we read, "So *elohim* created *adam* in his image, in the image of *elohim* he created him; male and female he created them. *Elohim* blessed them, and *elohim* said to them . . ."[9] In other words, at the very beginning of the Bible, we read of a God unlimited by sex, both male and female simultaneously. This story suggests that God is both masculine and feminine, just as human beings are both male and female. You can debate this—the Bible invites such discussion—but there's no avoiding the fact that this text suggests a deity that isn't strictly male but rather equally female and male.

But what of the "he" and "him" in the aforementioned passage? It's a function of rather mundane grammatical limitations. Hebrew has only masculine and feminine pronouns, no neuter. Add to that the fact that the Bible evolved and emerged out of predominantly patriarchal cultures and was finalized in definitively patriarchal circumstances. No wonder, then, that when faced with a choice between "him" or "her," "he" or "she," biblical Hebrew would choose the masculine. (There's no biblical precedent for our modern "he or she.") When gender is in question or when there's a mixed group, Hebrew defaults to the masculine. It's even less wonder that images of and language for God that prioritizes the masculine would dominate the texts. Yet, given this patriarchal cultural context, it's remarkable that, as Genesis 1 illustrates, the Bible also immediately and explicitly complicates the simple conclusion that God is male.

\*\*\*

Reading on from the first chapter of Genesis, it doesn't take long before we run into another name for God and another form of "lord." In Genesis 2, and throughout the story of the Garden of Eden, it's "the LORD God" this and "the LORD God" that. Readers might also notice that the whole perspective and tone of the narrative changes and that everything gets created all over again.

Some people interpret this Garden of Eden story as an extrapolation of the first chapter's creation of the world in seven days. However, a close reading, appreciating the literary and theological characteristics of the texts, might lead readers to agree with scholars that these two creation stories come from two separate sources and were only later combined into the longer narrative of Genesis. Indeed, the observation of such differences led scholars to develop the long-standing hypothesis that the first five books of the Hebrew Bible, called the Pentateuch or Torah, came from more than one person or group.[10] The names were far from the only evidence of this, but they were part of it.

Halfway through Genesis 2:4, we meet this LORD God. Those caps are there for a reason. The word represented in English translations as LORD—typically large cap L, small cap ORD—is from the Hebrew word transliterated YHWH. Remember, the earliest Hebrew Bibles didn't have any vowels. These four letters, then, functioned as consonants. This four-letter name for God is sometimes called the Tetragrammaton (from the Greek for "four-letter name"). We see it first here in Genesis, in the second creation story, down and dirty in the Garden of Eden (as compared to high and mighty out in the ether)—which, if you've read the next book, Exodus, is really weird.

After all, it isn't until Exodus—and a good number of generations after Adam and Eve—that we read of the "revealing" of God's Name to be YHWH. There, we read that it was only after much prodding and back-and-forth that God condescended to tell Moses God's name, or perhaps Name. This, YHWH, is the personal name that Moses wrung out of God. Yet we came across it already in the second chapter of Genesis and without any fanfare or flag-waving or explanation whatsoever. We're barely a millimeter into the tome that is the Hebrew Bible when we read of YHWH. So it might rightly strike a reader as odd that God's name, in blithe operation from the beginning of human beings, is "introduced" so much later.

And that's not the only remarkable thing about the four-letter Name. For one thing, it's far more wonderful than a mere "Lord." "Lord," after all, is simply a title—a grand and superior one, sure, but Hebrew has a (different) word for exactly that: *adon*, as discussed earlier. "Lord" is limited to evoking a relationship of hierarchy, and it's morally ambivalent. There are good lords and bad lords.

YHWH on the other hand, is different. Have a look at that episode in Exodus. Exodus 3:1–4:17 is the story of Moses's encounter with God in the form of a burning bush. God, or rather YHWH, as this narrator confusingly prefers (a name that supposedly hasn't been introduced yet), tells Moses that it's time to get God's people out of their Egyptian misery and that Moses is just the guy to do it. Moses is not so sure. Among his protestations—rather bold given how scared he is—is that when he, who was raised as Egyptian royalty, shows up among the Israelites declaring that the God of their ancestors has sent him, they're bound to ask, "What is his name?"

Moses asks, "What shall I tell them?"

Don't let the speed with which God answers lull you into thinking it's a simple answer. God answers immediately. But God's answer is a sentence, and there are a couple of possibilities for its translation. The most common translation is "I am that I am." But the range also includes "I am who I am," "I will be who/what I will be," and "I will cause to be what/who I cause to be." Thank goodness God was feeling garrulous because God continues on to say that Moses should tell the people that God's name is "YHWH," the same as the God of their founding ancestors. Finally, God says, "This is my name for ever and my memorial to all generations."

Hebrew builds most of its vocabulary on the foundation of three-letter verbs. In this passage, God plays on the verb "to be" in spelling out God's name. In other words, God's name is not so much a fixed thing as action: the act of be-ing. The implications are profound. For one thing, we'll find that this is a name of God that is defined by a relationship, a special you-are-my-people-and-I-am-your-God name. This is the name by which the Egyptians are to understand this particular God ("Go to the king of Egypt and say to him, 'YHWH, the God of the Hebrews'").[11] And this is the name by which God is to be known specifically to God's people, the oppressed Israelites who trace their identity back through the ancestors with whom God made a particular covenant. The text suggests that YHWH, then, is an extra-special, particular sort of name.

Although we have biblical precedent for people saying "Yahweh this or that," over time the four-letter name, so packed with power, became forbidden to utter. Hence the "translation" LORD, which we now know is no translation at all but a rendering conveniently composed of the same number of letters as the Hebrew. And hence the Jewish customs of referring to HaShem, which literally means "The Name," and of pronouncing "Adonai" when reading the four-letter name aloud. The word "Jehovah" was born from an effort to avoid articulating the Name. It is an artificial construct that combines the consonants of the four-letter Name, Y/J, H, W/V, H, with the vowels of the Hebrew *adonai*.

Our best guess for vocalizing the all-consonants name is as Yahweh, which shows up in shortened form all over the place: *hallelu-y/jah* ("praise Yah"), *elijah* ("my God/*el* is Jah"), and "Forever loving Jah" (Bob Marley).

If, like me, you were raised in a churchgoing home, you were instructed never to swear, which meant not only avoiding four-letter words—yes *those* four-letter words—but also exclamations such as "Oh, God!" "God damn it!" and simply "God!" This had something to do with the commandment forbidding "taking the Lord's name in vain." I thought, of course, that "Lord" was essentially God's title, because even if I was reading it in the Bible, I didn't distinguish between LORD and Lord. I had no idea they were different words. And *such* different words!

But if you look at the Hebrew for that commandment (which appears in Ex 20 and Deut 5), it's YHWH that you'll find, which makes things a whole lot more interesting than simply avoiding a certain word in exclamations. Understanding something about the Name with a capital "N" suggests this commandment has less to do with the casual use of a particular word and more to do with summoning the Holy One—the power that word connotes—for narrow, selfish, or trite purposes.

Considered in its greater biblical context, the commandment says that the Name that refers back to this extra-ordinary god of ancient purpose and enduring relationship, who is be-ing itself, is not to be associated by mere limited humans with that which is wrong-headed or disingenuous. This surely puts the lie to people who claim to speak for God for purposes that suit their own ideologies and interests, for haters who invoke God to crush, alienate, or otherwise undermine others. "According to the Bible," such people "will not be held guiltless" by the power of the very Name they invoke.

\*\*\*

Given the power of the Name in Jewish tradition, you can see why the earliest Christians would declare of Jesus, whom they described as having "the very nature of God," that "God . . . gave him the name that is above every name, so that at the name of Jesus every knee should bow, in heaven and on earth and under the earth, and every tongue acknowledge that Jesus Christ is Lord."[12] And so we come full circle. For the Greek word *kurios*, here translated "Lord," is the same as the Septuagint's Greek translation of YHWH as it appears in Exodus 3 and elsewhere. You'll remember that Jesus's followers used the Greek translation of their (Hebrew) Bible, so this association would not have been lost on them.

That they came to identify Jesus in this manner with none other than YHWH is arguably even more extraordinary than that they would call him *christos*, "christ," which is the Greek translation of the Hebrew *meshiach*, "messiah." That description, translated as "anointed," functioned in the Hebrew Bible to distinguish individuals set apart for a special purpose or service to God, namely priests and kings. Neither of these kinds of people was considered to be God. They had special duties vis-à-vis God as mediators between heavenly stuff and earthly matters, but there was no question about their utter and absolute humanity.

By Jesus's time, there were Jews looking for someone who would lead them in the tradition of the storied King David, someone who was, of course, descended from David, since God had promised that someone from David's line would sit on the throne in Jerusalem forever.[13] Over time, *meshiach* and *christos* became synonymous with Jesus's divinity. To speak of Jesus as "the messiah" was to speak of Jesus as the "son of God," that is, divine. To speak of Jesus as

"Christ," then, is to speak from faith. It presumes a particular religious perspective: that of a Christian.

Christianity has been around for so long and is so prevalent that we forget how terribly odd it is. That a particular human being would come to be seen as nothing less than God takes some real imagination and no small guts. A person can lose her life over that. Many have. The endurance of Judaism should show that it wasn't a given that first-century Judaism and the texts that came to be biblical (but still weren't fixed as such) would produce a movement that claimed Jesus as a divine messiah. Granted, the belief follows some solid ground-laying in the Old Testament, but even Jesus's followers didn't think all of it referred to him.

Given the long tradition of anti-Jewish persecution, it bears mentioning (again) that the texts of the Hebrew Bible are just as authoritative for Jews as they are for Christians; Christians simply read them in a much different way. Texts that Christians read in light of what they believe about Jesus had meaning centuries before Jesus's birth and death, and continue to have meaning apart from Jesus for Jews today. To insist that the only way to read the Hebrew Bible is through the lens of the New Testament is ahistorical and anti-Semitic.

\*\*\*

This topic—Jesus as God and biblical oddities as they pertain to the divinity of Jesus—is worth a book of its own. I'd hardly be the first to that party. Many such excellent books exist. For our purposes— to determine how the divinity of Jesus as portrayed in the Bible might be a bit stranger than we're given to consider—I'll focus on just a few points. The most striking is that the Bible doesn't speak with one, unified voice on the subject. Even if we take only the New Testament into account, the case is hardly cut-and-dried.

Consider the Gospels, the books that are explicitly and completely about Jesus as composed not by disinterested journalists but by persons who *believed*—they're called Gospels ("good news"), after all. Intriguingly, Jesus—who didn't write anything, or at least not anything that has survived—never claims in any of the first three Gospels to be God, not explicitly; even in John's Gospel, Jesus distinguishes himself from God while claiming to be one with God.[14]

Consider also the simple fact that there are four Gospels. In other words, even the most devout, groundbreaking Jesus followers didn't agree on the specifics. Their portraits of Jesus are really quite distinct. Matthew gives us the most "as the Bible says" moments, appealing to the Hebrew Bible (probably in Greek translation) for justification in believing that Jesus fulfilled divine intentions suggested by ancient prophecies. Mark depicts an urgent God-in-critical-times with an originally dark and rather uncertain ending. Luke features a recognizably messianic Jesus from before the babe was even born to be "Son of God," "holy," and king forever.[15] John gives us the most otherworldly, mystical Jesus.

It's really Paul, author of the earliest New Testament writings, to whom we owe the identification of Jesus with God, as it would develop in Christian theology. And that's kind of strange because, as we've seen, Paul never met Jesus, not in person, anyway. Yes, he met Jesus on the road to Damascus, but that was in a vision. Indeed, from what we have of Paul's writing, he was much less interested in Jesus the man than in Jesus the Christ. He believed that Jesus was the Son of God through whom people could be saved from sin and death. So we find meditations on theology, orthodoxy, and right behavior in Paul's writings much more than we find concern about Jesus's nativity, youth, or ministry.

It's worth reminding ourselves that in the historical and cultural contexts out of which the Gospels come, there were plenty of stories of gods becoming human and vice versa. Consider Greek and Roman mythology, in which Zeus took on human form to consort and cavort with human women; the Roman emperor himself was a god in life and/or upon his death. Strict categories of supernatural and natural, divine beings occupying an utterly separate realm than human beings, don't appear until a few centuries into the Common Era. Even within a predominantly monotheistic Judaism, there was room to think about the divine and human on a kind of continuum rather than as strictly non-overlapping categories. Think of angels, divine beings who could appear as human.[16]

Psalm 82, briefly noted earlier, is a particularly intriguing window into an evolution of thinking about the gods and God, including a demotion of the gods into mortal beings. And this is just in the Bible. Examples of such a blurring between the divine and human appear also in extrabiblical Jewish texts from the period.[17] The apocryphal book of Sirach tells of Moses ascending in divinity to something even higher than angels, "equal in glory to the holy ones."[18] And of course, in Hebrew Bible texts that would have been authoritative to Jesus's Jewish contemporaries, we find that the angel of the LORD could be God himself.[19] Philo, a Jewish contemporary of Jesus and a learned scholar of the Septuagint, concludes from a rather cryptic statement in Exodus that Moses "was gradually becoming divine" and "is changed into the divine."[20]

It was the belief that Jesus was raised from the dead that catapulted the poor Jewish preacher from Galilee into the stratosphere of divine beings.

\*\*\*

God in Christian traditions is a three-part affair: Father, Son, and Holy Ghost; Creator, Incarnation, Holy Spirit. Yet nowhere in the Bible is God explicitly defined or named as a Trinity. The Bible, New Testament included, never uses the word "Trinity," never spells out the three-in-one and one-in-three belief so foundational to Christianity. Rather, the concept of a "triune God" developed within an emerging and evolving Christianity after the texts had taken shape.

The "Holy Spirit" equated with God in Christianity has roots in the Hebrew *ruach elohim*, a term we encounter at the very beginning of the Bible, where we read that when the earth was still "a form-less void," there was the *ruah elohim*. The Jesuit priest and poet Gerard Manley Hopkins writes of hope in a poem of heartbreaking beauty—a hope that draws from a biblical beginning of things—claiming that still, even now, "the Holy Ghost over the bent world broods." He's drawing, of course, on an interpretation of Genesis 1:2 and a translation that favors "to brood" for the Hebrew verb *merachepheth* rather than the more frequent "to hover" over the waters. Two things are interesting here: the interpretation and the translation.

Hopkins, being a devout Christian, interprets the Hebrew *ruach elohim* as Christianity's third person of the Trinity, the Holy Ghost or Holy Spirit. Fair enough. It's easy to see how he got there. But notice that in the Hebrew, this force is the "breath/wind/spirit of God." It functions in a text equally authoritative to Jews (who do not have the Trinitarian theology we find in Christianity) as to Christians.

*Ruach* is a feminine noun in Hebrew. Here it is paired with a verb (the one that we usually read translated into English as "hovered") that elsewhere appears in the context of a mother bird protecting her young.[21] We'd say the bird is brooding over her young. Hopkins knew his Bible and evoked this rich association, so fitting in the context of a story of creation: that the spirit of God might patiently mother a hatching world, and that this brooding endures still.

Given this common Christian understanding of the *ruach elohim* in Genesis 1:2 as in some way the Christian Holy Spirit, one would expect the beginning of John's Gospel to pick that up. After all, it clearly depends on and echoes Genesis chapter 1. "In the beginning was the Word, and the Word was with God, and the Word was God," and its equation of Jesus and God in the phrase "the Word became flesh" would seem to be a good place to mention the Holy Spirit. But John doesn't. The doctrine's development depended instead on other texts. When the divine Jesus says his goodbyes, he assures his friends that "the Father" will give them this *parakletos* that Jesus calls "Holy Spirit" to be with them, "in" them.[22] The Paraclete (Greek *parakletos*), meaning "helper," "advocate," or "intercessor," could then stand in, ever-present, for the departing Jesus.

A Holy Spirit is described as the impregnator of Mary and comes upon Jesus at his baptism.[23] It is said to have inspired John the Baptist from before he was born and led Old Man Simeon to understand Jesus's exceptional nature.[24] Yet reading a text such as John 16:7–15 or Acts 1:2–5 makes it sound as though the Holy Spirit/ Advocate/Helper was to be available to people (or maybe even comes into being) only after Jesus is gone. Consider Pentecost—the dramatic moment when the Holy Spirit filled Jesus's disciples and enabled them to speak in many languages.[25]

\*\*\*

That God has several names in the Bible should tip us off to the fact that God is hardly a straightforward entity or character. We're dealing with a far richer theology than any simple term might connote. Investigating the question of God's name leads to matters of theology—who, what, how is God?—and shows how swiftly the Bible complicates our casual references to "God." We talked a little about the problem of God's sex and gender, particularly with simply assuming that God is male.

Since God is clearly bigger than the limitations of gender, we might assume that the God of the Bible is bigger than everything. We're inclined to describe God using such grandiosities as omniscient (all-knowing), omnipotent (all-powerful), omnipresent (everpresent). But the Bible often undermines even the grandest claims about God.

Take omniscience, for instance, that God knows everything. That may be true. It may be theologically accurate. But that's not the way the Bible tells it. Some stories and images of God in the Bible portray a God who is learning, has regrets, or hopes for a future that doesn't come to pass.

By way of example, in the Garden of Eden story, the narrator says that God, after creating a single human being, observes that the situation (which God made) isn't quite right. It isn't good for *adam* to be alone. God sets out to find a suitable partner for *adam*. God creates animals and parades them before *adam*, "but there was not found a partner." Only then does God anaesthetize *adam* and make *adam* into two, finally landing on an appropriate partner. (And only then are the gender-specific terms "man" and "woman" introduced into the story.) Reading on, the narrator of Genesis 6:6–7 says that God regretted making *adam* on earth, that it grieved God deeply.[26]

These are not images of an omniscient God. Neither does the Bible portray God to be consistently all-powerful or even necessarily omnipresent. That God gives human beings choice in thoughts and actions compromises claims of absolute power. The absence of God is punishment to Cain. Again, that the Bible calls into question absolute claims about God doesn't mean that they're theologically false. It simply shows how many, various images of God the Bible presents and, in so doing, how the Bible undermines our efforts to reduce God, to place limits on God, even limits as extraordinary as claiming God is all-something-or-another.

\*\*\*

There is a line of thinking, most common among Christians, that the God of the Old Testament is a god of judgment and wrath and the God of the New Testament is a god of forgiveness and love. There are a couple of problems with this. One is that it's wrong. God appears with both sets of dispositions in both testaments. The other problem is more subtle.

It has to do with nomenclature, which contributes to this erroneous line of thinking. Some Christians treat the Old Testament as, well, old, outdated, superseded by the New. To them, the person and significance of Jesus have rendered obsolete the ideas and expectations articulated in the books of the Old Testament. But the books of the Old Testament are just as much Bible for Christians as are the Gospels and Paul's letters. Yes, they come from times in some cases centuries before the New Testament. So they're older. But they are no more outdated and obsolete than are the books explicitly about Jesus. For that reason, besides the fact that a whole cohort of people (Jews) maintain that *only* the books of the Old Testament are the Bible, I use the term "Hebrew Bible" more often than "Old Testament" to refer to the collection. Besides, it's always worth remembering that the Bible wasn't written in English or Spanish or Korean or whatever language in which you may first encounter it.

Back to the problem of the disposition of God in the Bible. There is definitely not only one. God favors love in both sets of texts. It's in the Hebrew Bible where we find the commandment to love your neighbor as yourself, which Jesus cites as the second (or second part of the) greatest commandment, and in the New Testament the author of 1 John makes the equation of God with love straightforward and clear.[27]

But God is also really demanding and can seem emotional, if not a bit capricious, throughout the Bible. In the Hebrew Bible, God is torn up by deep sorrow such as comes from a parent's love.[28] In the New Testament, we find that command to pluck out your eye if it wanders, as well as Jesus's rejection of family and his outright anger.[29] Indeed, on closer examination, we discover a whole range of sometimes competing qualities and characteristics.

Before zeroing in on some of those qualities, another quick observation about the books of the Hebrew Bible by comparison with those of the New Testament. The former took shape over nearly a millennia; the latter about a century. The former talks back and forth with itself; the latter does too, but always with the Hebrew Bible as part of the conversation. Remember, it was texts of the Hebrew Bible that Jesus and his followers appealed to as authoritative. That and that alone was their Bible. The New Testament didn't exist yet. It was to the texts of the Hebrew Bible that Jesus appealed to make sense of his time, and even more critical, it was to the

Hebrew Bible that the authors of the New Testament appealed to make sense of Jesus. Finally, comparing the collections: the Hebrew Bible is a whole lot bigger; there's more stuff in there with all that entails, including more opportunity to present a variety of images of and ideas about God.

\*\*\*

Now for some specifics of the diverse ways that the Bible represents God. They're in full-fledged evidence from the start. Consider the theological chasm between Genesis chapter 1 and Genesis chapter 2. In the first, God is absolutely Other and Out There. God never appears. From out of the ether, a disembodied God simply speaks the world elegantly into being, and what becomes is exactly as it is, say no more. By contrast, in the second chapter, God walks around, fashions objects (including a human being), plants a garden (or an orchard), and actually considers that things could be better— that the human being shouldn't be alone, for example, which God addresses through a process of trial and error.

Monotheism, belief in a one-and-only God, is a hallmark of both Judaism and Christianity. Ask any Religion 101 professor, consult any *Introduction to World Religions* textbook, and that will be one of the defining characteristics cited. The Bible, then, one might reasonably surmise, is a book that espouses that there's one and only one God. Not so. At least not consistently so, as discussed briefly already.

There are several texts in the Hebrew Bible that take for granted, without argument, explanation, or apology, that there are other gods around. We saw this in Genesis 1. At the time Genesis 1 was written, edited, and collected, most people thought of the heavens as populated by a number of deities. Each had different attributes, even different jobs, and it was not uncommon to find hierarchies among them. The position of high god could change, but there was usually one. In the case of Babylonia of the sixth century BCE, when (and where) Genesis 1 may well have been written, Marduk was high god of a pantheon of deities. In Canaanite Ugarit, in the same geographical area as Israel, from texts dating to times likely earlier than Genesis 2 and 3, we read of El the high god, who presided with his long white beard from a throne on the clouds over the several other (also important) deities.

Psalm 82, noted earlier, shows an evolution of sorts in the theology within the Bible. Its opening, "God stands in the divine assembly," makes that clear. But as it continues, the gods in the divine assembly are demoted to mortal status, condemned to "die as men do." (The reason for their demotion is provocative. God strips them of their stature because they had failed to act justly and to help the most vulnerable members of society.) God says, "I had taken you for divine beings, sons of the Most High, all of you." If that's not a clear statement of the notion of a multiplicity of divine beings in the Bible, I defy anyone to find a clearer one.

The commandment "Thou shalt have no other gods before me," as well as all those texts that tell about the gods of other peoples, especially excoriating against their worship by Yahweh's people, reveal a worldview in which the Hebrews' or Israelites' god is simply one among many—the best one, and the only one worthy of their worship, mind you (according to those texts), but not alone in her or his divinity in the universe. The term for this, the belief in one god though there are many, is "henotheism." The Hebrew Bible reveals a good bit of henotheism within it.

Another example shows up at the beginning of the book of Job, where we read that "one day the divine beings presented themselves before Yahweh," as though "divine beings" are a perfectly predictable norm. Readers today get hung up on *the satan*, who's among those beings (Ah, Satan! such thinking goes. There he is—the favorite angel before his great comeuppance or downfall-ence, as the case may be), glossing over this transparent understanding of Yahweh, God *of gods*.

*\*\*\**

It behooves us to recall that the biblical texts reflect their historical and cultural circumstances. By the first century of the Common Era, Judaism had become decisively monotheistic while reflecting the prevailing dualism of its time. That is, one (good) God versus the supernatural personification of evil, Satan. Contrast such dualism to texts that deny even other such beings. The effect: no other deities on which to blame or with which to explain away trouble. Isaiah 45 (from the sixth century BCE context of Cyrus II's conquest of Babylonia) repeats, "I am Yahweh, and there is no other," and declares, "I [Yahweh] form light and create darkness, I make weal and create woe."[30] This is the cost of a radical monotheism. This kind of reasoning by extension provided devastating fuel for anti-Semitism. If there is only one God, and that God is utterly powerful and perfectly just and good, then whatever suffering a person or community experiences must be appropriate punishment for that particular wrongdoing. One cannot explain it away as some lapse in God's judgment, attention, or ability. Nor can one blame it on another deity.

One effect of the monotheism of first-century Judaism was complete and utter rejection of any suggestion from within Judaism of another God, much less (God forbid, literally) the suggestion of God in human form. Even that God might identify God's anointed ("messiah"), God's Son, and king of the Jews as an apocalyptic itinerant preacher facing ignominious capital punishment was intolerable to many. Hence the great rift between conscientious traditional Jews and those who became followers of Jesus, a rift that reaches a shrill pitch in texts such as Matthew's "his blood be on us" and in John's anti-Jewish rhetoric, with its legacy of anti-Semitism.

I'm not going to argue that God is not omniscient, omnipotent, or omnipresent. I'm not going to argue anything, but simply observe that those are not how the Bible portrays God. The who, what, and how of God are questions of theology. For people who "believe," those questions (and any answers, such as they are) don't necessarily depend on the Bible or on any other particular sacred text, for that matter. They are predicated on faith, informed by sacred texts, sure, but also by personal experience, imagination, a sense of morality, mystery, and circumstance. The Bible doesn't have the final word on theological issues—it's too messy. And thank goodness it's messy, since that should let a little air out of our high-flying balloons, and remind us that when it comes to the Bible, the only simple answer is that there are no simple answers.

The Bible's refusal to categorize or otherwise define God once and for all in concrete, sensible, scientific terms is a powerful corrective. For once defined, it's not so big a step to manipulate and control, domesticating and reducing God to nothing more than, well, not-God. But it's exasperating, too, this resistance to consistency and sense.

***

For one thing, in both testaments, God says, does, and commands unsavory things. We find that God hardened Pharaoh's heart so that he wouldn't release the Israelites; "an evil spirit from the LORD" torments Saul; God gives "bad" and/or "impossible laws"; God sends lying prophets; and following the metaphor of Ezekiel chapter 16, God is a wife-beater. Then there's God's and Jesus's demand to "hate father and mother, wife and children, brothers and sisters."[31]

What to do with this? Pay attention to context. The long history of the Bible's development is relevant here. People are responsible for the texts as we have them. Did God have a say in it? That's a matter of belief. But there's no denying that the texts come to us through human hands, humans every bit as invested in and informed by their particular circumstances as we are by ours. It's not unreasonable to say that a people whose faith in God had been challenged by the nation's defeat might want to say that God does even terrible things (think: plagues, the tenth in particular) in order to make people recognize God's power. Or to note that the texts come out of uncompromisingly patriarchal circumstances, so God naturally looks in them more like a man than like a woman. Or again, that in order not to blame God for failures of prophecy or promise, it became necessary to blame us the people.

The Bible simply doesn't portray a perfectly consistent, laudable, and powerful deity. In the Bible, even the nature of God is a messy affair. What's a reader to do? First, recognize that the Bible blows away any effort to stuff God into a box of human making, the better to tote around, show off, or presume to quote with definitive confidence. The Bible itself undermines the popular declaration "God said it. I believe it. That settles it."

What we *can* say is that the Bible portrays a God who is neither male nor female; who is both out there in cosmic neverland and right here, immediately, intimately present; who is punitive and forgiving, capable of experiencing a range of emotions, deeply interested and invested in the affairs of earth, and wildly, extraordinarily dynamic. In other words, the Bible's representations of God reflect the Bible's wide-ranging history, its literary diversity and the driving urge of human beings to find our place and purpose and to make some sense of it all.

# Chapter 4

# Angels, Demons, and a Talking Ass

In 1946, the holiday catalog of Indianapolis's Ayres department store was spare at best. American industry had focused its attention on the war effort, so there was little of general interest to sell. The store hired artist Virginia Holmes to fill the empty spaces with charming images of cherubs, and the catalog quickly gained popular appeal. The next year, on the morning after Thanksgiving, holiday shoppers were delighted to discover that a chubby-faced bronze cherub had appeared overnight and was sitting atop the store's clock tower. it turns out that Ayres had quietly commissioned a sculptor to fashion the piece. The emergence of the cherub became a beloved annual ritual in the years following. Said to watch over busy shoppers, the cherub, recently restored, still resumes its post each year from the day after Thanksgiving to Christmas.[1]

If there's one image that dominates the holiday card industry other than the Holy Family or Santa Claus *and* that can appeal to both kinds of recipient, it's the cherub. If you're looking for holiday cards to satisfy and delight both Christian and non-Christian friends, you can't go wrong with Raphael's mischievous cherubs. You know the one: two chubby baby angels in the bottom of the frame, chin on hands, eyes wandering up. Originally a small part of the lower register of Raphael's "The Sistine Madonna" painting, these "putti" are so popular that they've generated several spin-offs. There's the woozy-looking "Drunken Angel after Raphael" by Larry

Mintz; an "alien version," with egg-headed aliens standing in for the cherubs. Ron Keas did one with Bassett hounds.

Cherubs reappear in force in the run-up to Valentine's Day. Often depicted with bow and arrow, these little darlings hint of their origins in the ancient Greek story of Cupid and Psyche, which itself bears no relation to the Bible. Although cherubs are especially prevalent in December and February, they can be a year-round thing. We refer to sweet and charming children as cherubs; and although the practice is less common these days, some people address their romantic sweetie-pie as a lovely cherub like Othello did to Desdemona, "Thou young and Rose-lip'd Cherubin."

The truth is, there is little if anything about these modern cherubs—Christmas, Valentine's, or otherwise—that has to do with cherubs in the Bible. But their origins are as biblical as can be. The word itself comes from the Bible, from the Hebrew *kerub* (plural *kerubim*). What's more, "aside from Yahweh, the cherubim are the most frequently occurring heavenly being in the Hebrew Bible," writes Alice Wood (who wrote a whole dissertation on them and so should know).[2] The word appears over ninety times in the Hebrew Bible, though only once in the New Testament.

The word behind our "cherub" is Hebrew, but beyond that, the term is a bit of a mystery. The plural form is "cherubim" (remember *elohim*?—same masculine plural ending) though the word has made its way into English as-is, and so it's common for us to talk about "cherubs." No one can say for sure where the word came from or how it was used before showing up in the Bible. A couple of theories situate its origins in ancient Assyria. It may be related to the Akkadian word *karibu*, referring to a kind of guardian who could also intercede with the gods on behalf of humans.[3] Others hear in the word hints of the Hebrew word for chariot, *merkabah*, and note how it appears in the biblical book of Ezekiel, a Hebrew prophet famous in part for the fantastic vision that launches the book. As Ezekiel tells it, cherubim are an integral part of the flying vehicle transporting a mystical likeness of the throne of God.

Whatever their origins, the biblical cherubim are more daunting than darling, more fierce than friendly. Lest Adam and Eve try to sneak back into the paradisiacal Garden of Eden, God placed a "fiery, ever-turning sword" at the entrance—along with cherubim. A bunch of chubby babies, winged or not, would seem to be of little use in such circumstances. Contrary to popular opinion and many a Christmas card, the Bible's cherubim are ferocious creatures— hybrid beings not found in nature but probably informed by ancient Near Eastern iconography. They would have to be scary, serving as they did to guard the sacred. The outspread wings of cherubim atop the Ark of the Covenant formed the seat of an invisible God, *Yahweh sabaoth/tsevaot*, "LORD of hosts."[4]

Seraphim, often lumped in with cherubim, and credited with singing holy hymns, are often depicted as happy harpists whiling away eternity on fluffy clouds. In the Bible, they are more like fiery serpents. The Hebrew word *saraph* has to do with burning—again, hardly the innocuous heavenly musicians of popular lore. God sends seraphim to attack the liberated yet ungrateful Israelites, and a saraph (singular) fashioned by Moses at God's instruction would save them again.[5]

What's more, while both cherubim and seraphim fall under the category of "angel" in popular religious depictions today, neither is the same as the biblical divine messenger *malack*, usually translated into English as "angel."

And none of those terms shows up in what is popularly thought to be the origin story for the "fallen angel," Lucifer. That story actually comes from a poem about Nebuchadnezzar—in which the Babylonian king Nebuchadnezzar is the biblical *lucifer* (in Latin, see *more below*). Satan has a biblical life of his own, altogether separate from Lucifer, and indeed from any personification of evil.

The Bible's divine world is a crowded place. Along with different varieties of angels we also find medically prophylactic snakes, a talking donkey, and a curse-wielding box (the Ark). A study of all these and more could fill an entire book. Let's see how much we can cover in one chapter.

***

Serpents, snakes, adders, asps. For as long as we can tell from recorded history and even before writing itself, human beings have attributed to these slithering reptiles something more than the ordinary. Agents of both life and of death, insightfully wise and wickedly deceitful, sinister, erotic, and even divine, serpents have enjoyed complex and varied associations since ancient times. An enduring symbol of eternity is the ouroboros, an image of a snake eating its tail, the cyclical shape suggestive of that which has no end. Harry Potter is dismayed to find that he is a "Parseltongue," endowed with the ability to speak "snake" belonging only to dark wizards. And the American Medical Association's logo is a snake twined around a pole. As this chapter shows, all of those images and associations—and many more besides—have biblical precedents.

The Bible's references to supernatural snakes are intriguing and confounding, and many of those references and images lie at the root of modern portrayals. Perhaps the most famous, the serpent in the Garden of Eden, is popularly associated with Satan, though any such identification is not explicit in the story itself. There's that odd Old Testament story, mentioned earlier, about fiery biting serpents/seraphim. In it, God sends snakes to punish the desert-wandering Hebrews for their insolence. When Moses intercedes for them God capitulates by instructing him to make a stick carrying a depiction of a snake (*seraph*, in the Hebrew). It would magically heal any snake-bitten victim who looked upon it.[6] A later text calls the object Nehushtan, to reflect its brassy/brazen nature in Hebrew.[7] That story comes up again in the New Testament gospel of John as commentary for understanding Jesus's crucifixion: like Moses's snake raised up on a stick, so Jesus raised up on a tree saves from death.

Serpents with wings serve as God's attendants and celestial choir in Isaiah's image of the heavenly throne. And the Greek word for the preternaturally evil snake in the Christian book of Revelation, *drakon* the "dragon-snake," became a Romanian name (*dracu*) for the devil and ultimately a nickname for a cruel Transylvanian count named Vlad the Impaler in its Romanian diminutive form—*dracula*. By contrast, at least two early Christian sects actually associated the serpent with Jesus.[8]

Depending on how you count them, there are as few as eight or as many as eighteen Hebrew words for "snake" in the Old Testament. Only five of the forty-plus ancient Greek terms for "snake" show up in the New Testament. Many of the terms, both Hebrew and Greek, are onomatopoeias. They have a hissing-ness about them. For example, consider the Hebrew *nachash* (where the "ch" has a back-of-the-throat-clearing sound); or the Greek *ophis* or *aspis*. Not all occurrences of these words in the Bible have supernatural connotations. Some are simply snakes; yet even those straightforward creatures are sometimes identified with the extraordinary qualities. One such quality is intelligence or wisdom. Jesus is remembered as advising his disciples to be "as wise as serpents and as innocent as doves."[9] In the first few chapters of Genesis, we see how a supernatural serpent manifests that characteristic. It *knows* stuff.

In the biblical narrative, the supernatural serpent in the garden of Eden appears after the drama of division—that is, after God fashions a second human being from the *adam* who then joyously declares, "this one shall be called *isha* [woman] because out of *ish* [man] she was taken."[10] In a bit of wordplay, we meet the serpent, described in Hebrew as *arum* ("cunning, crafty, shrewd"), just after the narrator explains that the original couple was *arumim* ("naked"), yet unashamed. It's an intriguing juxtaposition not least because in Proverbs, the most wisdom-saturated biblical book, each occurrence of the adjective *arum* is favorably contrasted with stupidity or foolishness, sometimes specifically the naiveté of the young. Its Greek translation in Genesis 3:1 is the same word that Jesus uses to advise wisdom like serpents for his disciples. Should we then assume that the serpent in Genesis is a creature superior to the innocent young couple? Perhaps, but the word is as slippery as the reptile itself. In other uses of the Hebrew term, it describes a quality to be avoided.[11] And at the end of the narrative echoes in sound if not spelling relate *arum* to *arur* "cursed."

Just as the word describing the serpent isn't clearly good or bad, the snake itself continues to evade evaluation as the story proceeds. For one thing, it isn't the liar that popular tradition makes it out to be, but neither does it exactly tell the truth. The serpent opens the Bible's first dialogue with a question. It asks the woman (not yet named Eve), "Did God say, 'you [plural] shall not eat from any tree in the garden?'"

The woman's answer doesn't quote God's command verbatim. She tells the serpent, "We may eat of the fruit of the trees in the garden; but God said, 'You [plural] shall not eat of the fruit of the tree that is in the middle of the garden, nor shall you touch it, or you shall die.'" She doesn't get the command wrong so much as make it even more restrictive—even touching the forbidden tree is prohibited. Also, recall that God's original command was directed to the only human being around at the time—*adam*. There was no woman apart from *adam*. Its form of address was masculine singular (which makes sense because the noun meaning "human being" is a masculine form, not necessarily because *adam* was definitively and exclusively male). We can't appreciate that in English translations of the Hebrew text because standard English does not distinguish between singular and plural (nor between masculine and feminine) second-person forms. English uses "you" in all cases. Hebrew does make distinctions by number and gender. So as the woman accepts responsibility for observing the restriction we see how the narrator understands her—along with the man, together—to be *adam*.[12]

Plus, she gets God off the hook by deleting "on the day that you eat it" from God's original prohibition. We know how the story goes—the woman eats, shares with the man, and God kicks them out of Eden. So, we should pick up on the uncomfortable fact that the serpent's reply catches God in a lie and adds another truth. For although the woman and man do ultimately die (the serpent isn't *entirely* truthful), they don't die for several centuries—hardly what God's use of the Hebrew idiom "on that day" connotes (much less the phrase's literal sense). Also, the serpent's addition, "when you eat of it your eyes will be opened, and you will be like God [or "gods," depending on which ancient version one is reading], knowing good and evil" is confirmed by God at the story's end. "See, the *adam* has become like one of us, knowing good and evil," God declares.[13]

It would seem that the snake is privy to information about the gods that human beings don't (yet) have. Nevertheless, it is not described as divine but is rather categorized among "the wild animals that Yahweh God had made."[14] It is one of God's creatures but operates outside of and even counter to God's intention. The serpent in Paradise has special knowledge. The snake knows about knowledge that the gods have, but the story doesn't say whether the serpent actually possesses such knowledge. Does the snake know whether what it's doing is good or bad, knowledge of good and evil being a divine characteristic? Again, it's hard to tell. The narrator doesn't say.

The snake asks a question, listens to the answer, and corrects the facts. It doesn't cajole, seduce, or otherwise force the woman's hand as far as the story tells. Yet by sharing its information, the serpent in Eden mediates between humans and God, between earth and heaven. In "Graduation Day," the final episode of Season 3 of *Buffy the Vampire Slayer*, it is in the shape of a giant serpent that the evil mayor attempts to transform himself from a (sort of) human to divine. Joss Whedon may not have intended to illustrate the Eden snake's intermediary role, but in portraying the serpent as the shape of supernatural evil and an "Old One" (among the world's original beings), it becomes a bridge character between human and supernatural, between ordinary and divine, just like the snake in Genesis.

The way that the serpent in Eden tells the woman about knowledge makes it sound like a good thing. Indeed, the story raises an interesting question about the quality of the knowledge that the man and woman gained. For one thing, it implies that before they ate from the forbidden tree, they couldn't make moral judgments. We'd call that sociopathic today, like Dexter, in the television drama by that name, who is "good" in that he kills only the really bad people but who has no feelings.

Some people argue that there was no badness in Eden, and so no need for such knowledge. Or does it work the other way—that ignorance makes everything ok? Does knowledge change the shape of one's reality? It certainly can complicate things. Consider: isn't it a whole lot easier to think that God originally made humans in a perfect place, Satan tempted the woman to disobey the all-good omnipotent and omniscient God, man followed suit, and we've been sinful ever since than it is to entertain and wrestle with the ambiguities that exist in this story?

If we peel away the popular interpretations that have accreted over the centuries and look at just the story itself, it's tough to say definitively, based solely on the narrative, whether it's a bad thing that the woman and man ate the forbidden fruit. Yes, it is an act of disobedience, and God seems angry about it. But we tend to think of gaining knowledge as intrinsically good and strive to foster in children from their youngest ages a sense of right and wrong.

The story itself seems to work as a narrative of human maturity, a kind of coming of age story. The childlike innocence of the original man and woman (naturally, inevitably?) gives way to a more nuanced sense of their existence, place, and purpose. Their original naiveté is replaced by wisdom. They gain the quality of *arum* that distinguishes the serpent from all the other animals. Indeed, maybe the story is a commentary on how human beings became distinguished from other animals not only by their creation but also by their development into something more like God. Whatever the case, for good or ill, the serpent facilitates this transition.

While the serpent is midwife of sorts to the humans' passage from infantile innocence to the maturity of experience, its role in the story also leads to their death. Although the snake does not control human mortality, it is tied up with it. The serpent tells the woman that eating from the tree of the knowledge of good and evil is not fatal. Nevertheless, their doing so led to expulsion from the garden because God was worried that they would also "take from the tree of life, and eat and live forever."

This story shares with other ancient Near Eastern narratives an association of serpents (and plants) with immortality. It's an enduring connection. In the modern cult movie sequel *Anacondas: The Hunt for the Blood Orchid*, giant snakes guard the sacred flower that explorers think is the key to extending life. In the epic *Gilgamesh*, which circulated throughout the area preceding the Bible's development, and which shares other striking features in common with Genesis (notably a flood story featuring two birds), the human protagonist's effort to seize a plant conferring immortality is thwarted by a snake who steals the plant away. In the Genesis story, too, a snake is at least indirectly responsible for the reality of human death.

A final bit of serpent ambiguity: Did this supernatural snake have legs? It talks; did it walk? After the fateful snack and subsequent chain of finger-pointing, God chastises them all. The snake is cursed with going about on its belly, its face in the dust. This suggests that before that point it may have walked. The narrative isn't explicit on this point but leaves it up to the reader's imagination. Some early artistic depictions of the conversation between the woman and the snake show the snake standing on legs and feet; and of course when the snake becomes identified with the devil, well, anything goes. In this story, the snake isn't exactly evil, but it does stir things up. It is possible to interpret the story, as has been done throughout the centuries, as a commentary on the existence of an evil in the world, working to undermine God's good purpose for human beings and the earth itself. It is in that capacity that the serpent of Eden has, in the popular imagination, become one with the Prince of Darkness.

The snake in the Garden of Eden, infamous for its part in the original couple's undoing, talks and may even have walked. It is definitely supernatural, but it is not the devil, at least not as Genesis tells it—in the text it is simply "the serpent." Nevertheless, its reputation for evil and association with Satan is long and powerful.

*The Passion of the Christ*, Mel Gibson's film version of the fraught hours leading to Jesus's crucifixion, begins with an arresting scene. In a dark and gloomy wooded garden—Gethsemane, where Jesus desperately prays, a sinister robed and hooded figure appears and proceeds to confront him with whispered doubts. "Do you really believe," it hisses with an androgynous tone and cool cadence, "that one man can bear the full burden of sin? No one man can carry this burden . . . Their souls are too costly. No one. Ever. No. Never."

After Jesus nevertheless accepts his God-given charge and groans in prayer, "Your will be done," he collapses to the ground, and the camera pans to the hooded being. As s/he watches with piercing eyes, a snake slithers out from under its robe and glides toward and up onto the prostrate Jesus. Weak and gasping, Jesus rises, looks the hooded figure in the eyes, and suddenly, forcefully smashes the snake underfoot. At that, the sinister being disappears and the story resumes. It's not a scene that the Bible spells out as such, but it dramatizes popular ideas of what lies between the lines of the spare gospel narratives. Some viewers said of the movie, "it is as it was."[15] Others said, "Not so much."

There is no serpent in the New Testament's Garden of Gethsemane stories. As a matter of fact, only one of the four gospels calls the place a garden (John). Two (Matthew and Mark) say it's the place people call "oil press" (Greek *gethsemane*). And Luke simply tells that Jesus went, as was his habit when in the vicinity of Jerusalem, to the Mount of Olives. But several things conspire to make it sensible that a scene such as that in *The Passion*—a garden of trees, a snake, an evil tempter—would strike Christians as eminently true. Not only does the New Testament identify Jesus as a kind of second Adam, an Adam in reverse who would right the wrongs of humankind, but also the original temptation to challenge the will of God in the garden of Eden comes to be associated in both Jewish and Christian tradition with the Devil disguised as the snake.[16]

***

Speaking of the Devil, *satan* is not always Satan in the Bible. It's a Hebrew word, and in its earliest occurrences in the Bible, it is a description of a role, specifically an "adversary." Analogy to a prosecuting attorney seems appropriate. The best known example appears in the book of Job, where we read of the *satan* among a cohort of divine beings. The story kicks off when the *satan* poses a challenging question to God: is Job such a great guy only because you're so good to him and his life is so sweet? What would happen if . . . ? That "if" launches the drama: God gives the *satan* permission to do terrible things to Job in a kind of test: how would Job's righteousness hold up in the face of trial and tribulation? The premise is disturbing, to say the least. But for our purposes here, note that the *satan* is not God's archenemy, the personification of evil. Rather, the *satan* is among God's lackeys and responsible for pushing and prodding to determine Job's degree of righteousness. What's more, there are a couple of places in the Bible where God expressly sends a *satan*.[17]

The idea of Satan as a fallen angel named Lucifer, eloquently depicted in Milton's *Paradise Lost,* depends in part on a prophecy in the book of Isaiah in which Israel's arch-villain Nebuchadnezzar, the Babylonian king responsible for ending the monarchy and destroying the Jerusalem temple, is criticized for imagining himself to be above mere mortals. Turning Babylonian astral theology against Nebuchadnezzar, Isaiah says, "You, so high, a star of the morning, have tumbled to earth. See, you died." (I paraphrase.) "You, who imagined yourself ascending to nothing less than the throne of God are nothing but a decaying human corpse."[18] When the Hebrew Bible came to be translated into Latin, that "morning star" became "the light bringer," *lucifer*.

The more general personification of evil as an entity apart from God and in competition or at least opposition to God evolved with a theology that loosened up a bit on the matter of a radical monotheism. Responsibility for what was bad in the world could then shift to an alternative, other, supernatural being. This transition reflects the kind of dualistic thinking characteristic of Zoroastrianism, which spread in the ancient Near East in the last centuries BCE. This is the theological moment of Chronicles with its trouble-wielding Satan, the New Testament biblical reference to Satan falling from heaven, and Satan the person tempting Jesus in the wilderness, for example.[19]

Now, let's have a quick look at Numbers chapter 22. It actually brings together several relevant bits: about angels, about Satan, about the many shades of God, and about talking animals.

To recap, Balaam appears to be a kind of free-agent prophet (not Israelite), a prophet-for-hire with a reputation for effectual words. It's no wonder, then, that people who worried about the multitude of encroaching Israelites would seek him out to do his work: curse the Israelites back to the stone age. (The story takes place in the Iron Age, for the record.) Oddly, God appears to have some catching up to do, asking Balaam what just happened. Balaam fills God in: the king of Moab, Balak, wants Balaam to curse the Israelites. God says, in so many words, "Don't do it. They're blessed." Interestingly, Balaam understands God (named Elohim in this story) to be Yahweh, because he tells King Balak's emissaries that he can't do it—Yahweh has forbidden him to go and curse the Israelites. Balak increases the pressure, offering to reward him handsomely; Balaam says, "Even if Balak were to give me his house full of silver and gold, I could not go beyond the word of Yahweh." Adding to the intrigue, here he adds, "my *elohim*," my God, even though Balaam is not an Israelite.

That night God tells Balaam he can go, after all, but can only say what God tells him to say. Then, when Balaam does go, God (in a fit of what can only seem blatantly capricious, reading the story as we have it) is angry that Balaam would go.

God does not stop Balaam with speech, though Balaam seems to have taken God's words pretty seriously to this point, but sends a divine messenger, often translated into English as "angel," though the Hebrew *malakh* means simply "messenger" and is used in the Bible of human messengers as well. Balaam, the heretofore conscientious prophet, cannot see God's messenger trying to stop him. But his donkey can. The donkey tries to avoid the messenger-angel, doing as God wants, turning away. In the process Balaam gets bumped and bruised. This ticks Balaam off, especially when the donkey simply lies down.

Then, we read, Yahweh made it possible for the donkey to speak. She asks Balaam why he keeps hitting her.[20] Rather than expressing astonishment that his donkey is suddenly speaking full, sensible sentences, Balaam answers, leading the donkey to defend herself by calling Balaam's behavior into question. Balaam concedes that the donkey is usually compliant and therefore must have a good reason to disobey him now. Sure enough, suddenly Balaam is able to see the messenger of Yahweh, standing there, sword in hand. Balaam recognizes and repents while the divine messenger chastises him for mistreating the donkey. The divine messenger explains, "Because I [speaking as Yahweh] don't want you to go, I came out to be a *satan*." So now Yahweh expressly says that God is a *satan*.

The donkey did the right thing, which God tells Balaam saved his life. And Balaam does what seems sensible. He says to God, "Sorry, I didn't know you were trying to stop me. I'll turn around as you wish."

But the divine messenger says, "No, go on. But only what I say should you say." The narrator doesn't tell us, but it's hard to imagine that Balaam might not be a little confused or at least a little skittish. After all, we've been through this before: God saying don't go. Balaam not going. God saying, okay go. Balaam going and God getting mad at him for going. It seems reasonable that Balaam would wonder whether this is just the latest flip-flop from God, leaving Balaam to suffer the consequences. Balaam takes the risk and goes, and much to Balak's chagrin doesn't curse the Israelites but stays true to his commitment to speak only what Yahweh tells him, blessing the Israelites instead.[21] Now, lest you think that Balaam turns out to be a great guy in the biblical estimation, note that he still undermines the Israelites on Balak's behalf by getting them to curse themselves.

***

A talking ass may seem pretty weird, but the Bible is actually chock-full of stuff like that. Balaam's donkey is the least of it. Darren Aronofsky's movie *Noah*, based on the biblical hero of the Flood, contains any number of elements that have caused people to ask, "Is that really in the Bible?" Most perplexing to viewers were the six-limbed creatures that one viewer called "crazy giant rock monsters."[22] These "Watchers" do derive from a biblical story, but Aronofsky took quantum leaps of artistic license in portraying them.

Make of the movie what you will, the Bible is plenty weird enough. In Genesis 6:1–4, we read that after human beings began to proliferate, the "sons of God" were attracted to the "daughters of man." Let me stop right there for a second.

The story gets crazy so fast that a reader might miss the whole "sons of God" part. The construction in Hebrew that leads to this literal translation is a common idiom meaning just that: biological offspring. But "sons of X" can also mean (and frequently does) "belonging to group X," that is, a category not limited to genetic makeup. Either way, we've got another example of the presumed existence of divine beings in addition to any single God—complicating the whole notion of biblical monotheism. Hold that thought.

As the story continues, we read that these (masculine) divine beings found (feminine) human beings attractive and took them as wives. That it's a one-way action suggests that the women didn't have a choice in the matter (i.e., the godlings raped them), but the Bible, as is so often the case, doesn't clarify. What we *do* read is that children were born from this divine-human mash-up, hybrids whom the narrator of this story calls "mighty men who were of old, the men of renown."

What does this have to do with Aronofsky's Watchers? There's another ancient (third century BCE) version of the events in Genesis 5–6 in which fallen angels called Watchers mated with women. The story is attributed to the biblical Enoch, from "the seventh generation of Adam," remarkable for not having died a normal death.[23] Instead he "walked with God, then he was no more, because God took him."[24] Anyway, divine-human offspring, according to this book of Enoch, were "the heroes that were of old, warriors of renown." Enoch calls them Nephilim. In the book of Enoch, they cause all sorts of trouble and terror, fomenting corruption and evil to such a degree that God floods it all away. The book of Enoch is not biblical in most canons.

In the biblical account, in the middle of the strange divine-human romance narrative, we read, "The *nephilim* were on the earth in those days, and also afterward," after the hybrids came along.[25] Whether or not the nephilim were related to the hybrids, the Bible doesn't say explicitly, but you can see how Enoch would make the connection. The word itself means "fallen ones." Because the Flood story comes so soon after this, people infer that the nephilim or hybrid human-gods were part of the problem. (Enoch implicates them completely.) The actual biblical description is only (albeit briefly) positive.

Incidentally, there are no helpful rock giants in the Bible.

*** 

And yet. The Bible does have its own odd, supernaturally helpful-rock stories. Remember the extraordinary number of people liberated from Egypt who then set out into the Sinai Desert, heading for their new home in "the land of milk and honey"? The Bible tells how Moses led some 600,000 men, children, and a lot of animals.[26] Subsequent narratives assume that there were women, too. That's a lot of living things needing food and water. What's more, since God determined that that complaining generation would die off before entering the Promised Land, they needed food and water for forty years. If you've ever visited the Sinai Peninsula or have even seen pictures of it, you can imagine the logistical nightmare of providing for the reportedly hundreds of thousands of people who left Egypt along with livestock (which the text notes were many), for four decades.[27] Enter the rock.

When they stepped into the wilderness, at a place called Rephidim, the Israelites complained to Moses that there wasn't enough to drink. They grew angry enough that Moses felt his life was threatened, so he appealed to God. God directed Moses to strike a rock on which God was standing and water would come out of it. Sure enough, water flowed. At any rate, this was just the beginning of forty years in the desert. *Forty years*. But the next time we hear of Moses striking a rock for water, it's at the end of their time in the wilderness. (And proves fateful to Moses, who was then judged unfit to enter the Promised Land. He had overstepped his authority, apparently.) This rock, at a place called Kadesh, again yielded water. Weird.

Ancient rabbis, noting this oddity—the reappearance of a gushing rock at the end of the forty-year Sinai journey—concluded that the rock had traveled with them. It was a mobile reservoir of sorts. Centuries later, Paul (who knew these stories inside and out) reinterpreted them in light of what he believed about Jesus. Paul wrote, "For they drank from the spiritual rock that followed them, and the rock was Christ."[28]

\*\*\*

Like these rocks, the talking donkey, and the snakes, most superstrange beings in the Bible get barely a wink from the narrators to recognize their oddity. Take the fish that swallowed Jonah. Yes, fish—it's not called a whale in the Hebrew. We might expect, hope, to hear more about this extraordinary being that could swallow a man and then spit him up again, unharmed, three days later. But no. The story simply relates that after Jonah had convinced his fellow mariners (a righteous bunch, despite their foreign status, the narrator goes to lengths to point out) to throw him overboard, we read simply that "YHWH provided a large fish to swallow up Jonah; and Jonah was in the belly of the fish three days and three nights."[29]

Then there's Leviathan, a dragon-like, enormous sea-beast that shows up in the books of Isaiah, Psalms, and Job in the context of telling how powerful the creator God is. Probably related to the primordial Lothan of Ugaritic tradition, the biblical Leviathan is subject to defeat by God.[30] It's in Job that we also meet the awesome Behemoth, described in a way that has led some to think it may have been inspired by a rhinoceros or hippopotamus.[31] Neither the Leviathan nor the Behemoth are dinosaurs. There are no dinosaurs in the Bible, except by reading them into the text, as some do.

The Ark—not Noah's, but the Ark of the Covenant—was said to house the terms of the agreement that God made with the Hebrews. As such, it was a means by which the holy, un-image-able God could be present to God's people, first as they wandered the Sinai Peninsula, then when they settled in the land of Canaan, and finally after Solomon had built the temple in Jerusalem. Made of acacia wood and covered in gold, it was carefully veiled from direct sight as it moved with the people through the wilderness. Two golden cherubim stood guard over it, and from there, Moses spoke with God.[32]

The Ark was no mere precious object but shows up in several narratives as possessing extraordinary powers. It was somehow instrumental in bringing down Jericho's walls, proved fatal to its keepers upon capture, and was a source of painful hemorrhoids and a plague of mice to its Philistine captors.[33] Escorted into the new Jerusalem of David's monarchy, a powerful symbol uniting Israel's tribes, it once killed a man, Uzzah, who spontaneously reached out to steady it was promptly smitten dead, apparently for presuming to touch it without proper permission.[34] After Solomon built the temple, the Ark resided in that holy space's most holy space. It's a mystery what happened to the Ark when the Babylonians destroyed the temple in 587 BCE. There is no mention of it—its escape, capture, or destruction—in biblical texts, leading to all sorts of theories and stories, including, of course, *Raiders of the Lost Ark*.

\*\*\*

If you do an internet search on demons in the Bible, as I recently did, you'll unearth citations from both the Hebrew Bible and the New Testament (not as many from books of the Apocrypha, since most of these websites are for Protestants, for whom those books are not part of the Bible) and no small degree of warning that demons want *you*. A closer look at the particular texts reveals how people have—without appreciating literary, historical, or even theological context—lumped diverse supernatural beings or forces together under the category "demon," usually with the warning that these same malevolent forces continue to seek purchase in the modern world. Let the reader beware.

Recalling how the Bible developed and evolved over many centuries and reading these texts within their larger literary contexts makes it easy to see how misleading such treatment is. As I noted earlier, the very notion of a *satan*, as opposed to Satan personified, reflects vastly different times and places. Indeed, the strict dualisms we find in the New Testament—good versus evil, the difficult present versus the future redemption, heaven versus earth—were less pronounced when the texts of the Hebrew Bible were composed but became prevalent in the centuries straddling Jesus's birth. In the Dead Sea Scrolls we read about the war between the "Sons of Darkness" and the "Sons of Light." It's no surprise, then, to read in Paul's letters, the Gospels, and other New Testament books of wars between supernatural principalities and powers.

But this idea of demons as evil mischief-makers that could possess a person with malevolent spiritual forces and cause all sorts of trouble doesn't fit the whole Bible. For example, to call the evil spirit that tormented King Saul (many centuries before Jesus's time) a demon is not only anachronistic but misleading.

Note that unlike demons, which are thought to be distinct from God and stand over and against anything right and good, the evil spirit that tormented Saul is explicitly identified as coming from God. This is not a separate malevolent force. In the Hebrew, this spirit is named both *ruach elohim* (the same as the creative force in Genesis 1:2) and *ruach YHWH*, "spirit of the LORD." In Hebrew it is called unequivocally *ra'ah*, "evil, bad." To call it a demon, then, is to read much later ideas into this ancient text. Note that the Greek translation of 1 Samuel 16:14–23 likewise reads the tormenting spirit not as a *daimon(ion)* but as *pneuma poneron*, "bad/evil spirit" from God.

In the Hebrew Bible, we read of "false gods," idols, and false prophets, each of which poses the danger of leading God's people astray. But nowhere are they called "demons" or described as supernatural beings that stand against God or the people of God. They are to be avoided and ignored as terribly dangerous to the people's relationship to God, but not as separate supernatural entities that could get inside a person in the manner of New Testament demons.

The word "demon" itself comes from the Greek *daimon*, which connotes a divine being but doesn't automatically assign it moral status, bad or good. It's in the New Testament's Greek that we find the term *daimonion*, which personifies evil in the way we associate today with the word "demon." A named demon, Asmodeus, plays a significant role in the story the book of Tobit (apocryphal) tells. But in only two places in the Hebrew Bible does the Septuagint translate *daimonion*.[35] And in both cases, the Hebrew behind it is *shedim*, likely a loanword from the Akkadian *shedu*, a term for particular protective spirits that took on a more sinister sense in the Hebrew as the wrongful recipients of sacrifices.

By contrast, the New Testament has over sixty instances of the word. Mary Magdalene is said in two Gospels to have been exorcised of demons by Jesus, after which she followed him.[36] What was the nature of these demons? The texts don't say, and the demons' sometime association with the seven deadly sins is a much later Christian development.

Matthew, Mark, and Luke each have a version of the story of Jesus casting afflicting demons into pigs. In Mark, the "demoniac" is named "Legion" and said to be tormented by "unclean spirits."[37] Matthew tells of two demoniacs and calls their tormentors "demons."[38] In Luke, these characteristics are combined: there is one demoniac called Legion, and the afflicting powers are called both "unclean spirits" and "demons."[39] The stories toggle without explanation between referring to a single force and plural forces. Here, as in many biblical cases, demons are portrayed as responsible for particular ailments as benign as a fever that we today, with the benefit of modern science, can identify with medical diagnoses.

In Acts, Luke tells another possession story about a recalcitrant "evil spirit." The word *daimonion* never appears. Rather, the afflicting force is called *pneumata ponera*, "evil spirits." Even though the exorcists invoke "the name of the Lord Jesus," the evil spirit claims they don't have the proper credibility, resists their efforts, and attacks the exorcists in return. The narrator identifies the exorcists as Jews of a particular (possibly self-described) priestly family, suggesting that the "name of Jesus" doesn't work if the people wielding it are not genuine Jesus-followers.[40]

\*\*\*

But enough of evil. Let's end this chapter instead with angels. The English word is a transliteration of the Latin *angelus*, itself from the Greek *aggelos/angelos*, which is how the Septuagint translates the Hebrew *malakh*, which means simply "messenger." As noted in the discussion of Balaam's donkey, a *malakh* could be human or divine and wasn't necessarily anything out of the ordinary. Even more surprising to us, accustomed to thinking of angels as sparkly beings with wings and Satan as the personification of evil, a biblical "angel" could be a *satan*, simply an adversary functioning on God's behalf.[41] Some English translations and interpretations read cherubim and seraphim as "angels," though the vocabulary is distinct and their functions different from each other and from a *malakh*, too.

While individual angels behaving in ways familiar to modern readers appear within the Apocryphal books of Tobit and Enoch, it's only with the book of Daniel, the latest book in the Hebrew Bible (it dates from the second century BCE), that we get astonishing angels flying to human beings as divine intercessors in the Hebrew Bible and Protestant Old Testament. They also, for the first time within the Hebrew Bible, are individuals with names: Gabriel and Michael. Gabriel, meaning "God is my strong man/hero," interprets Daniel's visions, lending particular insight.[42] And Michael, meaning "Who is like God," is described as leading the battle of heavenly forces against those associated with Daniel's enemies.[43] Both of these characteristics are relatively late developments in the Hebrew Bible's historical and cultural contexts.

Angels of the sort we imagine today, clearly distinguishable from human beings, are more common in New Testament texts. An angel Gabriel (re)appears twice in the New Testament, in both cases in the Gospel of Luke: first to announce Jesus's coming to the elderly priest Zechariah and to say that Zechariah's wife Elizabeth would bear her own baby, John (the Baptist); the second time to tell Mary that she'll be the mother of Jesus.[44] Nowhere in the Bible does Gabriel blow a horn, though later art often depicts him that way.[45] There's an archangel Michael in Jude 1:9, and an angel of the pit named Abaddon in Revelation 9:11. That's it for named angels in the New Testament.

That said, unnamed angels appear throughout. They communicate through dreams, come from heaven, and attend to Jesus.[46]

In Matthew's Gospel, a terrifying shiny angel comes down from heaven, rolls away the stone of Jesus's tomb, and speaks to Mary Magdalene and the other women.[47] In Luke, it's two dazzling men, not called angels, who tell the women of Jesus's resurrection.[48]

Of the Bible's strange beings, even angels defy easy categorization.

# Chapter 5

# Good People Behaving Badly

I suppose you could say that it started with Eve—Eve and that darn apple. Everything was going so well, perfectly, even. But without trouble, there's no story. So, on the other hand, you could say that without Eve there'd be no Greatest Story Ever Told. Whatever the case, it's safe to say that the first good-people-behaving-badly that we find in the Bible are the first couple, created to live in an orchard of endless beauty and delight, reverently tending it and guarding its welfare. They couldn't be anything but good until Eve, after a bit of thoughtful debate and reasoning, ate the forbidden fruit, and Adam, without either thoughtful debate or reasoning, followed suit.

Like Adam and Eve in that story, other supposedly good biblical characters, even the greatest of the heroes of the Bible, have bad sides, too. It certainly keeps things interesting. And it ought to keep us from holding up any of them as a perfect role model without nuance and qualification. A quick caveat of my own: discussion of the following examples is necessarily incomplete—there is a lot of bad behavior in the Bible.

***

Noah is a popular boys' name these days, and it's not hard to see why. Genesis relates that Noah and his family were spared from an otherwise global eradication of earthly life because he was such a great guy. Noah was, as the narrative tells, "a righteous man, blameless in his generation; he walked with God."[1] It's hard to get better than that. The Hebrew behind that English holds no surprises. The word translated "blameless" comes from a Hebrew word meaning "completeness" or "soundness," that is, "with integrity." The idiom of walking with God usually functions metaphorically to describe a way of being and living that's in keeping with God's expectations and wishes.[2] Despite five centuries of life during which he might have misstepped in his walk with God or otherwise compromised his integrity, Noah was even at this hoary age still without fault.[3]

So when God came to regret creating human beings and determined to put a watery end to the whole bloody lot of them, God selected Noah, the one in whom God had "found favor," to build an ark, gather the animals, weather the storm, and eventually repopulate the earth. It's particularly striking, then, that after all that, Noah went off the rails.

As the story goes, once he was back on solid ground, and with the wine to celebrate, Noah overdid it. In his stupor, he got naked. When his son Ham happened upon the sight, and (it's hard to say exactly what happened next, if anything; the text doesn't explain) Noah was furious. He cursed the son of that youngest son soundly. Astute readers will wonder, why attack the boy Canaan if Ham's to blame? That Canaan is Ham's son hardly answers the question, but it has provided (weak) justification for arguing that the curse wasn't specific to that family in that moment but holds for generations to come.

Indeed, we're still dealing with the fallout today. Noah's curse has been interpreted as divine (itself a stretch, since this is Noah, not God) justification for enslaving people of African descent, since Ham's lineage is said (itself on thin evidence) to have populated Africa.[4] The logic (such as it is; it leaves much to be desired) goes like this: Because Noah cursed Canaan, saying, "Lowest of slaves shall he be to his brothers," so it should be. And for all time, even including the outrageous racial inequity that still exists today. Such interpreters conveniently overlook many details, not least the fact that the biblical curse says nothing about subjugation in perpetuity.

***

The next most significant character we meet in Genesis, and one of the all-time biblical greats, has a few foibles of his own: Abraham, or Abram, as his name starts out. God singled out Abraham for special favor that would extend into the indefinite future. It is to Abraham that Yahweh makes the threefold enduring promises said to extend to all Israel forever: upon getting up and going where Yahweh directs, God promises that Abraham will become the ancestor of millions, people who will have a country of their own, and who will be a means through which other peoples experience blessing.[5] (This last is just as convoluted in the Hebrew as that sentence makes it seem.)

So Abraham is really the first of the chosen people. And he's a good guy. For the most part. When hard times hit the land of Canaan, Abraham shuttles his family to Egypt, always the spot for a good meal in ancient times. (Thank you, serene and steady Nile.) Egypt is also always the spot for Israelite anxiety. Abraham is no exception.

With echoes of how Abraham has been singled out by God for this astonishing promise (including future children with his wife, Sarah) still ringing in our ears, Abraham takes a somewhat inexplicable turn.[6] Worried that the Egyptian king might take a liking to Sarah and kill Abraham to have her (quite a leap of logic, but worry will do that to a person), Abraham tells Sarah to pretend that she's his sister. Then, if Pharaoh wants her, he can take her!

And Pharaoh does. So it is that Abraham consigns his wife to sexual service in the Egyptian palace. The narrator says that Abraham acquires all sorts of bounty in the exchange, which hardly seems right. But rather than punish Abraham, God afflicts Pharaoh. So Pharaoh confronts Abraham, asking why Abraham duped him, and begs Abraham to take Sarah back. Abraham does, and they leave, with all the stuff Abraham had gotten in Egypt. The narrator tells *readers* that it was "on account of Sarah" (Hebrew: *al-devar*) but never explains how Pharaoh figured out that Sarah was the reason for his court's suffering, and it never shows a repentant Abraham.

Actually, Abraham does this again—passes off his wife as his sister in order to save his neck.[7] In chapter 20, it is King Abimelech of Gerar who is duped by Abraham's say-you-are-my-sister act. Again, God confronts not Abraham but Abimelech with dire threats should the unwitting king not return Sarah to her rightful husband. Adding to Abraham's censure, as far as we're concerned, both of these incidents occur before Sarah ever bears Abraham a single one of the descendants that God had promised. In other words, Abraham plays fast and loose with God's explicit promise. Note that in neither case did Abraham ever do anything of his own to get Sarah back.

\*\*\*

Speaking of Sarah, I wish I could redeem the stories of her relationship to her slave.[8] I would love to say that the relationship has a happy ending, that Sarah comes out heroically, having stood up for the humiliated and oppressed, that the lowly are raised up and those who suffer indignity or abuse are vindicated, and finally everybody gets along. Not so. It has its moments, this story, but the mother of all Israel, the great Sarah, wife of Abraham, isn't much of a heroine in these instances. If anyone emerges from the fray of that relationship carrying the flag of a reader's sympathy, it is Hagar, the Egyptian slave, belittled and abused. But even Hagar is ultimately stripped of autonomy and initiative by a resolutely patriarchal, hierarchical telling.

At this story's beginning, Sarah is an old woman and still hasn't borne any children, despite the promise God gave to her husband that he would have descendants more numerous than anyone could possibly count.[9] The narrator tells us that Sarah incites the subsequent dramatic action by reasoning, "Because Yahweh has prevented me from bearing children . . ." With such an intro, we readers should suspect that what follows is not exactly as God would have had things go. After all, Sarah would seem to be going against God (but in order to fulfill God's promise). What she does is tell Abraham (here Abram) to have sex with her slave, Hagar. "Maybe I'll be built up from her," Sarah says, expressly claiming that Hagar's children would legally count as Sarah's, since Sarah owns Hagar.[10] That ugliness is just the beginning.

Hagar does conceive, and it turns out that legality is not enough. Hagar looks down on the barren Sarah, who, rather than finding solidarity with Hagar or comfort that this surrogate mother has accomplished what Sarah had set out to do, seethes with antipathy for her slave. Sarah blames Abraham, who replies simply that she should do with her Egyptian slave what is "good in your eyes." The narrator continues, "And Sarah afflicted her."[11] Ironically, the verb, a hard one, is the same as the one used to describe the Hebrews' oppression by the Egyptians.

So brutal is Sarah's treatment of Hagar that Hagar runs away. It would seem that she's going to make it—she is near the Egyptian border and has access to fresh water—when a messenger from God meets her and tells her to go back "and suffer affliction under [Sarah's] hand," which sounds simply cruel.[12]

Hagar does go back, but not before this divine messenger makes her the first woman to receive an annunciation. The messenger tells Hagar that she'll have a son and that his name will be Ishmael, and she's told about his future. Then, she audaciously names God (El Roi, "God of seeing"). Hagar is the only person in the Bible to do so.

The women's story resumes in chapter 21, where we read that Sarah is again angry at Hagar because, it seems, of how Ishmael and Isaac play.[13] This time, Sarah demands that Abraham cast Hagar out. Abraham doesn't like the sound of it, but God sides with Sarah and tells Abraham to get rid of Hagar. God assures Abraham that

Ishmael will nevertheless become "a nation, for he is [Abraham's] descendant."[14]

Abraham sends Hagar and Ishmael packing. This time Hagar's circumstances in the wilderness are rather more grim. Things get so bad for her and for her son that she leaves him to die. Weeping, she removes herself, sparing herself from witnessing his death. God comes to Ishmael's rescue, and presumably Hagar's too, since she lives to find an (Egyptian) wife for Ishmael. We don't know the details, though, or anything more about this remarkable woman because the narrative returns, as it has so many times throughout these women's stories, to center on the fathers and sons.

\*\*\*

One of those sons, Jacob, is the next after Isaac to receive the three-fold blessing (of descendants, homeland, and a means of others' gaining blessing) that God first granted to Abraham. Jacob—he's alternatively called "Israel," whose twelve sons give rise to the twelve tribes that compose God's chosen nation—was hardly a consistently upstanding guy. On the contrary, the first we read of Jacob doing anything is when he deceives his father to steal the benefits that rightfully belonged to Jacob's brother, Esau.

As the story goes, Jacob and Esau are twins, but Esau emerges first, making him the eldest and so having special inheritance rights. When their father, Isaac, is old and blind, Jacob pretends to be Esau and tricks his father into giving him what should have been Esau's. It's an irrevocable blessing.[15]

What's more, the much-praised Rebecca, Jacob's mother, assists in the deception. Only the grimmer elderly, blind Isaac calls the act wrong and laments that he cannot make it right. Surely Esau's rage is understandable, though readers ultimately sympathize with the main character of this set of stories, Jacob, who runs away.

The deceiver is himself deceived when Laban sneaks his eldest daughter into Jacob's marriage bed rather than the younger, desired

Rachel (whom Jacob will subsequently marry, too). Before all is said and done, Jacob outwits Laban, this time manipulating the breeding pattern of goats in order to enrich himself before setting out toward the land of his birth, where, in a remarkable act of forgiveness and generosity, Esau welcomes his lying, cheating brother.

Along the way, readers learn that Jacob's wife Rachel has deceived everyone by stealing and hiding religious objects from her father's house. This without the knowledge of Jacob, who unwittingly promises the pursuing Laban, "Anyone with whom you find your gods [the religious objects] shall not remain alive."[16] In the ensuing search, Rachel successfully hides the objects, and that's the last we hear of them, which itself is odd given how much excoriating criticism "having other gods" and such religious objects gets in much of the rest of the Bible.

***

Judah, the ancestor of arguably the most important tribe of Israel—the tribe out of which King David comes with the enduring promise of God's favor on his monarchical line—was a bit of a louse. After all, he masterminded the plan to get rid of his brother Joseph, not caring whether it was by kidnapping or murder, when Joseph was just a boy. Sure, Joseph was an annoyance to his older brothers, and their father's favoritism toward this youngest son hardly endeared Joseph to the others. But dispatching the boy as Judah advised the brothers do—selling him off to passing travelers—is hardly an upstanding fraternal thing to do.[17]

Judah fails to do the right thing again, by his own admission, in a peculiar story embedded in the greater Joseph tale. There, Judah willfully neglects to see to the welfare of his widowed daughter-in-law, Tamar (#1; there's another Tamar later). Tamar takes matters into her own hands and catches Judah in quite a lie: he seeks to have her executed because she has gotten pregnant out of wedlock, but in a shocking twist, she reveals that the child is Judah's. Judah admits his guilt, even claiming, "She is more in the right than I."[18] Incidentally, Matthew lionizes this Tamar among the (only) four women named in his genealogy of Jesus at the beginning of that Gospel, each of whom was subject to questions about her sexual activity.[19]

\*\*\*

And then there's Moses, the only one ever to speak to God face to face, the great liberator, lawgiver, and all-around hero. Tradition attributes the Bible's first five books to him. He is the sea-splitting prophet par excellence. Yet the very first thing we hear about Moses after his infancy is how he murdered someone.

Our biblical Moses goes directly from his wicker hamper to assault and manslaughter. He beats a man to death and hides the body, hoping to get away with it. In a screenplay, that moment might be the crucial "inciting incident," the moment that really kicks off the story. But you'd never know it for how little attention that moment gets today.

Remember that Moses was born to a Hebrew woman at a time when, according to an executive order from the Egyptian pharaoh, all Hebrew boy babies were to be killed. Moses's mother secreted him as long as she could, then set him adrift (carefully supervised by his sister) on the Nile to be "discovered" by Pharaoh's daughter. Moses's sister suggested to her that there might be a Hebrew woman who could nurse him (what a coincidence!), and so Moses's mother got paid to nurse her own baby. But I digress. The point is that Moses, though Hebrew, was raised to be a good Egyptian royal.

Side note here. For all the Bible's man-centered-ness and general patriarchal assumptions sprinkled with passages of downright misogyny, it portrays some remarkable women as well. This story is chock-full of them. We read first about the Hebrew midwives Shiphrah and Puah. The fact that the midwives have names in the story is almost as remarkable as their heroic actions in defying authority to save babies. Moses's mother, his sister, and Pharaoh's daughter are each instrumental in preserving his life.

Then, immediately after the infancy narrative, we read another strange tale.[20] In it, Moses is already a full-fledged adult. Apparently Pharaoh's daughter had raised the boy with full knowledge of his Hebrew background because we read that he "went out to his kinsfolk" and saw an Egyptian beating a Hebrew, "one of his kinsmen." (Questions abound in these texts. For one, Pharaoh wanted to kill all Hebrew boys but acquiesces to raise one under his own roof?) The assault led Moses to kill the Egyptian, but not before Moses checked to see if the coast was clear.

Turns out, it was not. And when Moses confronted a Hebrew man for pummeling another Hebrew, the man said, "What, are you going to kill me like you did the Egyptian?"[21] Moses was right to be afraid. The news made it to Pharaoh, who deemed Moses's offense deserving of capital punishment. This time, Moses saves his own life. He runs away. There we have our great lawgiver.

Moses's committing murder really gets the story going. We see Moses siding with the Hebrews against the Egyptians, for one thing. Also, it ultimately sends him into the wilderness, where he'll meet his mentor, the Midian priest Reuel (alternatively called Jethro), meet his wife Zipporah (daughter of Jethro/Reuel), and happen upon the burning bush, whence God calls him to go back to Pharaoh and demand all the Hebrews' release. With so many dramatic moments, we rarely remember the murder part.

\*\*\*

Consider, too, Moses's brother. Aaron is so hugely important a religious leader that he's named Israel's high priest and ancestor of all subsequent high priests of Israel. Yet this is the same Aaron who is implicated in the great Golden Calf scandal. It is none other than Aaron who calls for the people to give him their gold jewelry for him to smelt into an object for them to worship.

According to the story, the newly liberated people felt abandoned by Moses, who'd gone up the mountain (Sinai, alternatively called Horeb) to get the famous stone tablets. Feeling forlorn and not a little impatient, the people down below ask Aaron to make a god for them. The narrator leaves wiggle room in the text for readers to conclude that Aaron was pushed into it, but it's hardly convincing. Aaron comes up with the idea, after all, and shows absolutely no sign of opposition.

Even when Moses confronts him, asking, "What did this people do to you that you have brought such great sin upon them?" (basically giving Aaron an out), Aaron simply says what we already know—that when the people asked for a god, he gave them one.[22] And he adds, "We all know they're bad people."[23] So much for religious leadership.

*\*\*\**

Abraham, Moses, and David might be considered the Big Three of Hebrew Bible–Old Testament heroes: Abraham, the one to whom God first made a binding promise to a particular people (Christians and Muslims also consider Abraham to be their original patriarch); Moses, the one through whom God forged a people-of-God; and David, the one to whom God promised kingship in his lineage forever. People, religion, nation—the biblical basis for each is on these three men, respectively.

Yet, like Abraham and Moses, David was not perfect. The best known example of his foibles, even failings, is his taking the lovely Bathsheba to bed despite the fact that she was married to someone else—to a righteous general in David's army, no less. David as good as murdered Uriah, Bathsheba's husband, by assigning him to the front line in a battle sure to be fatal. Adultery and murder. Add to that willful parental negligence regarding his daughter's rape by her brother, and you're flirting with the definition of a villain. Nevertheless, the biblical narrative tells us that David was beloved by God from the word go. He is remembered for defeating the Philistine giant Goliath (and later, by extension, the whole Philistine machine, even though he served as a mercenary in their army) and for really cementing the whole national enterprise.[24]

It was to David alone that God made the remarkable, unconditional promise of kingship for his descendants forevermore.[25] That promise came with no strings—God would see to it that it would always be so—which made the destruction of Israel by the Babylonians in the sixth century BCE especially problematic theologically. Later biblical editors would revise the story of God's promise to David, adding conditions that make the nation's defeat and loss of the land God's punishment for the people's wickedness.[26]

Later still, biblical writers revised David's profile in light of the Babylonian catastrophe by prioritizing his role in the temple over his monarchy. That is, it doesn't take a particularly close reading of the books of Chronicles to discover a quite different profile of David than we find in the books of Samuel and Kings. For example, Chronicles skips in deafening silence right over the whole Bathsheba episode.[27] What's more, Chronicles portrays David less as the nation's commander in chief and more as someone concerned with religious matters, especially the laying of the groundwork for the temple, even including the details of its choir.[28]

\*\*\*

The man who actually got that temple built—David's son and successor, Solomon—is yet another example of a superstar with issues. You may have heard the expression "as wise as Solomon." Maybe you already know that the biblical book of Proverbs is attributed to Solomon, as is the philosophy of Ecclesiastes. He's also remembered as quite the lover. Song of Songs, a biblical book of erotic love poetry, is attributed to him, and the Bible tells us that he married many women from a number of other countries.

This was shrewd politically—such marriages facilitated international alliances—but it was theologically problematic. It made God angry—not the polygamy so much as Solomon's hospitality. Solomon built "high places," where these foreign women could worship their (foreign) gods, gods whom King Solomon also began to worship. This did not go over well with Yahweh. As a matter of fact, it was enough to undo the nation, according to the biblical texts as they've come down to us. It's hard to say much for sure about the era during which Solomon was king, but some biblical texts suggest that building religious sites for his foreign wives was, at the time, more to be expected than reviled.

But centuries later, it became important to explain why the nation and the temple fell to the Babylonians. And the explanation, according to those responsible for our biblical texts, could not be that it was God's fault. Actually, God had to orchestrate it, and justifiably. In other words, logic required that the people had done some terrible things along the way to merit this final destructive act. So the originally unconditional promise made to David becomes conditional, thereby justifying defeat of the monarchy and loss of the land to the Babylonians.[29]

***

While we're on the topic of Israel's earliest kings: What about Saul, you might ask. After all, here's a guy anointed by God to lead, yet who behaves so badly that God removes God's spirit from Saul and replaces it with an evil spirit.[30] Yes, the greater narrative portrays a king chosen by God who nevertheless strays from the path of righteousness. The problem for readers today is that the thing Saul is expressly accused of (taking some spoils from battle, the crime that warrants this spirit swap) is something that later kings in the Bible will do with impunity. In the greater biblical drama Saul strikes me as a dramatically tragic figure. From the very beginning, when we read competing narratives of Saul being chosen king (standing out as excellent, tall, and bold, versus his less than impressively hiding among some baggage) to his making way for the great king David, Saul takes some pretty low blows.[31]

***

It was time for class, Introduction to the Hebrew Bible, which convened in a windowless room, packed to within a jot of the fire code, and as always with a diverse mix of students with widely varying interests and investment in the material. The student I'm remembering, in this case with a cringe, was an earnest youth, a dedicated student, who stopped me in the hall during the break (it was a long class) to say, "My wife delivered our first baby last night— a boy. We named him Jonah." My congratulations were pure, even as my gut churned. We stepped back into the classroom. On the syllabus, the prophet Jonah was next up. Bad timing.

Jonah is one of the Hebrew Bible's books of the prophets, among the twelve "minor" prophets, minor not in significance but simply in length. They include such heavy-hitters as Amos, "Let justice well up like water, righteousness like an ever-flowing stream"; Micah, "What does the LORD require of you . . . but to do justice, love kindness, and walk humbly with your God"; Hosea, "I will heal their affliction; generously I will take them back in love"; and Malachi, whose messianic anticipation brings the Christian Old Testament to a close.[32] One could be excused for thinking any book, any prophet in such a line-up, would be admirable enough to name one's firstborn after. But that's not the case with Jonah.

Unlike these other prophets, who launch immediately into their work with "Thus sayeth the LORD, '[This]'" and "Thus sayeth the LORD, '[That],'" Jonah bolted. Every other prophet, no matter how resistant they may have felt, delivered God's word as required. Not Jonah. He ran away, slipping onto a ship in an effort to get away from God. In his defense, when God sends a storm toward the ship, putting all its passengers in danger, Jonah *does* urge his fellow sailors, despite their generous protest, to throw him overboard to save themselves. It worked, as far as we know. The narrator turns our attention to the fish that swallows Jonah and, three days later, vomits him up on land, to try the whole prophecy business again. This time Jonah proceeds as directed.

But when Jonah finally gets to Nineveh, where God had originally ordered him to go, he rather listlessly delivers his prophetic message of repentance. It's the least persuasive bit of preaching that we've got among these books of prophets. Others ardently deliver speech after speech in efforts to sway, cajole, rebuke, and comfort. Yet Jonah, commissioned to prophesy to an enemy to rebuke their wicked ways (catnip for a biblical prophet), delivers a mere single line: "Forty days more, and Nineveh shall be overthrown."[33] And it works! Unlike the effect from every other prophet, Jonah's audience indeed repents, immediately and with nearly cartoonish enthusiasm, from the king on down to the lowliest citizen, and beyond even that to the cattle, who don apologetic sackcloth just like everybody else.

So God refrains from punishing the city after all. But Jonah, instead of seeing this as a success, pouts, complaining that he went to all this trouble and claiming that he *knew* God would forgive them. Jonah is so bothered by the whole thing that he says he wishes simply to die. The book ends with a gentle chastisement for Jonah's small-mindedness.

\*\*\*

By contrast to the name Jonah, Mary is a deservedly popular name. Yet of the Marys (and there are several, starting with the Hebrew Miriam), Mary the mother of Jesus is not without rebuke—and by none other than Jesus.

Equally surprising for those readers familiar with Mary's importance to Christian tradition, there's precious little mention of Mary the mother of Jesus in the Bible. She's a giant of a figure in Christian tradition (even "without sin," in Roman Catholic doctrine), yet in the earliest New Testament writings, she doesn't even have a name. Paul says simply that Jesus was born from a woman. In the earliest Gospel, references to Mary are few and contestable. Mark names her as Jesus's mother and includes a couple of references to a Mary who may or may not be Jesus's mother.[34] Matthew has a little more information in the context of Jesus's birth and includes Mary and Joseph's fleeing with the newborn to Egypt (though nowhere in Matthew's nativity story is Mary an agent of action, and mostly she's unnamed, called simply "his mother").[35] It's Luke and John who have the most stories about Mary, but even those are few. And in truth, the effect is mixed.

Luke tells the story of how Mary was chosen to bear the baby Jesus and calls her "blessed among women." In Luke's nativity story, Mary thinks for herself ("How can this be, since I am a virgin?"); actively decides ("Let it be with me according to your word," which has led some to call her Jesus's earliest disciple); "ponders these things in her heart"; worries over the youngster Jesus's absence (he's in the temple); and "treasured all these things in her heart."[36]

But the only other references to Mary in Luke's Gospel (two) show the adult Jesus essentially rejecting her.[37] The most explicit of those rejections appears in all three synoptic gospels. Luke's version: "Then his mother and his brothers came to him, but they could not reach him because of the crowd. And he was told, 'Your mother and your brothers are standing outside wanting to see you.' But he said to them, 'My mother and my brothers are those who hear the word of God and do it.'"[38]

John's first reference to the mother of Jesus similarly portrays Jesus silencing her. It happened at a wedding. In an embarrassing moment, they'd run out of wine when the feast was in full swing. Jesus's mother, sensitive to the social gaffe, asked Jesus to fix the problem. People often skip over the story to his doing just that, turning water to wine. But Jesus's first response was to tell his mother to mind her own business.

The last time Luke mentions Mary (though she may have been among the "women who followed him from Galilee"[39] and may also be "Mary the mother of James" at the tomb) is in the first chapter of Acts where Jesus's mother is named among those who had devoted themselves to prayer after Jesus's death and resurrection.[40]

Mary isn't mentioned by name in John's Gospel. As mentioned earlier, she's rebuked by Jesus at the wedding at Cana, where Jesus calls her simply "Woman."[41] And the dying Jesus assigns her to be mother to the "beloved disciple" also present at the foot of the cross.[42] These are hardly ringing endorsements of affection.

\*\*\*

Peter, *Petros* in Greek, *Petrus* in Latin, meaning "rock." If there's any larger-than-life disciple of Jesus, it would have to be Peter. Jesus gave him the keys to the kingdom and pointed his finger at Peter, declaring, "Thou art Peter [Petrus], and upon this rock I will build my church."[43] It is, among other things, a neat pun. Peter, then, is the disciple to whom every Roman Catholic pope traces his spiritual lineage. Premier leader of Christianity (according to them, anyway), the pope is the descendant of Peter. The pope walks in the shoes of this disciple. Never mind the celibacy part: Peter was married.[44]

Peter did not start out as Peter, but as Shimeon, son of Jonah (Hebrew), or Simon, son of John. Simon, a fisherman from Bethsaida, was among the first to follow Jesus. He witnessed miracles that not everyone saw and walked on water until his faith wavered and he started sinking. When Jesus asked his disciples, "Who do you say I am?," Peter replied by calling Jesus not only "the messiah" but "son of the living God."

By so identifying Jesus, Peter earns high praise. That's the moment when Jesus changes his name from Simon to Peter, "the rock on which I will build my church." And that's the moment when Jesus says, "I will give you the keys to the kingdom of heaven. Whatever you bind on earth will be bound in heaven and whatever you loose on earth will be loosed in heaven." Interpretation is everything and quite often snarly, but however you parse this, Jesus gave Peter unprecedented authority. So it's Saint Peter who Christians believe will be the first to meet them at the pearly gates, and Peter who will tell if you're fit (or not) for heaven.

In the Gospels, Peter is always named first among the disciples and was their spokesman when the occasion called for it.

But for all Peter's leadership and high praise from Jesus, he also got into some serious trouble. Jesus had told his disciples that he was to be arrested and crucified. When Peter says in so many words, "No way would that ever happen to you," Jesus rebukes him, even calling Peter Satan and a stumbling block who just doesn't get it.[45] Jesus accuses Peter of thinking only in human ways, not accounting for God's.

Then, on Holy (Maundy) Thursday, the night before Jesus's crucifixion, Peter initially rebuffs Jesus's efforts to wash his feet. Again, Peter doesn't get it—the big picture, the humble Jesus who defies human expectations and norms. But when Jesus equates that with rejecting Jesus altogether, Peter recants and doubles down, saying, "Then wash not only my feet but also my hands and my head." In the melee and confusion of Jesus's arrest, Peter cuts off a man's ear. (Jesus puts it back on.)[46] In all these cases, one could say that although Peter is missing the big picture, he meant well.

But the worst infraction is one that even Peter recognized as it happened. Although Peter had earlier professed that he was ready to be arrested and killed alongside Jesus, when it came time for Jesus's trial, Peter tries to save himself instead. Recognized as a follower of Jesus, Peter denies it. Three times. Just as Jesus had predicted and that Peter had protested would never happen.[47]

*** 

Today, more than two thousand years after the events of Christianity's founding, it's easy to assume that his followers simply picked up the mantle Jesus left—"Love one another" and "Go, now, and tell"—and soldiered on, spreading the gospel and making new Christians. To learn that they didn't all get along or always agree about how to proceed can be disconcerting. But there it is, in the Bible and elsewhere. Biblical accounts show that it wasn't perfectly clear to the people who survived Jesus how best to do what they believed Jesus charged them to do, and they argued about it.

The biggest recorded discord in the church's leadership occurs almost immediately, within the first generation. Just exactly how it went down is still a subject of some speculation, since the Bible (being what it is) doesn't give us an objective play-by-play. What we do read is Paul's reporting that he "opposed Cephas [Peter] to his face, because he stood self-condemned" by a "hypocrisy" (hardly conciliatory language) and "not acting consistently with the truth of the gospel."[48]

At issue: just how Jewish must a person be to become Christian? Did Christians need to follow dietary laws along with all the rest of the Jewish laws? Specific to men was the issue of circumcision. Jesus was a Jew, and the earliest Jesus followers were Jews. As men, they would have been circumcised as infants according to their tradition. Strange as it sounds to our ears today, it was a natural question then. In a nutshell: Did a person need first to become Jewish in order to become Christian? Jesus had been circumcised. All of them had been circumcised. Why, then, wouldn't any man who wanted to follow the risen Christ need also to be circumcised?

The debate was a sensible one. But as is the nature of debates in which the parties have real stakes in an outcome, this (which played out, as the Bible tells it, in Jerusalem and Antioch) seems finally to have been no gentlemanly argument from behind podiums.[49] Although later Christian tradition imagines Paul and Peter teaching together in Rome, the biblical evidence suggests that the rift may have been irreparably divisive. It was a personal and impassioned disagreement that resulted in no small bit of hurt feelings.

***

This chapter wouldn't be complete without at least a brief discussion of God. After all, one would think that if there's one perfect character in the Bible it would have to be God. But God does some *really* questionable stuff in the Bible. Take God's own admission of creating both good and evil.[50] Even accounting for the range of possible translations, there's no way around it. That's what it says. Or consider Pharaoh of Hebrew slavery and the exodus. The story, as we're inclined to retell it, emphasizes Pharaoh's cruelty and belligerence. Pushed to release the Hebrew captives, he resisted. What we conveniently forget is that the Bible says more than once that God "hardened Pharaoh's heart" so that he wouldn't release the Hebrew people.

Now, the thinking goes that God did that in order to show God's great might on behalf of the chosen people. But it doesn't take a giant of ethical reasoning to find some problems here. For one, that sounds a lot like exacerbating or at least lengthening the Hebrews' suffering so that God can flex God's muscles. That's apart from the elephant in the room: Did Pharaoh even have a choice in how he behaved? It doesn't sound like it. Rather, God made Pharaoh continue to mistreat the Hebrews so that (again) God could show how powerful God was in defeating him.

Similarly, there's God's inaugural directive to the prophet Isaiah: "Make the mind of this people dull, and stop their ears, and shut their eyes, so that they may not . . . turn and be healed."[51] Which sounds like exactly the opposite of what God wants from the prophets and people. Or this: Abraham, horrified by God's intention to obliterate the good people along with the bad, gets God to reconsider the plan to destroy Sodom and Gomorrah.[52] (The story tells that, in the end, there weren't enough good folks to save the place.)

Moses similarly cools the temper of an irate God by appealing to God's justice and earlier generosities.[53] Then think about Job, whom God calls utterly blameless, yet gives the *satan* free rein to subject Job to torture and abuse in order to win a bet.[54]

***

What's a Bible-believing person to do with this? For one thing, reading these stories about these characters urges us to think for ourselves, to learn about the Bible's historical and cultural contexts as well as its literary forms and norms. Rather than engaging in all sorts of gymnastics of logic to absolve the biblical characters of their questionable or blatantly wrong behavior, they remind us that the Bible is not always prescriptive. Some of its texts are stories working as stories do, with multiple layers and not a few befuddlements, but they are definitely *not* a blueprint for thoughtless application today in how we ought to conduct ourselves.

What's more, the Bible's descriptions, if you will, reflect the conditions and cultures of its stories' origins and transmission. Patriarchy is one immutable lens onto biblical characters' personalities and actions. Its images of God are so varied as to constantly remind us of their basis in human experience, in the human effort to make sense and go on. The Bible is not always prescriptive; on the contrary, in the case of some stories and some texts, if we are to take them seriously, *when* we take them seriously, they beg us to resist. Considering these accounts should encourage us to take care whom or which aspects of whom among the Bible's cast of characters we choose to emulate.

Finally, consider the glaring conclusion, upon reviewing some of these biblical "heroes," that according to the Bible, God does not require perfection of the sorts we might expect in order to contribute meaningfully to the story of the world. The New Testament champions divine forgiveness for any and all sins. And the Hebrew Bible is also preoccupied with justice, mercy, and forgiveness, with mending each rift between God and God's people. Admitting that the Bible portrays its greatest characters (even God) as engaging in questionable behavior or exhibiting flaws and foibles should remind faithful readers that taking the Bible seriously does not mean reading, much less applying it without thoughtful and informed critique.

# PART III

## Troubling Texts

# Chapter 6

# Impossibilities, Normalized

Punctuating the dramas of grand origins, catastrophe, domestic dispute, and travel adventures in Genesis are such attention-stalling bits as this: "Shem was a hundred years old, and he begot Arpachshad two years after the flood. And Shem lived after he begot Arpachshad five hundred years, and begot sons and daughters. . . . And Arpachshad lived after he begot Shelah four hundred and three years, and begot sons and daughters. And Shelah lived . . ."[1] You're about to nod off amid all this begatting when it hits you: Wait, he lived for how many years? But the recital continues, as if in listing genealogies it is perfectly predictable that a person would reach ages in the hundreds of years.

From the first pages of Genesis, the Bible presumes things that we identify today as downright impossible. People live for centuries; God chats with people the way we do with our neighbors; thousands of people along with thousands more domesticated animals wander for forty years in a small barren territory; people called prophets see all sorts of uncanny things (Moses's burning bush and Ezekiel's flying chariot, for example); God walks around in an orchard; Satan walks and talks with Jesus; Jesus walks on water; and Jesus is resurrected from the dead and appears to his followers after that. The list goes on.

What should readers make of these elements so basic to the biblical narrative and so outside of the laws of nature or modern human experience? Without resorting to one-size-fits-all scientific explanations or simply explaining away the Bible's oddities with modern arrogance, this chapter helps readers get a handle on the whys and wherefores of the Bible's miracles and its reason-defying assumptions, appreciating the roles they play and the ways that we might make sense of or simply accept them today.

There are two general categories of biblical oddity: the matter-of-fact weird and the admittedly weird. There are peculiarities and strange events that biblical texts report without any notice of the fact that they are extraordinary. Think of the talking snake in Genesis or the unanswered question of where Cain got his wife. There's God's speaking to people (and they back to God) in the same ordinary manner that we might speak with each other, and the prophet who spends three days inside of a fish before resuming his duties.

By contrast, there are also peculiarities that the Bible draws attention to *as peculiar*: the burning bush, which burns but is undamaged, for example; the Nile turning to blood; Jesus raising a man from the dead. In a way, this second category (odd things the Bible admits are odd), including miracles and plagues, is easier to understand because we can imagine God making a big show of coloring outside the lines of natural processes. That is, God, in all God's god-ness (i.e., extra-ordinary), does extraordinary things because God can.

There are so many individual examples of both categories that we simply can't address them all here. I've chosen to discuss those "impossibilities" that have come up most often in my experience studying and teaching the Bible. If your favorite oddity happens not to be represented here, I hope that the general discussion might nevertheless prove illuminating.

Let's start with those super-long lifespans. Extreme lifespans such as we find in the genealogies of Genesis chapters 5 and 11 are among those peculiarities that the Bible presents as simply matter of fact.

Astute readers may notice that lifespans are especially long in narratives that appear before Noah and the Flood story; after that, lifespans are less long. (In Bible-speak, these are the "antediluvian" and "postdiluvian" years.) Look closely, and you'll see that lifespans before the Flood flirt with a millennium: Such-and-so lived after the birth of Such-and-so eight hundred and some years. By contrast, after the Flood, lifespans are counted in more-than-a century decades. Abraham is said to have lived 175 years, Jacob 147—not nearly so long as people living before the Flood, but long enough to question.[2]

One way readers have handled these unrealistically long lifespans is to simply treat them as literally true. Those who subscribe to the "inerrancy of the Bible" say that that's just the way it was. God made it so that people lived ridiculously long lives, changed that after the Flood, but still let the leaders of God's people enjoy lifespans longer than ours. Some propose that God let people live longer back then, before sin started adding up.[3] And "Abraham, Isaac, and Jacob foreshadowed what will be the norm when the debilitating and aging effects of sin and the Fall are forever eradicated."[4]

As far as we know, people have been wrestling with this question for a very long time, trying to make sense of these logic-defying numbers. That alone should give us pause. It reminds us that these texts are *ancient*. And while we tend to presume that readers must try to read these texts literally or to rationalize what seems impossible, that way of reading may not have held the same sway in the period when these texts took shape.

For those of us who suspect there's something other than the literal going on with these genealogies, research suggests a few possibilities.

One possibility is that, maybe, in the postdiluvian period of the matriarchs and patriarchs, one biblical year was actually two modern calendar years. There's some evidence for this. There are places in the Bible where daytime and nighttime each count as separate days, and there are references to two agricultural periods in a year. In other words, divide postdiluvian lifespans by two, and that's the number of years as we would count them now.[5]

Some people have sought out and demonstrated patterns in the numbers. They take the lifespans seriously but not literally. This approach presumes some kind of mystical code at work, a sense that discerning readers are tasked to discover. Finding such patterns still doesn't necessarily answer the question "Why?," however.[6]

Comparisons with other ancient, nonbiblical literature helps. Take the Sumerian King List, for example.[7] Originating from the same general geographic area as the biblical texts but from an earlier period, the list demarcates lifespans before and after, get this, a flood. Lifespans before the flood are extremely long; after it, less so (but still centuries). Coincidence? Few scholars think so. Comparing these genealogies to the millennia-long lifespans of ancient, antediluvian Sumerian kings suggests that assigning lengthy lifespans was a way to lionize the heroes of old. Some of these ancient Near Eastern ancestors even became deified. Biblical ancestors before the Flood, which changed everything, were not gods but enjoyed mythopoeic lifespans nonetheless.[8] Adam lived 930 years, Noah 950. And still, important ancestors whom God favored are said, in these biblical stories of ancient times, to have lived an inordinate number of years.

In that respect, then, some literalists and others are not so far apart. From a literary and historical-critical perspective, lengthy lifespans in the Bible (and their difference before and after the Flood) may indicate degrees of favor by God and/or the community that transmitted the stories. The biblical scholar Claus Westermann concluded that the numbers are meant to illustrate "the power of God's blessings on his people," but they need not be taken literally.[9]

Finally, most scholars observe the oddity but see similarities with other ancient Near Eastern literature, that, like similar Mesopotamian mythologies, there may be more about each of the individuals listed than we presently have sources fully to discern. Indeed, references to extreme longevity appear within texts that aren't necessarily concerned with adhering to modern scientific expectations (arguing therefore against the literal). This larger-than-the-literal sensibility sees these lifespans as part of a greater narrative that doesn't presume historical reportage, asserting that the origin stories in Genesis have meanings apart from the literal and make that meaning by using hyperbole.

Taking the different theories and approaches into account, one can see that despite general scholarly consensus, not everyone agrees on how to handle the death-defying lives as told in the Bible's first (not necessarily earliest) book.

***

Another oddity of which the Bible takes no notice is Moses's curative snake-on-a-stick. As the story goes, anyone suffering from a soon-to-be-fatal snake bite needed merely to look at a bronze serpent that Moses had fashioned and mounted on a pole in order to be healed.[10] The Bible doesn't go into any explanation of how or why this could be so. Moses does this on God's instruction, so there's that. But still, in itself the miracle cure is not treated as such. And readers hardly notice because it's embedded in a still stranger story.[11] For one, as noted earlier, the serpent or snake of English translation is a seraph (plural: seraphim). Second, the ailment for which God directs Moses's cure is caused directly by God.

In the greater narrative, the people liberated from Egypt and making their way to the Promised Land complain yet again, criticizing God and Moses for leading them into what they are sure is a fatal journey. Yahweh's unmitigated response is to send seraphim that bite and kill a lot of the people, seemingly indiscriminately. They ask Moses for help; he prays to God; and God tells him to make the snake on a pole. Weird all around.

***

And then there's Jonah's three-day sojourn in the fish. The biblical book of Jonah, among the collection of prophetic books, tells that the prophet Jonah spent three days and three nights in the belly of a big fish. Not only does the story provide no explanation for this surely-even-then-unheard-of-event, but it includes a relatively lengthy bit from Jonah's time in said belly. He sings a long song (the bulk of chapter 2), which reveals not a whit of concern about the biology of the thing or how such a gastric environment might affect a man. Rather, it's a prayer (comprising bits and pieces from various psalms) that Jonah prays "from the belly of the fish," because of course a person might simply kneel down on the stomach lining among the acidic fluids and oceanic biomass in the process of getting digested, fold his hands, and talk to God.

It's hard to be literalist about this. In fact, there's much about the book as a whole that strains credibility (repenting ruminants— cattle in sackcloth—at its conclusion, for example), suggesting that there's something else going on here. There are many literary clues to suggest we should read this not as historical reporting but as something else—fiction for sure, maybe satire. (Consider the gender-bending fish. In Jonah 2:1 the word for "fish" is masculine; in 2:2 it's feminine; in 2:11 it's masculine again. Or that Nineveh, said to be a huge city, "three days' walk" across, has been excavated to reveal that in its largest period it would have been about three miles across at its widest point.)[12]

There's more aberration and oddity than can be discussed in this brief book. But for the purposes of this chapter, note the big fish, Jonah's three days inside it, and upon his emergence the swift resumption of his prophetic duties. There's no healing period or acknowledgment of what might have resulted from three days in the fish's belly.

To try to read the Jonah story as history, thinking that that's what it means to "believe in" the Bible, supposing that it must be factually and physically true, is to miss out on it altogether. The very preposterousness of it all is part of the point. Besides its narrative qualities (a striking two-part symmetry, for example), its very oddities invite us to consider more deeply what really is going on in this text *as text*, in this story *as literature*, in this tale *as theology*. The possibilities are rich: the grace of God; responsibility to purpose; God's concern for *all* peoples versus Jonah's narrow nationalism; the possibility that even the worst offenders might see their way to rightfulness. All this and a bit of humor, too. In other words, the text itself begs for a far richer reading than the flatly literal.

***

On the topic of impossibilities among the prophets: How could Daniel know exactly what was going to happen centuries in the future? Here he was, a captive of the Babylonians in the sixth century BCE, explaining what would happen on the world stage some four centuries later, in concrete detail.

Evidence suggests that the book of Daniel was actually written many centuries after the story it tells is said to have taken place. Daniel, in other words, is *set* in ancient times, but the events it claims to foretell were happening around the time the book was actually taking shape. The future events Daniel predicts had already happened.

It is commonly believed that biblical prophets told the future. That's not quite right. Biblical prophecy is indeed concerned with what lay ahead, but the prophets were not so much fortune tellers as astute observers of their times and places whose messages reflect deep concern for how the people's actions informed their relationship to God and what might then happen in response. So prophecy had everything to do with the present. Biblical prophets were spokespeople for God who often operated like social critics, warning people to behave as God commanded, "or else." They might also include words of comfort and balm, restoration and security.

In the case of Daniel, among other lessons and encouragements, the book showed its Jewish audience, who were suffering under foreign (Greek) rule, how a Jewish man under foreign (Babylonian) rule maintained integrity, courage, and faith. It tells that God is in charge of history and will care for God's own people, even when it may feel to those people as though they have been abandoned.

While we're on the topic of misconceptions, a common one among Christians is that Old Testament biblical prophecy was meant to predict the coming of Jesus. Not so. What is true, though, is that the New Testament writers used the widely accepted tradition of reinterpreting received texts in light of new ideas and experiences. Those Jewish Jesus followers looked to their inherited sacred stories for ways to understand what they came to believe about Jesus. And among the most important of those traditions were prophecies from the Hebrew Bible. So they retrofit them for Jesus.

\*\*\*

When it comes to miracles and plagues, what's a poor rationalist to do? By definition these are events that lie outside scientific explanation. Miracles are meant to demonstrate the extraordinary powers of those who perform them. That is at least part of the point. In some cases, the biblical text even offers that as explanation: "that they may know that I am God." Raising Lazarus from the dead, Jesus says several times (John 11:1–43, and only in John), is for the glory of God and of God's son, so that witnesses will believe Jesus was sent by God. The Egyptian plagues are called "signs." They indicate God's power to liberate God's people from serving Pharaoh in order that they might serve God.

In the Hebrew Bible, Moses either performs or is the instrument of numerous miracles, including parting the Red or Reed Sea, getting water from a rock and food from heaven (manna), and securing safe passage through the Sinai wilderness. Elijah and Elisha perform wonders of multiplying food and resuscitating the dead. Women such as Sarah and Hannah, definitively "barren," nevertheless go on to have children by the grace of God. In each case, God's ability to act outside of expectation is on display. The effect is to stimulate loyalty and service to God.

Years ago, I read a quite convincing study of the ten Egyptian plagues that sought scientific explanations for each, speculating on what natural process might lie behind them and how one could lead to the next: a great rain that eroded clay into the Nile (red like blood) that choked fish, causing (anthrax-infected) frogs to migrate into homes, where they died, causing lice and flies to proliferate, which led to cattle deaths and human boils. The next set of plagues are due to climatological conditions, and the final reflects infant mortality rates—not perfect, but an interesting theory.[13] Another explanation is, shall we say, symbolic: that the plagues demonstrated the Hebrew God's power over gods of the Egyptian pantheon, from the god of the Nile to particular guardian animal-gods to Pharaoh himself, understood as a god in Egyptian theology.[14]

But literary form suggests there may be still more at work. Astute readers have long noticed patterns in the plagues; the medieval French rabbi the Rashbam, for example, wrote of three sets of three types in the first nine plagues, indicating a thoughtful literary composition, not primarily an effort to record actual events as they happened.

Similarly, the episode in which the "sun stood still" so that Joshua and his troops could finish their fighting has been a matter of speculation. Did it "really" happen? A recent article reports that research has determined that a solar eclipse occurred on October 30, 1207 BCE, which could be the event behind the biblical story. And the Hebrew behind "stood still" could refer to a stopping not of movement but of function—that the sun quit shining.[15] Historical solar eclipse? Maybe so, maybe not.

Our impulse to find scientific verification for extraordinary biblical events is a modern one, and while some real geological, astronomical, or biological event may indeed lie behind some of the Bible's wonders, that those references appear in a text concerned first and foremost with God should remind us that those responsible for the biblical texts were writing out of faith. They saw, interpreted, and explained happenings through that lens, not from a disinterested scientific perspective.

Scholars of the intertestamental, or Second Temple, period (roughly the centuries between the latest Hebrew Bible's writings and earliest New Testament writings) note that there are many accounts of miracle-workers wandering around the Middle East doing extraordinary things. So, while the ability to do miracles was an extraordinary trait, it wasn't unique and was not limited to god-men. That Jesus performed miracles was but one of the qualities that made him special.

The stories of miracles Jesus performed do a few different things. The first such tale in John's Gospel, turning water into wine, Jesus executed with reluctance, apparently because his mother pushed him to do it. It shows Jesus to be set apart, to be outside the norm, and is like other miracles in John's Gospel said to demonstrate Jesus's "glory" and stimulate the belief that he was the son of God. John's Gospel tells of Jesus performing seven miracles, called "signs," each in order to publicly identify his extraordinary nature. The other Gospels show Jesus resisting doing supernatural things to prove his identity. Most of Jesus's miracles as reported in the Bible were to heal or cure people (including raising a few from the dead). Some were to exorcise demons, and some altered natural processes: walking on water, for example, or feeding far more people than paltry resources seemed to allow.

For the sake of discussion, consider these three events, each of which the New Testament treats as exceptional: the Star of Bethlehem, the miracle of the loaves and fishes, and the appearance of darkness plus an earthquake at Jesus's death. Rational, scientific explanations have been put forth for each of these. Yet none of them requires such logic in order to work within the narratives where they show up.

Matthew's nativity story treats the Christmas star, the Star of Bethlehem, as extraordinary.[16] (Matthew is the only Gospel that mentions such a star, the guiding light for the magi who journeyed from the East to meet the newborn baby Jesus.) For centuries, people have sought to identify an astronomical event that could explain how people many miles to the east of Israel, from the heart of ancient Persia, might have seen a star and followed it to Bethlehem. No single theory satisfactorily explains it, running into problems if not of astronomy then of chronology. Yet we know that there is a long tradition of ancient Near Eastern sages looking to the heavens for special information. Many of the gods were associated with specific planets or constellations. That a star might be identified with a king wouldn't have been odd. And we've seen how biblical writers recognized these associations, for example, in a critique of the Babylonian Nebuchadnezzar (the Lucifer prophecy discussed earlier).

While the star of Bethlehem appears only in Matthew's telling, stories of Jesus feeding far more people than his resources could sensibly provide appear in every Gospel, and in Matthew and Mark more than once. The (social) scientific explanation for how this could be possible is that when people witness a generosity, they're more inclined to be generous themselves. Seeing Jesus's willingness to share prompted others to share what they had, enabling everyone finally to be fed, according to this logic. Whatever the historical details that informed this memory or story, it's the theological explanation the biblical texts promote: Jesus could make miracles happen.

John's Gospel doesn't mention any extraordinary events at the moment of Jesus's death, but each of the synoptic gospels does. Mark and Luke tell of sudden midday darkness; Matthew adds an earthquake (and resurrection of the dead nearby).[17] People have looked for evidence of events that would correspond to the time and place of Jesus's crucifixion. For example, recent studies of seismic activity south of Jerusalem, around the Dead Sea, have led scientists to pinpoint an earthquake on April 3 in the year 33 CE.[18]

But nothing about those stories requires (or even asks) that we read them literally. On the contrary, remember that the Gospels are presented as exactly that, "good news." In other words, they're not disinterested reporting of historically verifiable fact but were designed first and foremost for the purpose of telling what the authors believed. They're stories of faith told in order to achieve a certain effect. Each of these extraordinary moments packs a theological punch. Consider the star. Besides the implication that Jesus was recognized even as a wee one by far-flung potentates as a person of great import (the adoring magi in Matthew), Luke's story provides a contrast to those wealthy foreign dignitaries in its murderous Herod, the wealthy Jewish king, to powerful effect.[19] Like the star, the darkness—whether or not it happened historically—would have meant something to early readers, namely that a very important person had just died or as the eschatological "Day of Yahweh," since both were part of the literary landscape of their audience's times.[20]

As for feeding multitudes from a few fish and a little bread, it's hard not to see the story as demonstrating the generosity and radical hospitality of Jesus. We would do well to remember that in each case, whatever lessons they may impart, these are stories first. And stories invite readers into worlds with multivalent potential. To reduce them to a take-home adage much less to hear them only as literalist reports is to make them smaller than they are.

When it comes to the Bible's miracles and plagues, "Did they happen?" is the question that dominates. I propose another: "Does it matter?" Or better: "What's the point? Why are they in there?"

Perhaps what the stories can tell us, when loosed from their literalist bonds, is more interesting, even more important, than whether or not they are "true" in terms of historical reporting.

***

Just as we get into trouble when we try to account literally for impossibilities alleged to have happened in some distant past, so we may be misreading by thinking that way about the future. That brings us to misconceptions about biblical apocalyptic literature, namely that apocalyptic literature is about the end of the world and properly decoded gives the where and when. Indeed, when we talk about apocalyptic this or that today, we're usually talking about some great cataclysm, a crisis of epic proportion. In modern parlance, "apocalyptic" is end-of-the-world stuff.[21]

It's important to note a couple of things. First, the word "apocalypse" in its original Greek means "revelation." It's an uncovering of what had been hidden. So the Apocalypse of John that concludes the Christian New Testament is the Revelation of John. (Note: not "Revelations"—the word isn't plural in the title.) Like biblical prophecy, biblical apocalyptic literature is concerned with what was going on in the present, at the time of its writing.

The book of Revelation's use of symbolism, starkly dualistic qualities, and wild imagery captivate the imagination and invite interpretation and reinterpretation. But again, like prophecy, its concern is less with predicting the future than with declaring how God was behind what was happening in the world of its author(s).

That an end is near is part of the apocalyptic paradigm, but it isn't necessarily the end of the world. Rather, it's the end of the difficulties its first-century audience experienced. Perhaps it's better to say that it is the end of *a* world and the beginning of a new (and better) one. God's dramatic interjection into the human sphere is integral to the genre, as is the distinction between a "now" of trial and tribulation wherein evil seems to have the upper hand, and an imminent "then" wherein God will put things to right on behalf of the righteous. So it's easy to see where modern readers get the idea that something very dramatic is afoot.

The Hebrew Bible has its own apocalyptic literature. (The genre flourished among certain groups in the Near East between 200 BCE and 200 CE.) The second half of the book of Daniel is the purest and longest example. But hints of a developing apocalyptic also appear in some other late (in terms of composition) texts, including sections of Isaiah, Jeremiah, Ezekiel, Joel, and Zechariah.

\*\*\*

One final impossibility: God's one-on-ones with individual humans. Why was God so chatty in biblical times, and why doesn't God talk to people like that today? Maybe you've asked or been asked (maybe both) this question yourself. Beginning in Genesis chapter 2, we meet a very hands-on God, who plants a garden, makes stuff, and walks and talks with people like an old pal. After a particularly surprising luncheon, where it is revealed that old lady Sarah will become pregnant, God tells Abraham that if God sees that things are as bad in Sodom as God has heard they are (odd itself, if you think God knows everything), then that city will be destroyed. Abraham argues with God—Abraham assuming the moral high ground, by the way. There are so many odd things about these stories, but to stay on topic: there is nothing ambiguous here about communication between humans and God. It's as direct, immediate, and physical as any we experience with other people. So what happened?

We do see evidence within the Hebrew Bible that it gets harder and harder as time goes on to have such personal interactions with God. That is, the earliest texts—in terms of date of composition—show such close give-and-take, but in later texts, God becomes more and more distant until, by the time of the New Testament, God is out there in heaven or otherwise only indirectly accessible—through prayer, prophets, or divine initiative, including the incarnation of Jesus and later the Holy Spirit. Literalists will say that once upon a time, the same God who sits in heaven today used to show up and talk, walk, and eat with regular folks. And that just doesn't happen in the same way anymore. From what we know of the Bible's development, it appears rather to be a simple case of evolving theology, which isn't to suggest that *God* has become less accessible (that's a matter of belief) so much as that people have changed their ideas about God over the millennia.

\*\*\*

How one reads extraordinary events and impossibilities in the Bible—those that the Bible presents without comment and those expressly noted as extra-ordinary—needn't be an assay of faith. Rather, these stories serve to remind us (again) of how the Bible unseats expectations, maybe the better to open us as readers to richer possibilities of interpretation and fresh ways of seeing than as static information to accept or reject at face value. They remind us of the inherent strangeness of the text, of its antiquity and foreignness, not as an excuse to dismiss or ignore it but as an opportunity to investigate, learn, and grow in dynamic engagement with the texts.

# Chapter 7

# Misconceptions, Misapprehensions

Pity the poor contractor tasked with producing robust carvings of the Ten Commandments for her client's front yard. She scours the Bible for a list so labeled. In vain. Nowhere in the Bible are the regulations commonly called the Ten Commandments so identified. What's more, there are actually three versions of what passes for them. The only list of regulations enumerated in the Bible as "ten" has little in common with those we call the Ten Commandments. Oh, and the contractor would be wise to ask whether her client is Jewish or Christian; and if Christian, of what stripe? This affects the way they'd want the commandments to be numbered.

This chapter highlights and discusses little-known facts to correct common misperceptions and add depth to simplistic assumptions. Among the most common missteps we modern people make is to oversimplify, taking the Bible at its most superficial word on matters of history, for example, or claiming to distill what the Bible says about sex, salvation, or Hell to match our present beliefs or purposes. We tend to speak as if "Israel" means only one partic- ular thing in the Bible, or that the Bible's wisdom literature speaks with one voice about the meaning of life and how one should live it, or that there is a single biblical list of Ten Commandments. Remembering that the Bible developed over a long period of time and in different places helps us to appreciate that it's a bit more complicated than we might first think. The issues addressed here hardly cover all misconceptions, but examining them can help us correct others, too, even if only by teaching us to guard against reducing the Bible to a pithy pocket guide.

***

For one thing, as I said, there are three biblical versions of Ten Commandments. They all appear in the Hebrew Bible: in Exodus 20:2–17, Deuteronomy 5:6–21, and Leviticus chapter 19. The first two are the ones most familiar to modern readers. The version as it appears in Leviticus includes yet more commandments, such as a prohibition against making fun of the physically disabled; treating the immigrant as a citizen with the same love as for oneself; as well as exactly how to offer, eat, and dispose of a particular sacrifice.[1] In total, it's a bit unwieldy. So the Leviticus version is usually ignored.

It is religious tradition, not the biblical text, that calls the regulations listed in Exodus and Deuteronomy "the Ten Commandments." In the Bible, they're not enumerated or otherwise labeled, and in both cases, they're introduced as "words," not "commandments." The only commandments actually called "ten" in the Bible appear in Exodus 34:10–27. These include such regulations as not offering a sacrifice with blood along with any yeast; not cooking a young goat in its mother's milk; and commands to observe Passover, the Festival of Weeks, and more. In other words, the Bible's "ten commandments" bear little resemblance to the regulations that have come to be called the Ten Commandments.

The Hebrew word translated here as "words" is a very common noun that can be translated "word," "matter," "thing," or "affair." In this context, I suppose we could call them "concerns." That said, they certainly read like commands—no ifs, ands, or buts about them. Scholars actually distinguish them from the hundreds of if-then commands that are found throughout Exodus, Leviticus, and Deuteronomy. Those (conditional) differ from these (apodictic) in their it-depends element. The ones called the Ten Commandments are absolute: "Thou shalt not."

The two versions of the Ten Commandments differ both in content and in reception. By way of content, they're pretty darn close. But if you're etching in stone for front lawn purposes, close doesn't cut it. In Exodus, the Sabbath command is intellectual: "to remember" (in Hebrew *zkr*); in Deuteronomy it is physical: "to keep, preserve" (*shmr*), and Deuteronomy adds a reason: "as Yahweh your God commanded you." Deuteronomy adds also that among those who get to take the day off from work are "your ox, your ass," and "any of" your cattle, and again supplies a reason: "that your manservant and your maidservant may rest as well as you." One could make a case, based purely on the literary nature of this verse, for wrapping the animals into the man- and maidservant identities, that is, a case for the personhood of animals.

It's in that Sabbath commandment that we find the greatest difference between these two versions. It has to do with the reason the different texts give for why its audience should keep this commandment. Exodus uses the seven-day creation story for justification: "For in six days, Yahweh made heavens and earth, the sea, and all that is in them, and rested on the seventh day; therefore Yahweh blessed the sabbath day and hallowed it." Deuteronomy uses the exodus for justification, saying, "You shall remember that you were a servant in the land of Egypt, and Yahweh your God brought you out thence with a mighty hand and an outstretched arm; therefore Yahweh your God commanded you to keep the sabbath day."

That's the greatest difference, but not the only one. While they agree on "Honor your father and your mother," Deuteronomy adds, "as Yahweh your God commanded you." And while Exodus explains "that your days may be long," Deuteronomy explains "be prolonged" and adds, "and that it may go well with you," before the bit about the land. Deuteronomy includes transitions between the commandments that follow "You shall not kill." A final difference of note: the coveting of "wife" and "house" are prioritized differently in the two versions (Exodus leads with "house," Deuteronomy with "wife"), and Deuteronomy adds "his field" to the lot. A modern engraver may elect to go with the Exodus version simply because it's shorter, unless she's getting paid by the word. Even then, though, there would be still more decisions to make.

The client's faith would determine whether or not to begin with "I am Yahweh your God," making that Commandment 1 (or "I," since I've noticed that people have a predilection for roman numerals when posting commandments). Jews begin with that, loud and clear. Christians argue that that's not really a command because it requires no action. Jews might rightly counter that it sure is and does: it's an act of intention to recognize this One, Yahweh, as your god. The Jews have got a point, especially in a world of competing gods, which seems to have been the context originally and so throughout human history.

Roman Catholic Christians consider "no other gods" plus "no graven images" as the first commandment. Lutherans agree, while other Protestant Christians make "no other gods" the first commandment and "no graven images" its own commandment, the second. To even out the numbering, Catholics and Lutherans separate the coveting into Commandments 9 and 10. The others keep all the coveting together.

Sometimes people are surprised by the fact that "Do unto others as you would have them do unto you" is nowhere among the Ten Commandments. That shows up in the New Testament, in Jesus's grand sermon on the mount (Matthew) or on the plain (Luke). With it, Jesus turns a historically rabbinic restraint into action.[2] That is, predating Jesus was a Jewish command to "*not* do unto others what you would *not* have them do unto you."

The story, in wide circulation in Jesus's time, tells of two esteemed rabbis, men from whom people sought the wisest counsel and best advice, presented with a challenge to explain the whole Torah while their questioner stood on one foot. Rabbi Shammai sent the fellow away in disgust, observing that the Torah was far more complicated and sophisticated than such treatment could allow. Rabbi Hillel, on the other hand, responded simply by saying, "Do not do unto others what you would not have done to yourself. That is the whole Torah; all the rest is commentary. Now, go and study it."[3]

And I have to say I like this negative "Do not do unto" version better. It gets around the sometimes meddlesome, if well-meaning and energetically "helpful" souls, who are sometimes so busy doing-unto that they can't see when that becomes its own kind of problem. Better still, note that Hillel didn't leave it simply at "Do not do unto others" but includes as part and parcel of the Torah the business of "commentary" and the responsibility to go and learn.

\*\*\*

Israel: talk about misunderstood. The trouble is, in the Bible the word refers to several quite different things. What's more, there's the biblical Israel-Canaan dichotomy. The way those terms appear in some of the Bible's historical books can make it seem that they're two very different places. In fact, the land of Canaan and the land of Israel refer to the same general geographical area: a strip of land along the eastern edge of the Mediterranean Sea.

The difference as portrayed in the Bible is one of culture and corresponding judgment: it's "us" Israelites versus "them" Canaanites; Israelites as the people of a God who promised that they should have that geographical territory versus Canaanites as pagan idolaters who have no business controlling any part of said territory (even though they were there first), according to the Bible. Never mind that many archaeologists and biblical scholars think that (at least some of) the Israelites actually *were* Canaanites, who came to identify with the community and traditions represented in the Hebrew Bible and therefore came to be called Israelites.

Further confusing matters in the Bible is the fact that, besides referring to that bit of land without national identity, the term "Israel" refers to three other things: a person, a nation, and the rebelling part of half a nation.

You will remember the Bible says that God made a special pact with a particular people beginning with Abraham and Sarah, then again with their son, Isaac, and his wife, Rebecca. That promise reappears with each generation. Isaac (unwittingly) transfers it to his younger son, Jacob, who marries the beautiful Rachel and the not-so-beautiful Leah. With them and with two female slaves, Jacob sires twelve sons and a daughter. When Jacob wrestles at night to uncertain outcome with a mysterious "man," that man leaves Jacob with a new name: "Israel," playing on the Hebrew verb "to strive" linked to *el*, the generic word for "god."[4] (Jacob identifies the mysterious man as God.)

In our account of the many faces of "Israel" in the Bible, this is #1: an alternative name for the man Jacob. That makes particular sense because Jacob is father to twelve sons whose offspring will come to compose the people of Israel (Israelites), who settle in the land of Israel, which becomes the nation of Israel, part of which becomes a smaller nation called Israel (as opposed to "Judah," the other part of the formerly bigger "Israel"). But I'm getting ahead of myself. Jacob-Israel is father of the twelve sons who become the ancestors of twelve tribes.

Fast-forward several generations to Moses. According to the biblical narrative, Moses leads the descendants of Jacob-Israel's twelve sons, the people who inherited a promise made first to Abraham and Sarah, out of Egypt and (finally) toward the land that God had included in that promise.

Over many years and many scrappy battles—the Israelites fighting with Canaanites and other non-Israelites in the land whose ownership and name they don't agree on—the Philistines emerge among the Canaanites as an increasingly troublesome problem to the Israelites. In light of such a threat, the system of individual Israelite tribes cooperating here and there (as per the book of Judges) to combat the native Canaanite inhabitants is no longer working out. There's some disagreement about exactly how to handle this, but the voice calling for centralized power to

which all the tribes would answer—a king—wins out. The books
of 1 and 2 Samuel chronicle the development of a monarchy in
Israel-Canaan. First and rather tentatively under Saul and then decisively under David, Israel's (Jacob's) descendants (called Israel)
execute the political transformation of a land (Israel) into a nation
(Israel).

We're almost there. The final "Israel" is also both land and nation, only smaller. After David's son Solomon dies and is succeeded
on the throne by a son with little of the diplomacy or charisma that
either his dad or grandpa had, that son, Rehoboam, so alienates
some of his own people that they go all tribal on him and defect.
All but Rehoboam's own tribe of Judah and one other (Benjamin)
break away to form their own, ten-tribe confederacy of a nation.[5]
At this point (922 BCE), the former nation of Saul-David-Solomon's
Israel becomes two nations. There is Judah in the south, led by a
descendant of David, with its capital city and temple in Jerusalem.
And in the north there is, wait for it, Israel. Israel in this case refers
specifically to the ten-tribe kingdom, led by a new king, Jeroboam,
and with a capital city of Samaria.

Judah is the smaller and weaker of these two nations. But it
survives for longer. After a couple hundred years, the northern
kingdom of Israel is defeated and overrun by the Assyrians and
ceases to exist as a nation for the time being. By contrast, although
Judah gets a bit bruised and battered by Assyria, it endures. This may
be because on the ledger of economic and political advantage Judah
wasn't nearly as valuable (read: attractive to powerful foreigners) as
Israel was. But to the people responsible for the Bible, Israel's defeat was no random occurrence or to be explained away simply by
appealing to the fact that Israel was a big deal by comparison with
Judah. No, to the biblical authors and editors, it was God's doing.
And as God's doing, there was divine reasoning behind it: Judah
was better in God's eyes. When the Babylonians come along some
150 years later and destroy not only the nation of Judah with its

Davidic monarchy but the temple in Jerusalem, too, theological reasoning is activated full-force again.

But that's another story.

***

With aphorisms such as "When pride comes, then comes disgrace; but wisdom is with the humble," "Bread gained by deceit is sweet, but afterward the mouth will be full of gravel," and the one that gave rise to "Spare the rod. . . ," one can be excused for thinking that the book of Proverbs offers straightforward advice for how we should live as "people of God."[6] Proverbs, together with Job and Ecclesiastes (plus several psalms), represent what scholars call "wisdom literature." Modern readers often approach them as roadmaps to life, a kind of how-to guide for righteousness, purpose, and meaning: a straightforward guide to life itself.

The trouble is these texts don't always comply with such expectations. Consider their obvious contradictions. For example, keeping Job's plight in mind, read Proverbs's "The righteous are delivered from trouble."[7] Or take Ecclesiastes's thinking it's better to be dead than alive, *and* it's better to be living than dead.[8] Proverbs finally directs its confident declarations to a very particular demographic: the upwardly mobile young man. Ecclesiastes is full of angsty questions and a weary accession to—if not downright pessimism about—the world.

I would argue that rather than offering a step-by-step guide to righteousness and success, the Bible's wisdom literature offers something much, much better. These texts offer the space to keep asking. And maybe that's where righteousness and the "fear of God" reside. What they offer are questions and meditations on possible answers in some times and places to those big questions. They model debate and offer correction to absolutes without falling into an endlessly qualified anything-goes prescription.

***

The Bible's authors and editors write of events through the lens of faith, with God an active agent in history. It shouldn't surprise us, then, that the authors' and editors' first priority was not a disinterested reporting of events as they happened. Among the most glaring departures from known history are events as told in the book of Daniel. As I explained earlier, Daniel supposes a setting in the sixth century BCE, but (for all sorts of concrete reasons within the text) scholars agree that much of the book was written as late as the second century BCE. An author writing in such circumstances could be excused for messing up a few historical details.

Relevant here: we know that Nebuchadnezzar II's son Amel-Marduk (king of Babylonia around 562–560 BCE) was murdered by Neriglissar (Nebuchadnezzar's son-in-law), who was succeeded by his own son (Nebuchadnezzar's grandson), a child so young and unpopular that elites quickly got rid of him and replaced the boy-king with (no relation) Nabonidus, who lost the throne for his son Belshazzar when the Persian king Cyrus II conquered Babylonia. Go ahead, take a breath. I will. Cyrus was succeeded by his son Cambyses, who was succeeded by his brother-in-law, Darius. If you find this dizzying, then you can sympathize with the author of Daniel, who was writing some four hundred years after the events he purports to report but millennia before Google.

If your faith is entirely invested in the Bible's factual accuracy, then you have to resort to some pretty fanciful reasoning to accept Daniel's assumption that Belshazzar was the son of Nebuchadnezzar, when we know for a verifiable, historical fact that Belshazzar was the son of Nabonidus. Plus, you'd have to accept that Belshazzar became king, though we know he never was (not for his lack of trying, even acting the part, however). And you'd have to accept a "Darius the Mede" ascending the Babylonian throne after Belshazzar (who, again, was never really on it), though there's no historical record of a "Darius the Mede" and plenty of historical records on the chronology of monarchy.

It would seem, then, that the point here is not historical accuracy but something else. In Daniel that includes showing how God can act in human history on behalf of God's people for a purpose that may not always be clear to people at the time. Daniel shows God's control over even the most powerful people and principalities, and demonstrates that God will defeat the audience's oppressors and their suffering will end. "Who cares if Daniel's author(s) got the names wrong?" seems to be the attitude of those who passed these texts along. Such historical details weren't the important thing.

*\*\*\**

Similarly, modern readers often bring assumptions about genre to their reading, assumptions that can mislead. For example, recall that Old Testament prophecy wasn't the kind of fortune-telling that a lot of modern readers treat it as. Most egregious among Christians is the direct equation of specific Hebrew prophecies with Jesus. In short, Old Testament prophecies are not simply predictions about Jesus. We have to be careful with this. While such texts can be interpreted and understood as prophesying about Jesus, Christians must also appreciate that these texts existed long before Jesus and continue to make sense without a New Testament filter.

For example, Isaiah 40:3–4 reflects the period just after Cyrus II of Persia had conquered Babylonia and issued an edict of release, a mandate for people such as the Jews, conquered and taken into exile in Babylon (587 BCE), to return to their native lands and rebuild their houses, temples, and businesses there. Not everyone wanted to go. Babylonia turned out to be a pretty cushy spot by comparison with what lay back "home." For many people, Babylonia was the only home they'd ever known. (After all, exiles didn't stop having children once they'd arrived in Babylon some decades earlier.) So when Cyrus liberated the exiles, they needed encouragement to make the trek back to Jerusalem and other points in Judah.

The prophet, then, served as "a voice crying, 'In the wilderness prepare a way for the LORD.'" For many Christians, this rings a bell of John the Baptist, "a voice crying in the wilderness, 'prepare the way of the Lord.'"⁹ Hebrew doesn't have punctuation, so a reader must judge from other things within a text where a comma, a period, quotations marks, and so on should go. Isaiah's "A voice cries, 'In the wilderness prepare'" becomes in the Gospels, "A voice cries in the wilderness, 'Prepare.'"

This section of Isaiah (chapters 40–55) likely dates to sometime just after 538 BCE, when the people of the LORD, the people of Yahweh, the Jews, needed urging to get up and go, to travel the many not-altogether-hospitable miles from Babylonia (modern Iraq) back to Judah (modern Israel). So the prophet adds that the mountains will shrink and valleys be less deep. In other words, it's going to be easier than you think. God will make it so because God wants you to get out of Babylon and resume your particular identity *in Judah*, with a reconstructed temple in Jerusalem.

Notice that this has nothing to do with Jesus. But then as now, the scriptures were living texts, subject to reinterpretation in light of contemporary events, and the events depicted by the New Testament writers were defined by a particular understanding of Jesus as the fulfillment of prophecies.

Another narrowly reductive reading concerns a prophecy frequently recited at Christmastime. Many Christians are surprised to learn that the Old Testament poem so frequently applied to Mary the mother of Jesus doesn't have the word "virgin" in the Hebrew, and it does have a very specific, concrete, non-Jesus historical context. Take a look. In Isaiah chapter 7, God directs the prophet Isaiah to speak to the distraught king of Judah, Ahaz, to calm him down. It was 734 BCE and King Ahaz was concerned that a coalition of armies (Israel and Syria) would attack. He considered asking the Assyrians for help. In this situation, he sought wisdom from Isaiah, an esteemed advisor, on what to do (though he didn't finally take Isaiah's advice). The way God told Isaiah to tell King Ahaz not to worry, that his attackers would fall away of their own accord, was with this particular poem.

Remember that we're working with translations here, and something to again keep in mind is that ancient Hebrew doesn't have punctuation. The Hebrew in Isaiah 7:14–17 reads something like "See that young woman? She's pregnant and will bear a son. She shall name him God-is-with-us [Hebrew: *immanuel*]. Before the boy is able to reject the wrong and choose the right, the land of the two kings you fear will be destroyed." In other words, it would take a little while for the enemies of Ahaz to be destroyed, but only as long as it would take for the child of that young woman, presently pregnant with said child, to reach the age of discernment—a few years at most. Many centuries after this oracle and the events it describes, Jews were reading this text in a Greek translation. The Hebrew word meaning simply "young woman" came to be specifically "a virgin" in the Greek Bible that Jesus and the literate Jesus followers used. Later still, only verse 14 got the love. In a popular English translation it became "Therefore the Lord himself will give you a sign. The virgin will conceive and bear a son, and will call him Immanuel."

So early Christians, looking to their scriptures for justification that Jesus was the Messiah for whom they had been waiting, found ways to understand received texts in light of new circumstances. Immanuel, by the way, is not another spelling for "Jesus" but a Hebrew word that means "God (is) with us." Within the books of the Old Testament prophets, children often bore message names. For the Jesus followers who composed the Gospels some seven hundred years after Isaiah's prophecy, Jesus *was* God in the flesh, God with us, and the virgin of the Greek version of Isaiah 7:14 that they were reading would be understood as none other than Mary.

\*\*\*

Let's talk about sex.[10]

First, does the following (or any part of it) sound familiar? "The Bible says that marriage is between one man and one woman, for uninhibited procreation, and should never be dissolved ('til death do us part'). Or this: Premarital sex disappoints our Heavenly Father, according to the Bible, and extramarital sex is even worse. God is absolutely opposed to ending a pregnancy (abortion). Oh, and although men and women should have sex, it's not exactly a good thing and has something to do with original sin, on which we're all a bit fuzzy, but suffice it to say it's in the Bible, something about the Fall and Adam and Eve's subsequent carnal relations." So endeth the Bible's word on sex.

Too bad none of that is quite right.

It's always such a relief to have things spelled out, to remove ambiguities and articulate a clear sense of what's expected and what's to be avoided. Good, God-fearing folk have adopted these absolutes, defended them, and (sometimes) tried to uphold them. But while this party line may be what some people believe is morally right, not a single one of those itemized statements is biblically accurate.

Take marriage. One of the biggest arguments against same-sex marriage has come from religious Christians declaring that the Bible defines marriage as between one man and one woman. As foundations of their argument they appeal to the beginning of Genesis, chapter 1, with its "male and female" creation of human beings, and chapter 2, with its man and woman, Adam and Eve.

Quick question: Does either text mention marriage? Look closely. Nope. No matter how many times we read these texts and no matter how one translates from the Hebrew in them, "marriage" is absent. When it comes to using the Bible in legislating about marriage specifically, this would seem worth noting. But what about "therefore a man leaves . . . and cleaves to his wife"? Isn't that about marriage? Consider: not only is there no wedding or explicit mention of marriage, but also the Hebrew word here translated "wife" is simply "woman" with the possessive pronoun "his." Not that the translation is wrong, just that this is not an argument for marriage as between a man and a woman, since there's no mention of marriage and the term here specified as a spouse is a general word meaning simply "woman."

For those who read these texts in the context of marriage, they're in good company. Jesus did it.[11] Still, Jesus didn't seem to be particularly crazy about marriage. The greater literary context of these texts and others suggests that he and Paul saw marriage as a way of managing the imperfect situation of human beings having two sexes. Paul also saw marriage as a stopover union of male and female on the way to (a perfect) restoration of androgyny after bodily resurrection (like God—both male and female—as per Genesis chapter 1).[12]

Then there's the pesky issue of number: one man, one woman, the defenders of "biblical marriage" claim. But the Bible is chock-full of polygamy—and not condemnation of it. Abraham had two wives (adding Keturah late in life). So did Jacob. The great King Solomon was a serial marrier. That is, polygamy is not frowned upon or discussed but simply assumed to be normal, and is even encouraged under some circumstances. A few late New Testament texts counter this tradition, but only specifically with regard to church leaders.[13] Then there's Paul, who in no uncertain terms judges it better never to marry at all.[14]

Which brings us to procreation and back to Genesis chapter 1. While historical context and cultural norms are crucial to understanding biblical ideas about men and women, in the case of procreation this is especially important. The mandate to have children and lots of them derives primarily from Genesis chapter 1's "Be fruitful and multiply." But let's think about this for a second. In a world where human beings are few, when your own particular brand of human (family, tribe, nationality . . .) is under threat, and mortality rates limit lifespans to a couple of decades at best (Noah et al. notwithstanding), procreation without restraint is a real plus. Where an entire demographic's value and even survival depends on having offspring, the stakes go up yet again—health, wealth, even survival depend upon it.

Such was the case in the world out of which our biblical texts come. General human population was low. Human activity was considered crucial to the welfare of the world, and there simply weren't very many humans out there. Life was hard and short—no immunization for children, pesticides for the crops, or widespread plumbing, much less prenatal nutrition and cholesterol medication. The specific population of Hebrews-Israelites was constantly under threat from both enemy tribes and natural causes. Adding to the urgency to make more people, consider that during the most prolific period of biblical development (Babylonian exile), which is the likely context for the authorship of Genesis chapter 1, the Israelites not only had been decimated by Nebuchadnezzar and his forces but had been taken into a foreign land where many of them simply assimilated into Babylonian society.

Back in those ancient days, it seemed that for individual communities and the planet as a whole, more children was an unmitigated boon. Add to that a patriarchal cultural system wherein a woman alone had little power or opportunity to build wealth (her social security lay in relationships—to parents, husband, and children), you'd better believe she'd want to have a lot of children, especially sons.

Compare those circumstances to today's, and you'll stumble on one of the most glaring examples of how adhering to the letter of a biblical text can yield exactly the opposite of its spirit. A humorous look at the inanity of taking procreation to its extreme is the musical interlude of Monty Python's *The Meaning of Life*, in which grossly impoverished and overcrowded families blithely sing, "Every sperm is sacred." The results of such an explosion in human population would undermine the Bible's first expectation for us: that we would have dominion like or in the manner of the creator God in whose image it declares that we are made to use those faculties to ensure the planet's well-being, in order that we as God's surrogates in the world would seek to maintain it to be "very good" as God had made it to be. The text allows "Be fruitful and multiply" to mean creative human endeavors other than literal procreation, endeavors that, in our modern times, reflect efforts to apply our dominion to being wise stewards of the earth, its resources and nonhuman inhabitants.

***

On the topic of extramarital sex, which would seem simple, there is nevertheless a gray area. Sure, Paul issues a pretty scathing judgment on what would seem to be extramarital sex (though the Greek makes it hard to be certain it isn't a more specific sexual immorality he's going after). But it's not correct to say that nowhere does extramarital sex meet with divine approval.[15] For one thing, recall how Father Abraham, our most illustrious patriarch, the first so "chosen" by God, slept with at least one woman who was not his wife. Nowhere is he chastised for it. His eldest son, Ishmael, is the son of Hagar, a slave. Jacob, too, conceives children from women not his wife, and they become ancestors of the tribes of Israel.

There's actually a whole story suggesting not only that extramarital affairs are acceptable but that they are morally preferable in some circumstances. Take Tamar. No really, the Bible says, take her. The Tamar to whom I'm referring here (there are a couple) appears in Genesis 38. She was Judah's daughter-in-law. The Bible says that Judah selected her himself to be the wife of his eldest son, Er. Then, in typically terse fashion, the text immediately and simply says that Yahweh didn't like Er and killed him. There is no explanation, no story detailing what Er did to displease God. Nothing. It tells us only that Er was at fault and killed and otherwise has got nothing to do with the story. With Er dead, the legal customs presumed by this story dictated that Tamar be married to the dead man's brother. Remember, we're talking here about a system of social welfare whereby individuals vulnerable to poverty and alienation required special protection. In this patriarchal context, a woman without a man had virtually no property or rights. Widows, especially those without children, were among the most vulnerable.

So Judah required that his next eldest son, named Onan, marry Tamar, which the young man did. Unwillingly, it seems. And can you blame him? There was little in it for Onan, and a lot to lose. According to the legal and cultural norms of the time, any child Tamar bore, even to Onan, would be legally considered Er's and get ahead of Onan in the line of inheritance. So Onan took some precautions of his own. He slept with her all right. But he made sure that he ejaculated somewhere else. The narrator says simply that what Onan did displeased Yahweh, who killed Onan too.

Digression: it's lacunae like these that have led to all sorts of theological and doctrinal conclusions over the ages. In this case, church leaders decided that masturbation, dubbed "onanism," was bad ("Every sperm is sacred," right?) and extended that also to birth control.[16] In truth, one can argue equally if not more strongly that what we have in the biblical story is concern for the woman's security. Just as Tamar was supposed to be married to her dead husband's brother in order that she not fall destitute, it's also not fair to deprive her of the children who could offer the same protection. It has nothing to do with birth control or masturbation. These were very different times and places than our own.

Back again to our story. I promise I'm getting to the extra-marital sex.

The whole narrative kicks off with Judah's wife Shua bearing him three sons. Two are now dead. The expectation is of course that Judah would marry Tamar off to his third and youngest son. He hesitates. This is now his last surviving son. We can only guess that he'd not been informed that God had killed them on purpose. Rather, Judah reasons that something about marrying Tamar must be fatal. So he withholds his only remaining son, Shelah, ostensibly because he's not old enough to get married. But the narrator makes clear that the real reason is "because he too might die like his brothers." Judah suggests Tamar go back to live in her father's house until Shelah grows up.

She does, and the very next thing the narrator says is that "a long time" passes. Still no marriage. Tamar takes things into her own hands, and in a wonderfully dramatic play on seeing and not seeing, Judah sleeps with her, thinking her to be a prostitute. She conceives. Just before Judah has her killed for her transgression, she proves that it's Judah's offspring she carries. He can't deny it and declares, "She is more in the right than I."

In other words, Tamar's sleeping with Judah—to whom she was not married—made her the more righteous of them because, Judah says, he had denied her marriage to Shelah. I know, it's confusing. Judah was ready to proceed with what seems to have been, at the time, an acceptable punishment: killing her for sleeping around when she was supposed to be married to someone in his family. But she definitely wasn't. She wasn't married to anyone, and yet sleeping with Judah was the right thing for her to do, as he is quick to admit. Incidentally, Tamar conceived twins, one of whom becomes an ancestor of David—and of Jesus, too.

\*\*\*

Original sin originates in Genesis. Or not. It depends on whom you ask. To be clear, the notion of original sin does not appear in the Adam-and-Eve story except by an interpretation that appears first in the New Testament and became doctrine only thanks to later church deliberations. So Jews don't "believe in" original sin. Most Christians do, thanks to Paul and a bunch of early church fathers, such as Augustine, Tertullian, and Ambrose. Paul started it all with his letter to the Romans, in which he wrote that just as Adam introduced sin into the world, so Jesus introduces a way out.[17]

The church fathers took this text and ran with it, extrapolating that original sin, then, is both a particular act of which Adam was guilty and something that has been passed on to his descendants, revocable only through the grace of God in Jesus. Add a Christian rereading of Psalm 51:5, in which the speaker (David, after getting called out for the Bathsheba affair for which he had her innocent husband killed) decries his chronically sinful state by saying he's been so thoroughly guilty and for so long that his guilt must have started in the womb, and you get the logic of original sin as conception itself. Augustine further twinned it with sexual desire, since the church fathers judged Eve to be complicit in the disobedience in the Garden of Eden, and other church leaders, such as Martin Luther and John Calvin, concurred. Misogynistic suspicions and judgments of women as leading men into sin and transmitting original sin to their babies has persisted ever since.

***

Two issues that get far more attention in the sexual politics of our time than the Bible's coverage of them would seem to merit are homosexuality and abortion. There are several excellent and detailed treatments of what the Bible does and doesn't have to say about homosexuality. I refer readers to those for in-depth discussion and analysis.[18] Suffice it to say, there's virtually nothing in the Bible concerning homosexuality that's relevant to our times: there are precious few texts of arguable relevance in the first place, none of which addresses love, much less commitment, between people of the same sex.

Similarly, there's arguably nothing in the Bible about abortion. Nowhere does the Bible prohibit terminating a pregnancy. Despite echoing (in English translation) the modern idiomatic parlance of debate on the issue, Deuteronomy 30:19, in which Moses exhorts the Hebrews to "choose life," is not about abortion. Its literary, historical, and theological context clearly anchors its concern in keeping the commandments. Those, Moses says, are life-giving; breaking them brings down the fatal wrath of God. (In other words, Deuteronomy 30:19 has nothing to do with abortion.)

The other biblical texts to which people appeal to argue that God forbids terminating a pregnancy are embedded in metaphorical language serving a very different message: that God "knew" the speaker all his or her life, even in the womb.[19] In the case of the prophet Jeremiah it's a way to legitimize his role as a spokesman for God.[20] The texts don't forbid abortion. That's not itself a judgment one way or the other about abortion; it's just a fact. Only by interpretation and extrapolation might such texts be taken to inform an antiabortion agenda. And that's an exercise that works both ways.

The only biblical text that might seem to deal with abortion is Exodus 21:22–23, but it has to do with the involuntary loss of a fetus due to violence against the woman carrying the fetus. What attention the event gets is focused on the relative value (to its male audience) of the woman and the baby. Embedded in numerous legal commandments, including "Whoever curses father or mother should be put to death," this text details the consequences in which fighting men inadvertently injure a pregnant woman. If the woman miscarries, it says, but that's all, the guilty party must pay a fine to the husband of the woman; if the results are worse, "if any harm follows," the "law of retaliation" is enacted: life for life, eye for eye, tooth for tooth.[21] But look closely, it's the woman, not the fetus, whose welfare is at issue here. Remember, the text already said what to do if the fetus is killed: a simple monetary payment is due from the fighter to the husband of the woman. Christians whose Old Testament is based on the Septuagint's Greek translation of Hebrew texts distinguish between whether the miscarried baby is "completely formed" (then "eye for eye, . . .") or not (a simple fine).

By contrast to the Bible's surprising silence on such issues of passionate modern concern, one topic that *does* get a lot of attention and in both Old and New Testaments is adultery. There are oodles of explicit laws in the New Testament Gospels forbidding adultery, and Jesus clearly states that adultery is wrong. Funny how so many of the people in our time who get up in arms about gay marriage and abortion so easily whitewash and "forgive" adultery (if they note it at all), though it is adultery that comes under excoriating judgment in the Bible, clearly and explicitly, over and over again, from the Hebrew Bible right through the entire Christian scripture.

If you're wondering how that squares with our discussion of premarital and extramarital sex, two things: first, the Bible is a book, a collection of many voices, not all of which are in agreement; second, "the devil's in the details," as they say (no, not the Bible; "they" as in "we"). Not all sex outside of marriage is judged equal by biblical standards.

***

A particularly dangerous kind of misunderstanding takes the Bible at its word in judging others, even when those others are, if not the people who gave us the texts, then related to those people. There's a popular belief that the Jews killed Jesus. After all, each of the Gospels describes the Jewish establishment—its leaders, its people in general—calling for Jesus's execution at the moment of trial. Pilate exonerated, the Jews implicated. But the biblical texts betray another story. They demand a second look, especially some two thousand years later.[22]

First, there's the pesky business of context—that the times out of which those texts come are very different from our own and that the Passover occasion of Jesus's trial and crucifixion would have made Pilate's allowances even less likely. Second, the biblical accounts don't all agree, and the ways they differ cast suspicion on the simplistic claim that the Jews killed Jesus. Third and finally, we already know who *did* kill Jesus: the Romans. "Yes," you may counter, "but it was the Jews who called for it." Which brings us back to number one: context.

It's easy to forget, even for the most seasoned biblical scholar, that at the time these stories began to circulate, there were not "Jews" and "Christians" so much as different kinds of Jews, including those whose beliefs about Jesus put them at odds with some basic tenets of the Judaism(s) of their day. The stories circulated among Jesus's followers, of course. Those followers were compelled to defend themselves, believing that the man Jesus from Nazareth was the long-awaited messiah, through whom God conquered death itself. In other words, when these stories began to be written, it was under antagonistic circumstances: Jesus's followers had challenged basic tenets of Jewish tradition—that the messiah for whom the Jews waited would be a king, for one thing. What's more, the Gospel accounts (where we read about Jesus's trial in Jerusalem) were composed after Jesus's followers came to believe that Jesus was a savior for gentiles as well as for Jews.

A cursory look at the different accounts in the order of their composition actually shows an increasingly innocent Pilate. Mark, the earliest Gospel, says simply that Jesus says Pilate calls him king of the Jews and that when Pilate offers to grant clemency to only one prisoner, the Jews demand Jesus be crucified and Barabbas released.[23] Matthew ups the drama. In Matthew's Gospel, Pilate's wife sends him a message alleging that Jesus is innocent, but the Jewish crowd is riotous in demanding Jesus's death. Pilate literally washes his hands of the matter, saying he's innocent of Jesus's blood, while the Jews call, "His blood be upon us and our children."[24] Luke begins the trial with Pilate saying he can't find any guilt in Jesus, but the Jews are unassuaged. Pilate learns that Herod is in town and tries to foist the problem off on him. Herod sends it back, finding no reason for a charge. Pilate adds another two claims of Jesus's innocence, but the Jews are unrelenting, so Pilate gives Jesus "up to their will."[25]

John, as usual, departs markedly from the other Gospels, but not on the question of Pilate's innocence. For one thing, the trial takes place before the Passover meal in John (afterward in the synoptic gospels), and in this case, it takes place at Pilate's office. But only Jesus goes in before Pilate because, the text explains, the Jews would have been rendered unclean to eat the Passover meal were they to go join him there. So, in this telling, Pilate trucks in and out of his office to visit with Jesus and consult with the Jewish leaders. He does so no fewer than six times. Given Pilate's powerful position, this strains credibility. Pilate tries to release Jesus three times (as in Luke), but "the Jews" consistently demand execution. Pilate asks if they're really serious about that. They claim no king but Caesar, and Pilate hands Jesus "over to them to be crucified." The "them" is a little hazy, since the crucifiers would have been Roman soldiers, but the grammar suggests it's "the chief priests" of the narrative.[26]

Finally, consider that as the representative of Roman governance and leadership, Pilate would hardly have stood for the potentially incendiary nature of a man claiming to be king of the Jews. Jerusalem at Passover was a nightmare for the Romans: Jews gathered en masse from all over Judea and beyond to recall through sacrifice, recitation, and community a moment of radical liberation from foreign political rule (Egypt). It was crazy enough already without entertaining an inflammatory miracle-worker with a breakaway band of passionate followers. Any death penalty in the Roman style of crucifixion was issued by a governor. Pilate would hardly have ceded that responsibility.

But the story that comes to us comes not from Roman journalists or secular Jewish historians. It comes from Jesus followers, a community that was both reaching out to gentiles and had become disenfranchised and persecuted by "Jews," who would not, nay, could not accept the sect's claims. Is it any wonder "the Jews" come off as distinct from Jesus and his followers (who were themselves Jews, remember) and guilty of the crucifixion of Jesus? When Jews still did not accept the Jesus followers' belief that Jesus was the Messiah, the Jesus followers, responsible for the Gospels (and thus stories such as this), showed the Jews' rejection of Jesus as original and actually leading to Jesus's crucifixion. Therefore, in their telling, the Jews killed Jesus.

Unfortunately, without nuance, without seeing what lies behind these stories—aided by observing how they differ and knowing history—and plopped into a modern context with a well-established Christianity of far greater numbers and power than Judaism, we have the seeds of anti-Semitism in its purest form.

*** 

What happens after we die and how we are to live in order to improve our afterlife odds are endlessly intriguing, even urgent questions. Here, too, the Bible bucks many modern assumptions. How is a person to be "saved" and have "eternal life"? Christians are quick to answer with creedal statements of faith and belief in Jesus as the incarnation of God who "died for our sins" and was resurrected that we might live forever. So it can be surprising to find little or no such language from Jesus, not as told in the Gospels, anyway. While the latest Gospel, John, does portray a Jesus who identifies himself as divine and belief in him as the means of relationship to God even as an antidote to dying in sin, still we do not find Jesus saying that belief in him as the Son of God and in his crucifixion and resurrection as conquest over sin and death is the means of salvation and eternal life for the whole world. That's Paul. By contrast, consider this—Jesus's own statement on the matter of gaining eternal life. It's much more personal, prosaic and down-to-earth. And as with much of Jesus's teaching, it's embedded in a story. That the story appears with the most minor of variations in all three of the synoptic gospels suggests we ought to take notice.[27]

In each version, a man approaches Jesus, who has been out with his disciples teaching among crowds of people. The man asks Jesus what he must do to attain eternal life. Jesus responds that he should keep the commandments and specifies the following: don't murder, don't commit adultery, don't steal, don't bear false witness, and honor your father and mother. (Mark adds "Don't defraud"; Matthew includes "Love your neighbor as yourself.") In each case, the man protests that he already keeps these. Jesus responds that then there is one thing more: Sell all you have, give the money to the poor ("you will have treasure in heaven"), and follow me.

The man goes away despondent because he owns a lot of stuff. For the benefit of his disciples and the crowd, Jesus makes his famous observation "It's easier for a camel to pass through the eye of a needle than for a rich man to enter the kingdom of God." That elicits the question "Then who can be saved?" (thus linking "eternal life" with "salvation"). Jesus answers that what is impossible for mortals is not impossible for God.

Notice there is nothing here about Jesus's death, nothing about his resurrection, nothing whatsoever about "belief," but everything about being decent and radically generous. There are two other elements crucial to Jesus's idea of salvation that we find here. One is that giving everything away isn't the end; "Follow me" is. The second is that "for God all things are possible."

Consider John 5:28–29 on the resurrection of the dead. It applies to everyone—everyone is resurrected, the text says. But depending on how you lived, it will go either well or badly for you after that. "Those who did good will come forth to resurrection of life; those who did evil, to resurrection of judgement." Whatever exactly any of that means—such resurrections, even good and evil—even John's Jesus is clear that one's actions affect one's afterlife prospects.

\*\*\*

The flip side of salvation is, of course, Hell. Again, traditional Christian teaching has historically come with a good dose of fire and brimstone. It issues the threat that failing to be a good Christian— the specifics vary, but lack of "belief in" Jesus is always part of it—will consign a person to eternal damnation. Given this, it can be surprising to discover that Hell as a discrete location in mytho-geography is absent in the Bible.

The Hebrew Bible makes scarce mention of what happens after a person dies. It's much more concerned with how one lives. That said, a reader occasionally happens on mention of Sheol, "the place of the dead," "the pit," "the grave." Sheol is never described as a punishment. In the rare cases where it is mentioned in the Hebrew Bible, it would seem Sheol just happens, and that's that. Ideas of Heaven and Hell such as we encounter them today evolved, and the Bible hardly marks the end of that evolution.

Indeed, still in the New Testament, Hell is never described as a place where people who don't believe in Jesus go. It's not even, really, an afterlife place at all. The word "hell" is a translation of the Greek *gehenna*, which actually *was* a place. That it was a place one could visit, though no one would go for kicks, suggests that Jesus's use of it in the context of suffering punishment was metaphorical, not to be taken literally.

*Gehenna* was where Jerusalem burned its garbage, and since the city and the surrounding communities generated a lot of gar-bage, *gehenna* was always burning. So when Jesus warned that a person might end up in *gehenna*, he probably didn't mean the literal, incinerating *gehenna*-dump outside of Jerusalem. Rather that's the kind of miserable condition that murderers (or those who, just as bad, humiliate others), adulterers (or those who, just as bad, objec-tify others), or those who use their privilege and standing to drag others into oppression would suffer on account of their bad beha-vior.[28] In no case does Jesus claim that the problem for which one might end up in Hell is a lack of "belief" or "faith." It's for doing (or not doing). Early Christians wrestled with this relationship of belief and deeds, faith and works. The New Testament includes both "jus-tified by works and not by faith alone" and "justified by faith apart from works." So maybe the wrestling itself is worthwhile.[29]

# Chapter 8

# And General Befuddlements

God loves Moses. From infancy, it was Moses, the baby in the bulrushes, saved from murderous intent and raised to be great. God commissions Moses out of all people on earth to lead God's people into the next great chapter of God's relationship to humankind. And then God tries to kill Moses. What?! But Moses's wife saves him with a bloody flint. What?! It sounds like fan fiction, a spin-off of biblical characters into a whole different set of stories. Except it's not. That episode is in the Bible. Nobody's completely sure what to make of it.

Thus far, we've focused on biblical peculiarities and mis-understandings that nonetheless have some explanation. This chapter discusses some of the oddities that even scholars don't know quite how to understand. We're so far away—in time and place, culture and language—from the Bible's origins that even among the most learned scholars, questions remain. Some of these puzzling texts may assume familiarity with customs or stories well-known to the authors but lost to us now; others may be cases of stories missing significant parts; in still other cases, we might simply want to know more than the texts reveal.

But before we throw up our hands in surrender, it's worth revisiting some of the ways we might at least contextualize the things that we can't completely figure out. After all, these questions don't go away just because we don't know what to make of them. And recognizing them has its own worth, if nothing else, in fostering a healthy humility. A warning: this may be the most dissatisfying chapter to read, for it includes those enduring questions and oddities that we haven't yet made reasonable sense of. These are things that can't help but leave one feeling a bit uneasy.

***

Let's start with that bizarre business of Moses's wife Zipporah and her flint. The episode takes place over a mere three verses.[1] As always, it's good to ask about a text's situation in the greater literary unit: the story poem, list, law, .... Most of the time, when we consider this greater context, we can better understand the text at hand. In this case, the effect is quite the opposite. The literary context sets us up with a certain comfortable understanding entirely at odds with the text itself.

In the verses preceding Zipporah's act, Yahweh is in cahoots with Moses. Not just cahoots; it was God's idea to join forces with Moses, out of all the people God might have picked. (And remember, Moses *did* try to dissuade Yahweh, suggesting someone else would be a better choice.) God treats Moses as a trusted partner in a particularly significant and dangerous endeavor: getting Pharaoh to release the Hebrews-Israelites. God gives Moses a magic staff and the power to execute signs of a miraculous nature and promises a mouthpiece (again because of Moses's protestations that someone else would be better, this time on the matter of public speaking), his brother, Aaron, though it would be God, of course, who was really doing the talking.

Sure, the drama is tense, the situation a bit nerve-wracking. But this is the prelude to a showdown whose heroes and villains are clearly drawn: Moses with God (and Aaron) on behalf of the beleaguered Hebrews-Israelites versus the heavy-hitting superpower of the day, Egypt, with its rich and mighty pharaoh. So when Moses heads off "with his wife and sons" to confront the king of Egypt, the alliances couldn't be clearer.

Which brings us to Zipporah's flint. The episode starts with a statement delivered in a typically bland biblical tone, the more remarkable for its spicy content. "At a night encampment on the way, Yahweh encountered him and sought to kill him."[2] Astute commentators have noted how blisteringly shocking this is, coming on the heels, as it does, of the intimacy that God and Moses shared and the setup of alliances I just mentioned. This is one of those moments in the Bible that should remind us how very old the text is. And the Old Testament most of all. A lot can happen to a story, especially the written-down text of a story, over the years, decades, centuries, millennia of its existence. Aside from the foreignness of its author's concerns, preoccupations, worldview, and more, things can get mangled or even lost.

Many scholars wonder if what we have in this episode isn't the truncated remains of a much larger (and more comprehensible) narrative. We've assumed that Moses is the subject of the "him" in "Yahweh encountered him and sought to kill him." Indeed, your translation may actually not have "him" at all, but spell it out as "Moses." If so, the modern translators have simply gone ahead and attributed the pronouns of the Hebrew original for you in an effort to clear things up. But that is an interpretive move. And note, especially considering the possibility that this isn't the opening at all but follows on some unexcused absence of text, that that's not a given. The Hebrew "him" may not actually have had Moses in mind. After all, the next thing that happens in the story is that Zipporah cuts off her son's foreskin. "Her son," the text says.

In other words, we've been reading the person behind the "him" of "Yahweh encountered him and sought to kill him" in light of what immediately preceded—all this stuff about Moses. Indeed, Moses has been the only real, human character in the text for quite a while now. In the text we have, that is. But maybe we're missing something, and the "him" actually refers to Zipporah's (and presumably, but not necessarily, Moses's) son. Zipporah does take some pretty dramatic action toward her son. So maybe.

Or maybe, reading on to consider also that she "touched his feet [alternatively, 'legs'] with it, saying 'You are truly a bridegroom of blood to me!,'" it is Moses, after all. I think we can agree that calling her own son a "bridegroom of blood" is a little creepy, even for the Bible. Still, even if we go with Moses as the object of Zipporah's declaration, that doesn't necessitate that it was Moses's feet (or "legs"; the Hebrew can go either way, but translators usually opt for "feet") that she touched with "it." The pronouns liberally sprinkled throughout the text are hardly clear in their referents. Maybe it was her son's feet . . . or legs. The next sentence does nothing to straighten it out. It begins, "And when he let him alone . . ." Note again that some translations (maybe yours) capitalize "he" to indicate that the referent is God. But biblical Hebrew doesn't have upper- and lowercase; there's no difference in the way the letters look, so that distinction is thanks only to modern interpreters, translators, and editors.

That final sentence does clarify something else, though, that this whole business has something to do with circumcision—the flint on the foreskin.

Not only are we unsure how to attribute the plethora of pronouns, but just what the heck is going on, anyway? There's little more we can say other than that Zipporah took a circumcising action that appeased God and so saved Moses's—or maybe her son's—life from a murderous God. And the most likely chain of events is that Zipporah understood (somehow) that God was seeking to kill Moses (or her/their son) and acted accordingly—probably circumcising her son and then touching the gruesome bit to Moses's "feet," likely standing in euphemistically for genitalia (as in Isaiah 7:20 and elsewhere). And something about that moved God to leave Moses alone.

But wow, there are a lot of questions that remain unanswered, even if we go with this somewhat reasonable reading. Maybe one day, some dusty archaeologist, shepherd, or tech escapee will happen on an older, dare I say more original, version of this story that will put to bed the questions it raises. Maybe. But in the meantime, this is what we've got. And somehow it came to us as Bible. So we tuck the possibly-part-of-a-larger-story-no-longer-have-explanation-of-this into our caps and press on.

Incidentally, the very next verse picks up where we left off, with God's promise that he will assign Aaron to be Moses's spokesman, confirming how very incongruous is the episode of Zipporah's flint.

***

If Moses is such a great guy, the one whom God commissioned to bring God's people out of slavery in Egypt, the one who dictated the law code that would define Judaism (and indirectly Christianity) for all time, the one who led the Hebrew people to the Promised Land, the one and only person in the Hebrew Bible who saw God face-to-face and lived to tell about it—the one who is even called "the friend of God"—then why the horns? Visual depictions of arguably the most celebrated biblical figure before Jesus make him look to our eyes more like the devil than anything else. Yet in paintings, tapestries, stained glass, and marble, there's no denying it: horns sprouting from the prophet's hoary head. What's with that?

It's a question that's rankled and puzzled modern Bible scholars, not least because there's only one place in the Bible where the word "horns" occurs. More specifically, it's the only place where the verb form appears of a word that otherwise appears as a noun.

The text at issue appears in the context of Moses's meeting God atop Mount Sinai (or Mount Horeb, depending).[3] After the forty days and forty nights of said meeting (during which Moses neither ate nor drank, according to the text), with the tablets of "the words of the covenant, the ten words" in hand (as discussed earlier, *not* the Ten Commandments we think of, but ten requirements having to do more with the mechanisms of worship), Moses's visage was transformed. It was strikingly peculiar to those who saw it; he himself had no idea of the effect.

Specifically, we read, "Moses didn't know that the skin of his face something-or-another-ed." The effect of whatever happened was awesome or terrifying to those who looked at him, so terrifying that Moses had to put a veil over his face. Most modern translations say it shone or some such synonym. But that's a guess, because the word, *qaran*, doesn't appear anywhere else in the Bible. And the more probably accurate is just too strange for modern sensibilities.

The Hebrew *qaran* is related to a fairly common noun, *qeren*, meaning "horn." Jerome's Vulgate (his translation from the Hebrew into Latin) adopted the word "horn," and the rest is history. Much medieval artwork—as well as earlier and later work—depicts a Moses with horns. Consider Michelangelo's *Moses*, illuminated manuscripts, and stained-glass windows. Nevertheless, it struck many biblical scholars as too strange to be true. For a long time, people figured this was some kind of mistranslation, that by an otherwise unknown twist in the Hebrew the text told of Moses's face emitting something to a particularly piercing effect. But "Horns"? Couldn't be, this line of thinking went.[4]

But Jerome was no idiot. And it's clear that he gave this some hard thought. In his commentary on Ezekiel he spells this out, writing that Moses's face had "become 'glorified' or as it says in the Hebrew 'horned.'"[5] Turns out, "horns" may be exactly what the Hebrew "intended." Analysis of the text in light of its literary, cultural, and historical context shows how powerful was the attribute of having horns, particular to deities. Odd as it is to our modern sensibilities, "horns" may be exactly correct.[6]

Even a cursory glance at iconography of the ancient Near East shows the prevalence of horns on gods and goddesses, the association of horns with exceptional beings and special power. In the text's literary context, the reference to horns follows the second (this time successful) effort of Moses to bring God's regulations to the people— the first effort having been ruined by the whole Golden Calf episode, wherein a human-fashioned, horned bovine stood in for God. Perhaps "Moses took the place of the golden calf, of the bull, of which horns are characteristic. In a sense that was indeed the case, for Moses was the visible mediator between Yahweh and Israel."[7] It makes a kind of sense, then, that Moses, unique among biblical characters in having seen God and lived, the mediator between God and God's people, might have been said to appear to have sprouted horns.

Over the centuries, Moses's noble horns became associated with the devil, Satan. What's more, without knowing or appreciating the nuances of Hebrew, the historical and cultural context out of which that passage in Exodus comes, without understanding how radically unique the Bible portrays Moses to have been, suspicious Christians came to associate the horns of Moses with Jews in a worldview that sees such horns only as sinister markings of the Devil. The anti-Semitism such ignorance has fostered is chilling.

*** 

Zipporah's flint, Moses's horns. While we're on the topic of puzzling objects, what's the deal with Boaz and the sandal? Apparently, it was a bewilderment even when the biblical book of Ruth was written, since even the narrator is forced to explain, "Now, this was the custom in former times."[8]

As the story goes, the widow Ruth pledges loyalty to her bereaved mother-in-law, Naomi, and so ends up in Naomi's family land. There, Ruth happens, fairy-tale-style, to catch the eye of the eligible bachelor Boaz. The smitten Boaz determines to make Ruth his wife, even after discovering that there exists another bachelor with right of first refusal. That is, if the other guy wants to marry Ruth, she's his. (Don't get me started on a feminist rant. It's actually a lovely story in which Ruth takes some courageous and intelligent initiative.)

The next of kin forfeits his right (or obligation) to marry Ruth by symbolically taking off his sandal, thereby opening the way for our romantic hero Boaz to marry her. It's tempting to see the practice as a reflection of a law in Deuteronomy, but there, a spurned sister-in-law grabs the refusing brother's sandal, spits in his face, and leaves him with the odious reputation of being the one "whose sandal was pulled off."[9] Needless to say, this is neither the tone nor the effect of the book of Ruth, with its happy ending.

\*\*\*

In the case of Lot's wife, who is transformed into a pillar of salt, it's tough to know what we're missing. Is there a custom or (now) unfamiliar mythopoeic trope behind this, or is it simply a colorful way of portraying how oddities in a particular landscape took shape? Whatever the case, discussion of Lot's wife also bears a brief recap.

When Abraham and his nephew Lot go their separate ways, Lot elects to stay in the lush Jordan plains and "pitched his tents toward Sodom."[10] If that city name rings a bell, then you might predict what happens later: Lot's family gets caught up in God's destruction of Sodom and Gomorrah. An angel tells them to flee the impending disaster and warns, "Do not look behind you."[11] When Lot's wife does look back as she runs, she is turned to salt. Weird. And that's about all there is to say.

We can moralize: she was told not to; she did anyway; she got punished (though the punishment seems a bit harsh, to say the least). And we can add a(n undeserved but not uncommon) sexist twist: just another shallow woman longing for a former life of sinful excess, and disobedient to boot. One problem is that Hebrew grammar indicates that only Lot received the warning. The relevant pronoun in the statement is masculine singular: "Do not you [single male] look behind you [single male]." Lot's wife may never have heard the angel, or if she did, assumed, as was grammatically justified, that it applied only to Lot. The most likely (though not entirely satisfactory) explanation for the whole turning-to-salt business is as etiology, explaining why the environs of the Dead Sea, the likely setting for the biblical story, are "peopled" by tall mineral salt structures.

\*\*\*

Another matter of some bewilderment is how exactly the book of Esther got into the Bible. It never once mentions God. Ancient sources suggest that it just squeaked by into the canon that we have. The book of Esther alone, among all the books of the Hebrew Bible, has no representation among the thousands of scraps and scroll-bits discovered at Qumran, where the Dead Sea Scrolls were found. Indeed, its inclusion among books that would become the Bible was still a matter of debate well into the first few centuries of the Common Era.

Likely originating some few centuries before the year zero, Esther tells of the challenges of being Jewish under a foreign power (Persian, in the story; Hellenistic-Greek, historically). Carefully composed as a story of symmetric reversals, it is finally the Jews who effect a slaughter originally intended against them. The violence it tells is off-putting but necessary to the story's structure—of such mirroring halves as to underscore that its plot is not based in history. The book provides an explanation and justification for the Jews' adopting an originally Babylonian or Persian festival of upside-down-ness, Purim, that is otherwise not mandated by the Torah.

Those of us who are accustomed to seeing the story as biblical are inclined to overlook the fact that this Hebrew Bible book never once mentions God. It's a striking absence when you notice it. It was troubling enough to the Greek-speaking Jews of the first century CE that they added episodes and prayers that would beef up the level of piety among its leading characters and also make explicit that God was involved all along. The Greek additions are included in Roman Catholic and Orthodox Bibles. In Protestant Christian Bibles, following the Jewish canon of the Hebrew Bible, they appear only as part of the Apocrypha. Most scholars think that Esther slipped into the canon on the basis of interpretations that place God behind the events, an agent of inspiration and coincidence. The later, godly additions probably helped, too, as they show this belief that God was involved all along.

***

While Esther lacks God, the Gospel of Mark in its earliest versions lacked the "good news." This, too, is chronically bewildering. In the original ending of Mark's Gospel—*gospel*, mind you, meaning "good news"—the news never gets out. Witnesses to Jesus's resurrection (his absence, to be precise) from the tomb, who were instructed to "go and tell," ran away instead and "said nothing." The End. Why?

Scholars agree that Mark's is the earliest Gospel. They generally date it to around 70 CE (a good forty years after Jesus's death), which is when the Romans sacked Jerusalem and destroyed the temple there. Small wonder that early Christianity was so consumed with the end times. It would seem to the Jews of that time and place, and so also to the small sect that believed Jesus to be the long-awaited messiah, that the world as they knew it was indeed coming to an end.

The tone of Mark's Gospel is consistent with such sensibility: everything happens in a rush. Even the language itself, scholars of the Greek have long noted, is hurried, terse, abbreviated. What's more, the disciples regularly fall down on the job, miss the boat, and generally come off as wrongheaded, even doltish. With all of that, and reflecting a rather tragic outlook, it probably shouldn't surprise us that its original ending was "and they said nothing to anyone for they were afraid."[12]

As time went on and the message of Jesus's resurrection spread, it makes sense that a happier ending was appended to the first (and then another, even more satisfactory and more in tune with the other Gospels), an ending reflecting the good news the Gospels tell.[13]

But how are we to explain that original downer of an ending? After all, it's still in there. Maybe the earliest authors or editors were content believing that Jesus had been taken straight to heaven (without a resurrection sighting) and believed that somehow the written Gospel would communicate what the Easter-morning witnesses had not. It certainly is in keeping with the style and tenor of the Gospel as a whole. Wouldn't it be great to be able to ask those people responsible for giving us the original ending and then adding more? Finally, of course, the other endings didn't replace the original, but they did shift its context, defanging the episode of the tragic tone the original had cast.

\*\*\*

Among the list of Things to Ask Biblical Authors in Heaven, should one get the opportunity, is why Matthew would choose to literally apply an Old Testament prophecy to the life and times of Jesus of Nazareth when it makes no sense. We've seen that it was understandably de rigueur for the New Testament writers to reach back into their scriptures and reinterpret the texts in light of what they understood and believed about Jesus. Clearly well-versed in the Hebrew Bible's "law and prophets," Matthew does this more than any of the others. What's surprising here is how the authors or editors responsible for the Gospel of Matthew missed the most elementary convention of Hebrew poetry, with a hilarious and incredible result.

I'm talking about the Palm Sunday "Hosannah" scene initiating the last week of Jesus's life. The Gospels say that when Jesus entered Jerusalem, where he would be crucified, he was met with an enthusiastic welcome. People lined the streets, waving palm branches and calling out part of a Hebrew psalm, "Hosannah . . . Blessed is he who comes in the name of the LORD [or 'Lord']."[14] Jesus himself arrived not in a grand chariot or astride a dazzling stallion but in a manner reflecting a humble prince of peace. In Matthew, the scene's inspiration is a prophecy from the book of Zechariah: "Speak to the daughter of Zion, 'Behold the king is coming to you, humble and seated on a donkey, and upon a colt, the foal of an ass.'"[15] The trouble here is with that doublet. A basic convention of ancient Hebrew poetry is construction in a series of parallel lines. In its most common iteration, demonstrated here, line A says one thing, then line B says the same thing in different words. (Another technique is to reverse the meaning; yet another is to expand upon it.) Nearly all prophecy is poetry, so it's no surprise to find it here.

In both Mark and Luke, Jesus sensibly rides into Jerusalem on a colt that a couple of disciples found for him. But Matthew takes the poem literally: Jesus rides into Jerusalem simultaneously atop two animals. Imagine that. Matthew is so well-read, so informed about the Hebrew Bible that it's hard to imagine he would make such a seemingly ignorant and childish mistake, if a mistake is what it is. It's even more baffling as a choice. Then again, maybe Matthew was so determined to show Jesus's action to be no-doubt-about-it literally fulfilling an earlier prophecy that he created a deliberately bizarre scenario that would leave no doubt as to its inspiration. We simply don't know.

\*\*\*

Neither do we know nearly enough to satisfy our modern curiosity about individual people we meet in the Bible. Among the many questions that persist (none really gets a biography extensive enough to satisfy modern readers), one of the most intriguing is, just who *was* Mary Magdalene? Author Dan Brown shot to the top of the bestseller lists with the imaginative and provocative (though not unique) suggestion that Mary Magdalene was Jesus's wife. To be clear, nowhere does the Bible make such a claim. Then again, nowhere is such a suggestion denied. The Bible simply doesn't say.

Oodles of questions about Mary Magdalene remain. What's especially intriguing to me is what the Bible *does* say about her. For one, she is said to be from a particularly interesting city. She is "of Magdala" or "the Magdalene." Miriam/Mary was such a common name that the Gospel writers further identified her by referring to her town of origin. In other words, Magdalene is not her last name but a reference to where she came from. Mary's Magdala, the Aramaic word for "tower," was probably where the modern town of Migdal (Hebrew for "tower") stands on the coast of the Sea of Galilee.[16]

Recent archaeological excavations there have revealed a town dating to Mary's time, with intriguing religious elements, not least among them a synagogue with a mosaic floor, colorful frescoes, room dividers, and accompanying ritual baths. Most intriguing of all: a small square object, carved from a block of stone that uniquely represents the Jerusalem temple, including the temple's most holy space.[17] This audacious representation within such a setting suggests a dynamic religious community that may have believed in a kind of democratization of the divine, a community that might have imagined having access at their Galilean synagogue to a holiness traditionally considered unique to the Jerusalem temple.

In other words, within the broader historical context of a proliferation of Judaisms (think: Pharisees, Sadducees, Zealots, Essenes, and more),[18] Magdalene community open to the Jewish Jesus's potentially revolutionary message.[19] And with Migdal/Magdala not far from Jesus's base in Capernaum and en route from there to his hometown in Nazareth, it's easy to imagine Jesus visiting (and revisiting) that very synagogue. And it's easy to imagine him meeting there a forward-thinking woman of means who was so captivated by his manner and preaching that she'd want to tag along.

So. This Mary was intriguingly "of Magdala." The Bible says even more, and it's even more tantalizing.

In the Gospels of Mark and Luke we read that Jesus cast seven demons out of her.[20] Just what were those demons or the nature of this possession, the Bible doesn't say. It doesn't say that these were seven sins, deadly or otherwise, though you can imagine the heyday artists have had depicting them. And the Bible doesn't say what effect the demons had on her, physical or emotional, though modern readers have speculated that they may have manifested as what we today would diagnose as varieties of illness, mental and otherwise.

Luke tells us that Mary Magdalene was among the women who joined Jesus's group of travelers, women "who provided for them out of their own resources," contributing wealth to support Jesus's community.[21] This upends some long-standing assumptions about women in the first century Mediterranean world, not least that they had no independence, much less the right to liberty and property. In the case of these Jewish women from first-century Galilee, the Gospel writer is nonchalant about both Mary's freedom to follow Jesus and her wealth. This has led to a long tradition of artistic depictions of Mary from Magdala clad in luxurious garb.

Most intriguing of all, the biblical narrators are unanimous about the Magdalene's presence at Jesus's most theologically significant events, the crucifixion and resurrection. If you agree that Mary Magdalene was among Luke's otherwise unnamed "women who had followed him from Galilee, standing at a distance," then we can say that each Gospel claims that she was present at Jesus's crucifixion.[22]

Many artistic depictions of Mary portray her with a vial of some sort. Whether or not this has a biblical basis depends on whether she is using it to wash Jesus's feet (not biblical) or to anoint his corpse (biblical). So it is that Eastern Orthodox iconography situates the Magdalene among "the Myrrh-bearers."[23] The Gospel writers thus place Mary in a select band of only two (in Matthew and Mark), or of only those unnamed women from Galilee (in Luke), or of three who see Jesus's burial place (in John).[24]

Out of all of Jesus's followers, including his innermost circle of twelve (well, eleven, since Judas has betrayed him), it is only Mary Magdalene whom every Gospel names as witness to the empty tomb and to the risen Christ. In Luke, Mary Magdalene is with other women who find the tomb empty except for "two men in dazzling clothes" who tell them that Jesus has risen from the dead.[25] In Matthew, Jesus's first appearance after his resurrection is to Mary Magdalene, among other women.[26] In the Gospels of Mark and John, it is to the Magdalene alone that the risen Jesus reveals himself.[27]

This is a big deal. Witnessing the resurrection, the risen Christ, would come to be a defining characteristic of the first generation of Christian leaders. It was why Paul, who had never met the living Jesus, was so adamant about saying that the risen Jesus had revealed himself to him, so that Paul could be considered among those who would lead the movement after Jesus's death. It also makes Paul's exclusion of Mary Magdalene (indeed all women) from his list of the risen Christ's appearances sound suspiciously misogynistic.[28]

What the Bible does *not* say about Mary Magdalene is that she was caught in adultery, was a prostitute, or otherwise behaved in sinful ways. These common misconceptions derive from the conflation of Mary of Magdala with unnamed women and with Mary of Bethany, a friend of Jesus's (together with her sister, Martha) who lived in a village near Jerusalem. She shows up only in the Gospels of Luke and John. Contributing to the confusion, the Gospel of John identifies Mary of Bethany as the otherwise unnamed woman who anoints the living Jesus's feet with precious ointment.[29] A Roman Catholic pope from the sixth century made this composite Mary a popular reality in one of his sermons, and it's had believers ever since.

\*\*\*

Filling in the Bible's silences about individual characters is one modern preoccupation; another is filling in referents to the symbolism that appears throughout. The book of Revelation may be the thickest with symbolism of any biblical book. We're still not sure to what every element refers. In truth, the question itself may be misplaced because the very use of symbolism invites endless reinterpretation.

Although we may not know exactly to whom or what some of Revelation's symbolism refers, we can be confident that the book arose out of particularly challenging circumstances for its author(s) and audience and that it sought to encourage the faithful to stay true to their community and beliefs in the face of persecution and attack. It is apocalyptic literature at its purest, literature that emboldens its audience to believe that, all evidence to the contrary, God is not only good but also powerful enough to prevail over the presently dominant forces of evil. Then, in a dramatic upheaval of their present reality, God will reward the faithful who have endured the pressures of an evil time.

The bulk of Revelation is John's (whoever this John was) address to seven Christian churches at the end of the first century, probably dating to a time immediately before or after the fall of the Jerusalem temple to the Romans. As such, while it tells of a cosmic end, brought about by God's immediate intervention into human affairs, that end is anchored in its author's time and place.[30] Consequently, modern attempts to read the book as a recipe for predicting an end of the world that has not yet come regularly prove to be wrongheaded. Revelation's author believed that the world would end within his lifetime. When it didn't, the symbols that refer to aspects of Roman rule and life for Christians under it lived on. Over the centuries they have been misinterpreted as signposts predicting the end of the world rather than taken for the encouragement the texts might provide to people facing extraordinary oppression and a world in which injustice appears to have prevailed.

Among the most famous symbols, and one that scholars aren't quite sure what to do with, is the "mark of the beast."[31] This reference shows up in a prophecy rich with evocative symbolism. A seven-headed, ten-horned, foul-mouthed feline composite arises from the sea and is granted extraordinary authority by yet another beast, who makes people wear the (first) beast's name or number on their right hand or forehead in order to buy or sell anything. That "mark of the beast," much discussed among modern Christians concerned to find in their own modern circumstances patterns and signs that match Revelation, was probably meant metaphorically. After all, Romans didn't have a physical sign of belonging to Rome, any more than the faithful who bore "the seal of God" had some physically evident divine stamp.[32]

Revelation says that the mark is the beast's name or number, and the number is "the number of a person." Its calculation, John says, is (depending on which ancient version of the book you've got) either 666 or 616. This assumes familiarity with the system of assigning numerical values to individual letters. Nero, dead at the time but with the horror of his rule still fresh in the early audience's minds, meets the criteria in its Hebrew forms both long (Nero Caesar = 666) and short (Nero = 616). In Revelation, this villain could stand in for all Roman rulers. Still, the matter of people branded in order to participate in a market economy remains a puzzlement.

*** 

As the preceding discussion suggests, even in those cases where the Bible's oddities defy experts, the possibilities for understanding, interpretation, and even application aren't without limit. It takes work, but the Bible, by its very oddities, demands such responsible and respectful treatment. After careful investigation of the text's range of translation possibilities; its literary context (what the Bible says both before and after the text in question) and form (is it a prayer, a story, a poem, a law, or some other genre?); its historical context (in all three of the kinds discussed: history of, in, and behind the text); and the particular theological assumptions at work, including the fact that all the texts were collected and presented by "believers," not disinterested reporters—whew!—a reader will discover that some possibilities for interpretation and understanding are stronger than others.

Among the oddities is the fact that so many modern readers, professing to love and "believe in" the Bible, nevertheless dispense with any such rigorous investigation (and the respect for this Word of God that it reflects) to draw facile conclusions that more often than not involve critical judgment of, even injunction against others. And declare them to be the Word of God. You can now see the problems with that.

# PART IV

But the Bible Says . . .

# Chapter 9

# Arguments behind Closed Doors

"Who slew Goliath?" the camp counselor asks, and the campers shout back, "David slew Goliath!," fists pumping the air. The excitement isn't misplaced. I mean, what a story. It doesn't get any more dramatic than the bare-chested shepherd boy with his measly slingshot taking down the professional warrior, a giant in stature, and covered in armor. Fist-pumping aside, it's no wonder that (biblically minded or not) people still refer to entities so big and strong as to seem indomitable as "Goliaths" and that David's improbable victory remains one of the best-loved (and best-known) episodes in the Bible. Who killed Goliath? "David killed Goliath!" we shout; everyone, that is, except some smart-alecky kid in the back who mutters, "Or Elhanan." She's right, of course.

This chapter addresses inconsistencies and disagreements within the Bible, the sorts of things that sometimes lead people to dismiss the Good Book out of hand. In the process of discussing both broad differences (the fact that there are four Gospel narratives of Jesus's life, for example) and specific inconsistencies (such as its opposing declarations about divorce and the number of animals on Noah's ark), this chapter also asks readers to temper their haste to toss out the Bible altogether. By bringing background information to bear, we can, if not make sense of these oddities, then accept them for what they are.

In no way an exhaustive list, the examples here illustrate different sources or categories of contradiction among biblical texts. In general, we can identify at least four kinds of disagreement. One is a function of the Bible's disparate literary sources—that it didn't come from one hand in one time and place. Another is that our Bibles reflect an evolving theology or worldview; events or information represented in some texts demanded (and received) reinterpretation in light of new experiences. A third shows how a particular issue considered in different contexts might generate conflicting claims. Finally, in some cases, we find late biblical texts wrestling with received texts that were simply wrong but by then were immutable. Yet another kind of disagreement may not be one at all, but is more a function of modern readers' interpretations than contradictions within the texts themselves.

*\*\**

Differences between the creation stories in Genesis chapter 1 and Genesis chapters 2–3 (wildly different styles, distinct names for God), including outright contradictions, helped scholars begin to articulate what would become the Documentary Hypothesis of the Torah's development. The hypothesis is not perfect, but it goes a long way to making sense of one of the most striking strangenesses of the Bible: that even a seemingly single narrative can be the product of many voices. If we fail to appreciate the multiple-source nature of these texts and try instead to read them as a uniform document, we are forced to engage in some pretty tortured threads of logic. For example, when, where, and how were human beings created? Or animals? Answering those questions on the presumption that Genesis chapters 1–3 are a seamless whole, derived from a single hand in a discrete moment in time requires overlooking some pretty glaring inconsistencies.

In the seven-day creation story in Genesis 1, Elohim creates *adam* at the end of all of Elohim's other creating. This *adam*, the text says, is or are indeed created (no more description than that) in the image of Elohim, as male and female.

In the Garden of Eden story in Genesis 2, before there was virtually anything else, at the beginning of "creation," there was a problem: nothing grew because God hadn't sent rain and there were no people. So Yahweh-God fashioned (the Hebrew word is different than the one for "created" in Genesis 1) *adam* out of *adamah*, the soil, land, ground, or dirt.[1] Nothing else is described as being in existence at this point. Animals come along later in an effort to find a suitable companion for the human being.

Unlike in Genesis 1, in Genesis 2 we have a description—rather poignant and intimate—of God's making *adam* and bringing the new being to life. Many literalist apologists say that this is simply a more developed description of the creation of a human being. Okay, but do remember that in this story, *in contrast to* Genesis 1, God hasn't created anything else yet. Oh wait, literalists say, of course He (always "He") has—just read Genesis 1. To which the discerning reader might ask, Then why in Genesis 2:5 are there yet on earth no plants, no rain, no human beings?

This is hardly the only contradiction within these first few chapters in the Bible. God made "all the wild beasts and all the birds of the sky" only after Yahweh-God observed that *adam*'s solitude was "not good," in an effort to find a suitable match for *adam*. Recall that in the original Hebrew, the term can apply to human beings or a human being, generically (as in Genesis chapter 1): neither male nor female, man nor woman, but a human. In other words, however you understand or translate *adam* here, the distinction in human beings between man and woman doesn't exist until some time after the creation of *adam*. You remember that in Genesis 1, by contrast, the male and female versions of a human happened simultaneously with the creation of *adam* as told. So herein lies not just a difference (like the business of the rivers and the garden) but yet another contradiction.

These contradictions, located within the first few chapters of Genesis, are beautiful examples of the Bible's internal rebuke against efforts to flatten it, to read it "literally" and apply it prescriptively. They bear witness to the rich possibilities of allowing competing narratives to inhabit the same sacred space. They would certainly seem to undermine interpretations that read the text as a singular reporting of events—"eyewitness accounts," some people claim.[2] Well-meaning as these efforts appear to be—by people desperately trying to defend the Bible—they succeed only in twisting and perverting what richness of meaning can be found when you take the competing narratives all together. By their very nature, absolutist literal reductions of these texts ironically can yield *mis*readings. The coexistence of diverse, even contradictory stories invites the kind of humble and open-minded engagement that demands ongoing learning and encourages spiritual growth.

*\*\*\**

In addition to cases of theological and mythopoeic disagreement such as we find in Genesis 1–3, we don't have to look far for disagreement on facts presented as historical. Consider Noah's menagerie. Just how many animals did he take on that ark, anyway? As a kid, I loved singing those "two-by-two" Sunday school songs. "Seven-by-seven" is much less lyrical, but it's no less biblical. Have a look. The specifically relevant texts appear over a couple chapters in the Genesis Flood story.[3]

Unlike the Ten Commandments disagreements, these are all embedded within a single, mostly unified narrative. Given that, this can be a great example of the did-you-see-the-gorilla party trick. You know, that video of a psychological experiment in which the narrator tells you to count how many times the ball is passed between two teams of people and then, at the end, asks if you saw the guy in a gorilla suit who ambles in and out.[4] The first time I watched it, I, like nearly everyone else, didn't see the gorilla. (I also lost track of the ball.) Like that, this story can prove a humbling reminder that even when we're reading, really reading, our minds will reconfigure what our eyes have seen.

Rarely does a first-time reader of the Flood story notice that God commands Noah first, "Of all that lives, of all flesh, take two of each into the ark," but a few verses later commands him, "Of every clean animal you shall take seven pairs . . . and of every animal that is not clean, two, a male and its mate."[5] Some people, unsettled by this contradiction, explain that the second simply gives more detail, specifies more completely what God has in mind. But in the next accounting (vv. 8–9) we read, "Of the clean animals, of the animals that are not clean . . . of everything . . . two of each, male and female, . . . as God had commanded Noah." Same in verses 15–16: "two each . . . male and female." (Genesis 8:19 narrates their exit not in numbers at all but "by families.")

Scholars debate details, but one of the best working hypotheses for the development of the Bible's first five books is that there are at least a few author-editor groups and possibly many original fragments of texts involved. According to the long-standing Documentary Hypothesis, the final product, the version that we have, is a mash-up of these. The latest of those sources, and also the one credited with putting it all together, is what scholars refer to as the Priestly writer-editors—"P," for short. Signature traits for P include concern with order (and by extension rules), with Sabbath (and by extension sevens), with what's clean and unclean—in short with things concerning what we would today call "organized religion."

What it seems we have in the Flood narrative is an ancient story with some Priestly concerns sprinkled in. What's astonishing to me is how later editors preserved details, even whole ideas, that ran completely counter to their own version of a story, even to their own preoccupations and concerns. Those responsible for the final form of the Bible we have were not, I strongly believe, stupid. They were not careless or illiterate. We have every reason to believe that even as they changed things and added things and moved things around, they took the business of transmitting the texts they'd received conscientiously—whatever the result. In other words, this was a conservative bunch. And the product of their conservative attitude is a disparate and multivocal, multifaceted, at times blatantly contradictory text.

***

If you turned to the Bible looking, very carefully and conscientiously, for details about how a pious person should deal with the sacrifice of animals, which was ubiquitous in the ancient world, you'd run into some puzzling inconsistencies. Take Leviticus chapters 7 and 17 and Deuteronomy chapter 12, for example. Reading from front to back, you'd run into Leviticus before Deuteronomy. Leviticus 7:19–21 states, "Flesh that touches anything unclean shall not be eaten" and carries the whole unclean/clean distinction over to the eater, too: a person who is unclean should not eat "from the LORD's sacrifice," on pain of banishment. It would seem that Deuteronomy changes all that: "Whenever you desire, you may slaughter and eat meat in any of your settlements. . . . The unclean and clean alike may partake of it, as of the gazelle and the deer," both animals that aren't fit for sacrifice.[6]

Even though Leviticus appears before Deuteronomy in the order, hence story, of the Torah, there is a very real possibility that Deuteronomy was written earlier than Leviticus. Most scholars think that Deuteronomy dates to the periods of religious reformation under the kings Hezekiah and especially Josiah, kings of Judah after the fall of the northern kingdom but before Babylonian conquest and Judean exile. Leviticus, on the other hand, is part of a collection that in the form we have today dates to no earlier than the exile. That said, some of its regulations may go back to Judean priests active before the nation's defeat, but still later than Deuteronomy.

In the matter of slaughter and sacrifice, where such activities should take place is instructive, too. A couple of things are at issue here. First, note that nowhere in the Bible is there a discussion of "religion." That's a category that simply would not have made sense to the people of the time. It's fair to say that everything was religious to those responsible for the biblical texts we have. It shouldn't surprise us, then, that before Deuteronomy (and way before Leviticus), there was no real distinction between sacrifice and "slaughter"—killing an animal you'd raised for food. Even if you killed an animal for food, you would still do so in recognition of and gratitude to God. The blood of said animal belonged to God. So, in texts that reflect those early days, we see a proliferation of altars; people built altars all over the place to sanctify the killing of animals.[7] In fact, a person might be criticized for slaughtering animals "on the ground."[8]

Deuteronomy, by contrast, shows a signature concern with centralizing sacrifice, that there should be one and only one altar where such activities should take place. Deuteronomy chapter 12 again: "Take care not to sacrifice your burnt offerings in any place you like, but only in the place that the LORD will choose in one of our tribal territories."

Leviticus shares temple-specific ritual concerns, whether for the author-exiles expecting or hoping to return and rebuild, or even later Priestly writer-editors after the Jerusalem temple had been rebuilt. But it takes distinctions to another level, further defining acceptable practices and observances after the Babylonian conquest of Judah and subsequent exile of its population. After all, distinctions of practice and belief kept identity alive when there was neither nation nor temple to do that. These authors-editors critique a natural impulse to give up and give in, to become Babylonian or at least forgo the Israelites' distinctive identity as People of the LORD. We see these things, the central location of sacrifice and the concern with distinctions (in Leviticus chapter 17, for example), as part of a subcategory of Priestly writing especially concerned with "holiness." In these chapters (Lev 17–26), priests and places must be holy, of course, but even if the temple is gone and its priesthood defunct, the people of Israel at large can (and should) also be holy, according to these texts.

These matters of sacrifice and acceptability for consumption by people of (the) faith return again in the New Testament among Jesus's followers when, after his death, they worked out what it meant to become what would later be called "Christian." Those concerns, many centuries after Leviticus and Deuteronomy, would share commonalties with those texts, including worries about distinctiveness and about how the religious practices of neighbors could compromise their own. Just have a look at debates about food sacrificed "to idols," as the New Testament writers describe the gods of the other peoples.[9]

***

One would think that in matters of law, the Bible would be clear and consistent. It's not. In addition to these examples are many other. Both Exodus and Deuteronomy allow Israelites to keep other Israelites as slaves; Leviticus unequivocally does not and gives a lofty reason for it: "You were once slaves in Egypt."[10] Leviticus disagrees *with itself* on whether or not it's permissible to have sex when a woman is menstruating. One part of the text says, essentially, Yes, but.[11] Another says, Absolutely not, and the result if you do is nothing less than to be "cut off"—both man and woman.[12] Concerning the Passover lamb, Exodus insists on roasting with explicit instruction to avoid boiling, while Deuteronomy *requires* boiling.[13] Exodus says it should be eaten at home; Deuteronomy insists on the central sanctuary.

If the Bible's rulebook is inconsistent, what does that say about the rules? Excellent question. Maybe we need to rethink our assumptions about their function. Since we don't have any extrabiblical evidence that these specific "laws" were kept as such, it's possible that they had a general, instructive function. It certainly undermines efforts to pluck a legal text here or there to apply literally to modern experience with no regard for the sum of all the laws. Perhaps, at the least, these rules declare that in everything and with every encounter, one should remember that this God of order has a vested interest in the choices one makes. And that people must apply their own thinking and judgment.

\*\*\*

There are equally striking discrepancies among the "historical" books. Take Joshua and Judges. We don't know all the details, but we do know that things didn't go down as Joshua says they did. Even parts of Joshua admit as much.[14] Besides the fact that archaeologists have determined that Jericho, so famously destroyed, according to the Bible, by Joshua and his army—the perambulating around, the trumpet blowing, the walls a-tumbling down—was actually a ruin at the time that would have been Joshua's.[15] That is, despite the story's drama of Joshua and his army razing Jericho's great walls in a single moment of divine intervention, scientists have demonstrated that there were no walls in Jericho at that time.[16] What's more, the book of Joshua concludes that, per God's instruction and with God's support, the Hebrew Israelites got rid of all the native inhabitants of Israel-Canaan in order to have this Promised Land for themselves.[17]

Not so fast, Judges cautions. Or rather, the book seems to be utterly ignorant of the wholesale victory so carefully detailed in the preceding book. Judges, which picks up the narrative chronology where Joshua leaves off (the tribes have just settled the land), talks about the native peoples who still inhabit the land as if the glorious events of Joshua had never happened at all. And those natives in Judges are not incidental but actually a huge part of the story, crucial to the narrative that follows (and illustrate a broader biblical theme). Judges doesn't seem the least concerned about this. There's no caveat, no explanation, no backtracking.

Judges simply begins with the assumption that there were still a lot of native peoples in the land. Judges or God needs them. The author of Judges or the editors who put the books next to each other seem to be mocking modern readers: "You actually read Joshua as *history*?!" they might as well be asking. In Judges, the natives of Canaan-Israel are the reason the tribes go astray, justification for God's punishing the Israelites' disloyalty, and the actual means God uses to punish the tribes.

If that's still not clear (and it *is* hard to wrap one's head around), it goes like this: In Joshua, we read of how God's people, the twelve tribes of Israel, dramatically and successfully rid the land (Canaan) that they understood to have been promised to them (as Israel) by God of its pagan inhabitants—diverse peoples who had lived there for generations. By the end of Joshua, those people were gone. And this was exactly as it should be, goes the biblical logic, because God had ordained that it should be so and God fought alongside the righteous Israelites to see that it came to pass.

Then along comes Judges, which begins, I kid you not, "After the death of Joshua, the Israelites inquired of Yahweh, 'Who shall go up first for us against the Canaanites, to fight against them?'" Now, if you're taking the Bible at face value, this is a bit of a shocker because these things cannot be reconciled. So there's more going on here. And that more might be how we find our way out of the moral conundrum of Joshua. (Not excusing Joshua, mind you, but understanding it, anyway.) God had absolutely and unquestioningly delivered on God's promise of a homeland, asking only for the people's exclusive loyalty in return, thus laying the foundation for a logic that could exonerate God when the nation was defeated. In other words, the defeats and indignities God's people subsequently suffered could be explained as the result of their own wrongdoing, a failure to maintain that exclusive loyalty. This is the power of a story carefully edited.

\*\*\*

Another such story is that one much beloved, of the shepherd boy David. The famous story of how, as a boy, David took on and defeated Goliath the Philistine, who had intimidated the entire Israelite army, appears in 1 Samuel chapter 17. If it's unfamiliar to you, have a look now and come back after you've read it. It's fun. Go on.

Now have a look at 2 Samuel 21:19. Yes, you read correctly that Goliath was felled by a certain Elhanan—a member of David's band of fighters, sure, but not David himself. It's all a bit fishy until you remember that the Bible didn't develop in the manner of modern books, with a single story line controlled by a single author. By all scholarly accounts, we have here a great example of an early story (Elhanan's killing Goliath as per 2 Samuel) reworked in later years so that the great deed went to the hero of the bigger story, David.

It's only natural to want to smooth over the differences and obliterate the contradiction. Actually, the earliest such effort is itself biblical. Chronicles doesn't tell a story of David killing Goliath, but in 1 Chronicles 20:5 we read that Elhanan killed a brother of Goliath.

First Chronicles, by all reckoning, is a late book, that is, composed much, much later than the Samuels, on which it leaned even as it smoothed out inconsistencies. Even a cursory read-through will make clear that Chronicles' primary goal is to lionize David. (And given Chronicles' postnation, postmonarchy origins, it would prioritize David's association with the temple over the bit about him being a king.) It appears that while Chronicles doesn't go as far as 1 Samuel 17 in attributing Goliath's death to David's slingshot, it doesn't give Goliath's death to Elhanan, either. It reflects the Elhanan story but makes his foe the brother of Goliath instead. And then it simply moves on.

And I get it. I understand the impulse to seize the story for David and explain away the pesky Elhanan. But Elhanan persists in the biblical narrative as the assassin of Goliath, suggesting that that story was already known by the time David came along and was probably closer to how things went down historically.

It can be difficult for modern readers of faith to appreciate that biblical truth needn't be fixed according to exactly what did or didn't happen. Over and over again, we see how the biblical writers and editors cared less about so-called accurate reporting of facts such as we expect from on-the-ground journalists than about impact, meaning, and message, always as they bore theologically.

So it's okay if Elhanan is the hero in the historical germ of the story. David's story in 1 Samuel 17 is still wonderful, a story of inspiration in all the best ways while also adding dimension and appeal to one of the most important biblical figures. And 1 Chronicles chose to keep the door open to the 1 Samuel story without completely ignoring its roots. In other words, there isn't any reason we can't allow that a certain Israelite by the name of Elhanan once killed a Philistine by the name of Goliath while also finding the portrait of a young David to be everything we'd want a great king-in-the-making to be *and* experiencing a boost of energy, even confidence in our lives by comparison. Isn't that the power of a good story? And surely stories can have at least as much weight and resonance as their factual counterparts. But they shouldn't be confused—facts as fiction or fiction as fact. That strips both of their inherent power.

While we're on the topic of Chronicles' differences from the earlier Samuel and Kings, consider the well-known story of David and Bathsheba. Where 2 Samuel 11 begins, "At the turn of the year, the season when kings go out to battle, David sent Joab. . . . David remained in Jerusalem." Therein the trouble begins. David sees Bathsheba, takes her, she gets pregnant, and so on—trouble and more trouble for David and "David's house."

By contrast, in 1 Chronicles 20, we read, "At the turn of the year, the season when kings go out to battle, Joab led out the army. . . . David remained in Jerusalem." It begins word-for-word the same with one hint of difference, and then takes a wildly different (and far more boring) turn: Joab succeeds in battle, David gains another crown, there's more fighting in which David's troops prevail, and that's about it. Nary a word about Bathsheba, David's infidelity, and subsequent murder of her husband; no mention of the infant's death and the sword ever hanging over David's house thenceforth. Chronicles works very hard to tell a history that reflects its beliefs and needs. Since there was no monarchy at the time Chronicles was written, David, the famous King David, must become David, the famous temple-designer, planner, organizer. After all, the temple had become the most important site and institution of Chronicles' time, and the less said about a monarchy that was no more, despite God's having promised David that someone from his line would be on the throne in Jerusalem forever, the better.

***

Among the Bible's most striking disagreements is the product of what we can only imagine to be a purely theological revision. It, too, is evident when you compare and contrast the accounts of Samuel and Chronicles. In this case, the earlier text may have so disturbed early readers by what it suggests about God that a newer version subbed in Satan instead. The very last chapter of 2 Samuel is odd in a number of ways.

The narrator says that God became angry at Israel (without any explanation as to why) and "incited David against them" by telling him to count the population of Israel and Judah. David tells Joab to carry it out, but Joab resists. For some reason, which the narrator assumes readers know, it was a very bad thing to conduct a census. In this case, there's some military implication—determining how many among the population are qualified to fight. Despite the counsel from Joab, ever the voice of reason, David overrides him and Joab carries out the kingly command. No sooner is it done than David regrets having conducted the census. Too late. God is angry. (Yes, you remember correctly that the narrator says both that *God* actually "incited" David to take the census and now God is angry that he did.) The punishment is terrible: a pestilence enacted by an avenging angel of God kills seventy thousand people before David pleads that the people be spared. The story ends with David setting up an altar where the Jerusalem temple will later be built, and God ends the plague.

But for our purposes here—how the Bible sometimes disagrees with itself, and sometimes quite blatantly—note that 1 Chronicles chapter 21 tells the same story. Almost. That story, composed some centuries after 2 Samuel, long enough for the 2 Samuel story to be fixed in the corpus of ancient Israel's literary tradition, "corrects" 2 Samuel by blaming Satan for inciting David, which also gets rid of the pesky business of God's seemingly incongruous anger.

Just whom the authors meant by "Satan" is unclear. Whether the kind of divine adversary *satan* that we saw in Job, for example, or a human being pushing David to act badly, it doesn't say. The nature of Chronicles (which shows David constantly bowing to divine power) makes the former less likely than that the authors meant some person pushed David to make this devastating move.[18]

***

Throughout the Bible, there's a sense that different times and places call for different behaviors, even different beliefs. One of the best-loved passages in the Bible appears in two places, Isaiah and Micah, word for word: "They shall beat their swords into ploughshares and their spears into pruning hooks."[19] Micah and Isaiah were contemporaries, both of them living and preaching in Judah in the late eighth century BCE. They'd seen the protracted fighting of Israel against Assyria, which Israel finally, truly lost in 722 BCE. But the fighting didn't end there. Assyria assaulted Judah in the same ways and won terrible victories against Judean towns and communities, dangerously close to the capital in Jerusalem, with its precious temple and the monarchy that God had promised would endure forever.

We don't know who said it first, but both the urban sophisticates who composed Isaiah's audience and the country folk to whom

Micah ministered suffered battle fatigue. Surely they welcomed these words of God. Incidentally, note how Micah (appreciating the rural context of his audience) tacks on a bit that doesn't appear in Isaiah's prophecy: "but they shall all sit under their own vines and under their own fig trees, and none shall make them afraid."[20] Most of us today also admit a weariness of war, the endless battling to which we're privy thanks to a communication system the ancients could hardly have imagined, and conflicts that they surely could have imagined: belief against belief, the insatiable desire for more driving attack against whoever or wherever has the goods, simple cultural misunderstandings gone out of control. Isaiah's and Micah's prophecy of a coming peace when instruments of violence would be transformed in the service of agriculture is as welcome now as in their time.

So it's a bit of a shocker, and a buzzkill at that, to discover in the biblical book of Joel a prophecy that promises a coming time when "they shall beat their ploughshares into swords and their pruning hooks into spears."[21] Yes, exactly the opposite, using the very same vocabulary and the very same literary structure but turned exactly 180 degrees. Biblical scholars note that much about the book of Joel suggests a later date of authorship than Isaiah and Micah and familiarity with earlier prophecies. What can we make of this intentional reversal? At the least, that Joel's circumstances called for a different message.

We, inheritors of this diverse collection, get them both. With this, once again, the Bible reminds us by its inherent contractions that we cannot, must not blindly apply any given text as the Final Word but must instead be thoughtful and measured about how we read, what we adopt and adapt, and how we treat these ancient texts within our own historical and cultural contexts.

To put it another way, the Bible doesn't require a one-size-fits-all approach to being a person of faith. After taking in the Bible's own internal disagreements and contradictions, one could conclude that belief, practice, even theology should be open to review and enrichment to allow thoughtful reconsideration in light of specific circumstances. As in the case of the contradictory prophecies of Joel compared to Isaiah and Micah, the Bible itself witnesses to the importance of appreciating historical context when interpreting texts.

***

Yet another example of contradictions within the Bible that point to the importance of considering historical context is the case of divorce.

In the Hebrew Bible, we find several texts that severely limit the conditions for divorce.[22] Do note, we have only particular circumstances, nothing in general nor any universal statements about divorce in the Hebrew Bible. Remember that for most of the Bible's many centuries of authorship and development, a woman's circumstances depended on her male relationships. Consider all those passages urging care for "widows and orphans." A woman without a husband, like children without parents, was terrifyingly vulnerable to all sorts of privation. Add contexts that deny a woman equal rights to property, and you can see that it could be cruelly irresponsible to divorce her, never mind who left the toothpaste uncapped. To divorce a woman was to make her economically vulnerable. Limiting conditions for divorce was thus a form of protection for her. In Malachi 2:16 we find divorce paired with violence as anathema to God's wishes: "I hate the putting-away [divorce of a woman]," God says, and "covering one's garment with violence." Jesus's strong criticism, even prohibition, of divorce as portrayed in the New Testament's synoptic gospels ties it to adultery and so adds the kind of moral element familiar to most modern readers.[23]

What a surprise, then, to find that the Bible also demands, actually commands divorce in the name of God.

How do we make sense of this disagreement, much less the particulars? Context, historical and social. The passage that demands divorce appears in a late book, dated to the fifth century BCE. By that time, the number of Israelites, God's chosen people, was sorely reduced by war and the circumstances of exile. It seemed crucial to the faithful remnant that they not risk the dissolution of their community, "the holy seed," by intermarriage.[24] In such circumstances, it showed a different kind of irresponsibility to marry a non-Israelite. So we have the heart-wrenching scene of a biblically mandated mass divorce. At the urging of the very people affected, and with much weeping all around, the priest Ezra mandates that to make things right with God, the men must divorce their foreign wives. The story ends with the men sending away those women with their children.[25]

***

Besides these cases of blatant disagreement within the Bible, we also find evidence of biblical writers wrestling with texts that had proved to be inaccurate by the time they'd received them. Since the Hebrew Bible developed over such a long period of time, some of its texts were accepted as fixed and authoritative long before others. The case of prophecy is particularly problematic because what happens if a "true prophet" turns out to have been wrong?

The author of Daniel chapter 9 had to deal with the fact that Jeremiah's much earlier prophecy about the restoration of Israel after seventy years of Babylonian domination didn't come close to being true.[26] Even hundreds of years after the Babylonian destruction of Jerusalem, in Daniel's historical period, Israel still had not been restored as Jeremiah had prophesied. The person Daniel is said, in chapter 9, to have undertaken intensive soul-searching and prayer (much of it focused on determining what level of sinfulness could explain the justice of such a long period of national punishment). We read that by revocalizing the existing Hebrew consonants, the angel Gabriel explains that Jeremiah meant seventy *weeks of* years.[27] That's one way to solve the problem.

***

As we've already seen, disagreements between biblical texts aren't limited to the Hebrew Bible, despite the fact that the New Testament is a lot shorter and developed over a much shorter period of time. Actually, the Christian New Testament embraces disagreement and difference as beneficial, even necessary to holy scripture. After all, it begins with four—count them: four—Gospels. Its first four books each purport to tell the "good news" of Jesus, each in the context of a faith-based biography. Why four and not simply one? It was important to those responsible for the Bible's final form to include, without apology, differing accounts.

The Gospels disagree in tone and general concerns. Matthew is especially interested in tying Jesus to the Hebrew scriptures; Mark is so fast-paced as to be nearly abbreviated; Luke's inclusion of gentiles and women is striking by comparison to the other synoptics; and John gets downright mystical. But they also disagree on specifics. These include such weighty matters as Jesus's divinity. John's Jesus is openly, repeatedly identified as divine, including by Jesus himself. That doesn't happen in any other Gospel. They also differ on such seemingly mundane details as the sign that hung over the crucified Jesus's head; in no two of the gospels is the sign exactly the same.[28]

The matter of Jesus's birth is particularly confusing. It's easy to overlook inconsistencies between the Gospels' nativity stories because each one works on its own. But consider that Matthew has Mary and Joseph dashing down to Egypt with the newborn Jesus to escape Herod's murderous intent, while Luke has them staying around for forty-day-old Jesus's "presentation" in the temple, after which they head straight up to their hometown of Nazareth. John tells of Jesus's beginnings from the beginning of the world, while Mark doesn't even mention Jesus at all until he is an adult.

Consider also the competing biblical claims about Judas's death: that he gave the money he got for betraying Jesus to Jewish authorities and hanged himself (Matthew), or that he used the money to buy a field on which he later fell and died (Acts).[29]

Over and over, the Bible resists facile treatment, rejects our efforts to dip in for an applicable gem of wisdom or a chastising corrective (usually of someone else). Taken seriously, it pushes readers to take themselves seriously—to learn well, think hard, consider the circumstances, and even bring a bit of compassion and humility to bear.

\*\*\*

There's been a great deal of attention in the past several years to the notion that if you are faithful, devoted to God, and simply ask for it, God will make you rich—that God *wants* to make you rich. And I mean rich in the glitzy, bejeweled, sports-car-driving sort of way. Materially rich. This approach has come to be called "the prosperity gospel" and depends on biblical texts such as "See if I will not open the windows of heaven for you and pour down for you an overflowing blessing" and "that they may have life and have it to the full."[30]

There's plenty in the Bible, whatever version you prefer, to suggest that good things come to those who recognize the biblical God as God, that is, to those who "believe." Consider the whole of the Deuteronomistic history (Joshua, Judges, Samuel, and Kings), for example. It's based on the premise that God wants Israel to be healthy, wealthy, and wise, starting with Moses's charge to the Israelites that if they would but keep to Yahweh-God as their God, things would go well for them in the land of milk and honey. Forsake the LORD, however, and they'd face destruction and exile. Truth is, it doesn't take much digging to find strong ammunition to launch a counterargument. Indeed, thick as this "gospel" may be in adherents, it's finally on pretty shaky biblical ground.

Take Jesus, for example. Although he was, according to the Christian interpretation of biblical accounts, *God* (and so could be and have anything he wanted), he chose to be the poor son of a carpenter and spent his adult life without material goods, much less an upwardly mobile job in, say, finance.

According to the Christian scriptures, poverty is the face of God.

Consider, too, that some of the Bible's most significant believers, biblical characters held up as models of faith, faced hardship; some even wished, on account of the strain their relationship to God put on their daily lives, for death. Ironically, the poster child for pro-lifers, Jeremiah, wishes that he had never been born and curses the person who "did not kill [him] in the womb."[31] Jonah, admittedly not much of a hero but a biblical prophet nonetheless, was so disappointed by God's actions—refraining from destroying Nineveh after the whole city repented—that he wanted to die. God showed mercy on the Ninevites, which really irked Jonah. He was so upset by God—the nerve!—and by the fact that God made him go all the way to the Assyrian capital, even though Jonah claims that he knew they'd repent, that he asked God to kill him right then and there. This is definitely not a case of "Ask and you shall receive." Jeremiah lived a long, long life. Jonah, too, lived to see another day—and possibly another, more merciful way.

Then there's Job, famous for his terrible suffering. Remember that before the onslaught of attack, pestilence, and all that, none other than God had declared Job to be super-righteous and therefore a special case for attention and affection. Job's righteousness got him exactly the opposite of prosperity; he lost everything—children, material wealth, and his health, too. He also wished to die. Sure, at the end, after tremendous suffering and untold loss, God gives Job a bunch of stuff, a long life, and new kids. Such a road from wealth to ruin to prosperity is hardly the path proponents of the prosperity gospel espouse.

Then we're back to Jesus, fully human and fully God, who oriented his entire adult life toward getting killed, which, if you're a good Christian believer, was the whole point: sacrifice for our sins.

This brief review of good guys whose goodness vis-à-vis God, whose "belief," if you will, brought them a whole bundle of trouble puts the lie to the prosperity gospel. Their goodness got them suffering, which, if it didn't kill them, made them want to die. The Gospels embed "Ask and it shall be given" in the context of giving and receiving what is deeply good—you don't give pearls to swine.[32] God will give what is good, but what exactly that is up to God to determine. Besides, ask anyone—having piles of money doesn't ensure a strong spirituality, much less happiness. Indeed, read on: it would seem to be that *giving*, not getting, and taking the harder way bring ultimate satisfaction.

# Chapter 10

# Biblical (Im)Morality

The best way to deal with interpersonal conflict is to run away; lying, cheating, and stealing really do pay; and my goodness, don't get so upset if you've worked super hard and a shirker receives as much or even more than you. If one reads the Bible without any critical analysis, seeking only to apply its texts directly to one's life, these would be a few of its take-home lessons. By contrast, there is relatively little textual support for moralizing about homosexuality and even less about abortion, as I noted. The Bible makes no judgment, yay or nay, about love and commitment between people of the same sex and says nothing about a woman choosing to end her pregnancy.[1] While the Bible says little about some of the moral issues that preoccupy people of faith today, in some cases the Bible actually and unapologetically espouses truly questionable ethics. From ethnic cleansing to owning human beings to not-so-Christian family values, the Bible is hardly a transparent model of righteousness through and through.

This chapter discusses some of those texts, contextualizes them where it's helpful and appropriate to do so, suggests ways besides the prescriptive to think about how we treat those passages, and simply acknowledges that their existence shows that the Bible may not always be what we expect or wish it to be.

How about enslaving women, who are then forced to bear children they can't call their own to satisfy a more powerful couple's desire? You're thinking of *The Handmaid's Tale*, aren't you—that dystopian novel by Margaret Atwood that engendered an enormously popular television series. Yes, well, it has a lot in common with (and draws from) Genesis. In the Bible, not only does Abraham have a child (Ishmael) for his wife Sarah with Sarah's slave, Hagar, but Jacob has several children for his wives through their female slaves. Jacob, also called Israel, fathers four children with women who are the property of his wives, Rachel and Leah. Those "handmaids," Bilhah and Zilpah, bear Gad and Asher, Dan and Naphtali.

About Jacob: consider that the man whose name becomes Israel, the patriarch who engenders the twelve tribes who become the people of God, lies, cheats, and steals with impunity. Jacob actually gained his esteemed position as the father of all Israel by duping his blind dad into giving him the birthright that should have gone to his older brother, Esau. When Esau got understandably angry, Jacob didn't talk it out with him or ask for forgiveness or otherwise offer to work through it together. No, he fled, on the urging of his mother, because Jacob was her favorite son, the Bible tells us, without judging whether or not such parental favoritism is problematic. He goes on to marry not one but two women and to have children with two others besides. These are hardly the biblical family values that modern people of faith champion. Yet there they are. In the Bible, Jacob prospers and continues to be blessed by God.[2]

Indeed, there's so much questionable (by today's religious standards) sex! Consider the whole Song of Songs. Interpret it as you wish—the love of God for Israel, of Jesus for the church—this evocative collection of poetry is entirely a celebration of erotic love, and it's utterly unconcerned about whether or not the lovers are married. It's worth noting that the book is also called the Song of Solomon, recalling the wealthy and wise son of David who had many wives. After all, marriage in the Bible is *not* only between one man and one woman, as modern moralists are in the habit of saying. In the Bible's historically patriarchal cultural context, a man might well have more than one wife.

The Bible often upends modern expectation. While the Song of Songs invites readers to consider that the sexually embodied nature of human beings, mutually desirous, can be a good and even beautiful thing, texts beg us to take a step back and acknowledge that just because it's in the Bible doesn't make it right. Sources indicate that it wasn't uncommon in the ancient Near East for a sterile couple like Abraham and Sarah to use a slave to round out their family. The situation with Leah and Rachel and Jacob is different. Leah had borne the family children straight away, so Jacob had heirs. Instead what we see is both a drama of sibling rivalry played out on the defenseless slaves (a competition to see which wife could have more children) and a convenient way to end the narrative with the requisite number of twelve sons-tribes.

*** 

Fast-forward to America in the eighteenth and nineteenth centuries CE. There, the Bible proved to be one of the most powerful documents providing justification for slaveholding. It's not only to the Hebrew Bible, with its ancient cultural norms, that people appealed but also New Testament texts such as the whole book of Philemon, in which an escaped slave is urged to return to his owner and to servitude. There are obvious moral reasons why these texts couldn't, shouldn't be applied directly today. But there are also reasons embedded in the historical and literary contexts of these texts for rejecting their use in such a way.

In the ancient past that these biblical texts reflect, people might be temporarily enslaved by economics or war (Hebrew Bible); the end of the world was believed to be just around the corner, maybe tomorrow, so better not to change one's status today (New Testament). When the end didn't come, Jesus's community struggled to figure out how to organize itself, for better or worse. This doesn't absolve the Bible of such ugliness, but it might explain it. Thankfully, abolitionists found plenty of biblical texts to argue for the moral bankruptcy of owning people and for the full humanity of each human. Still, we can wish that the Bible would be more consistently straightforward about the absolute wrongness of slavery.

***

Let's face it, ethnic cleansing is pretty common in the Bible. You'd think that anyone reading the book of Joshua would find at least a wee bit troubling the unapologetic, not even slightly nuanced goal of ridding the land of its original inhabitants, actually killing them all. This is undertaken on God's orders so that "God's people," the tribes descended from Jacob's twelve sons—the people who would become Israel—would have it for themselves, as God promised them generations earlier. To understand what these texts might be doing in the Bible and what people today might do with them, even as people of faith who "believe in" the Bible, takes as much rigorous learning *about* the Bible, its languages and historical and literary contexts, as it does familiarity with relevant biblical passages.

But it's so much easier to take the texts at face value, in English (never mind that whole pesky translation thing), and assume that you've got a mandate from God. We wouldn't be the first to make such an assumption. This impulse is how we got "manifest destiny," with its terrible legacy. European settlers saw America as the land of milk and honey, the Promised Land that God had determined their righteous selves should have and hold for their very own. They saw themselves as God's chosen people, and what would become the United States was in their eyes nothing less than the land of Israel. It was their *destiny* as dictated by God to take the land and get rid of its inhabitants.

And the Native Americans? Easy: they were Canaanites to the European settlers' Israelites. That is, those people who looked, acted, and spoke so very differently from the Bible-toting European settlers, those people who didn't believe in the biblical God were "pagan" just like the Canaanites of old. Extrapolating from the Bible, the settlers saw Native Americans as blind to God's truth. What's more, with their other gods and goddesses, they were a temptation to be eradicated—and their evil ways with them. It was a manifest destiny straight out of Joshua.

I'd like to assume that any reader would simply accept as a given that ethnic cleansing is bad. Taking other people's land in blatant disenfranchisement is wrong. I'd like to assume that readers encountering the biblical book of Joshua would be troubled by its program, find it unsettling as biblical text, and yearn for some kind of sense, which we might then try to ferret out together. The ugly truth is that these texts have already served to justify exactly the same genocide for material gains and fear-driven deportations that we face today.

So it's even more important to understand something of the historical and literary contexts of these texts. Again, this doesn't absolve them of their hatefulness, but it can provide some perspective. First, most scholars today think that at least some of the people who would come to compose Israel were actually themselves Canaanite, that is, natives of the land. Although they did not participate in a physical exodus from Egypt, they nevertheless came to identify with the god Yahweh and the traditions of a core people descended from a common ancestor.

Second, and related, another way to read Joshua is as an explanation, in hindsight, for failure. The greater story of Israel, as it's come down to us in the Bible, makes sense of its defeat and destruction by claiming that it was God's doing. Remember that the Bible's ordering of texts does not reflect the chronology of their authorship, and many texts were written and/or edited well after the events that they describe. Joshua was likely composed well after the destruction of Israel at the hands of the Babylonians. The final form of Joshua, Judges, Samuel, and Kings demonstrates a faith-based history reworked to exonerate God.

The books' final forms reflect a logic that could make sense of the nation's destruction. The logic in the Bible's final form goes like this: Despite God's giving them the land and helping get rid of all the people who had been living there—people whose beliefs tempted God's people to worship other gods and goddesses—despite all that God had done for them, asking only their loyalty in return, the Israelites nevertheless turned away, giving their attention, their devotion, their adoration and loyalty to the gods and goddesses of the people who had lived there (or still did, if you're looking at Judges). God had to follow through. This logic required that God had to destroy God's own people as punishment.

Remember, in these books' final forms, we read that God's people could have the land as long as they remained loyal to God. That was the deal. So here's Joshua, showing how God made good on the promise, even removing the temptation from their midst, that Israel would be completely loyal in its devotion to God. But Israel sinned anyway, the stories tell, and so came great destruction at the hands of Assyria, and later Babylonia, orchestrated by none other than the Israelites' God.

Rather than reasoning that God couldn't protect God's people from foreign attack, the biblical witness concludes that God had made it happen. God determined that Israel and Judah should be defeated and God's people lose the land that God had promised them, not as an act of capricious injustice but because the people deserved it. The reasoning goes that they deserved such punishment because they broke their promise to God to be loyal exclusively to God and instead adopted the ways and beliefs and gods of the "people of the land." The biblical texts, edited in light of the destruction by the Assyrians and Babylonians, portray Israel as voluntarily agreeing to God's promise that as long as they had no other god before the LORD God, God would enable them to prosper in the land. This is the context of Moses's plea to the people to "choose life" by accepting the terms of God's agreement.[3] But if they break their side of the deal, they'd lose everything.

God's good-faith effort to help them get off on the right foot in the Promised Land meant helping them obliterate the threat to their keeping the promise—ridding the land of the temptations posed by its inhabitants. Of course, the historical reality was something different, which Judges, with its many remaining Canaanite groups (as well as stories featuring Canaanites in Samuel and Kings), shows. The ethnic cleansing as portrayed in Joshua and elsewhere is described as a divine imperative. The native peoples and things that were obliterated were subject, the texts say, not simply to unbridled violence but to the control of the *herem*, "the ban," whereby people and their things were understood to have been dedicated to God. Again, this is not to excuse the texts but to understand them.

The Bible's ethnic cleansing, like its normalization of slavery, poses a conundrum that can be addressed by modern people of faith only by understanding and respecting the Bible's ancient past and history of development, and only by allowing for ways of faithful reading besides the literalistic application of those texts to today. Without understanding some of the Bible's historical and literary contexts and without allowing nonliteral ways of reading and appealing to the texts, the Bible's take on slavery and ethnic cleansing would seem to be downright immoral.

***

Abortion, on the other hand, which pro-life people of faith argue is immoral to the point of criminalizing the people who seek and provide it, is actually nowhere condemned in the Bible. Despite the passion of well-meaning Christians on this issue, the Bible doesn't ever say it's wrong for a woman to end a pregnancy.

So how did such passionate antiabortion politics become the "Christian" position? Election after election, politicians court a huge swath of Christian voters by declaring their opposition to abortion. In 2016, when the presidential election was yoked to the specter of several Supreme Court vacancies, many people advocated voting for Donald Trump not because they thought he would be a good president or was even a good person but simply because they said their

Christian beliefs dictated they vote for a man who promised to ap-point justices seeking to overturn *Roe v. Wade*. "God uses even bad people" was the refrain.

How did this happen? In the vice-presidential debate, Mike Pence appealed to the Bible in stating his position on the issue in just the way that Christians have been doing over the years. He said, "The sanctity of life proceeds out of that belief—that ancient prin-ciple that—where God says before you were formed in the womb I knew you."

Let's talk about that. That quotation comes from the beginning of the book of Jeremiah, the ancient source for what Pence calls a principle. At the beginning of the book, the first words out of the prophet's mouth (in this case, speaking for God) are "Before I created you in the womb, I selected you; before you were born, I consecrated you; I appointed you a prophet concerning the nations."[4] Think for a minute about the relevance of this text. Jeremiah was a prophet who lived and worked during tough times. In the name of God, he said harsh things to powerful people and was punished again and again for them. Personally, he took it hard. The book is peppered with complaints—Jeremiah's lamenting his vocation, that it alienated him from a community he loved, that friends and family reviled him. He was beaten and left for dead for preaching about God's dis-appointment and determination to punish a wayward people. So desperate was Jeremiah to convince his community to change their ways, to repent and so to avoid the destruction he anticipated, so desperate was he to protect and preserve them, that he said the very things that made them hate him.

All Jeremiah could claim in his defense was that *he* didn't want to say those things, they weren't even his words, but that *God* had made it impossible for him not to. God had called him to this work, had given him the difficult things to say. Jeremiah did not wish for the loneliness and brutality his message brought upon him. But God so loved this people, Jeremiah said, that God told him to preach repentance and an unpopular message of impending prosecution and punishment. Jeremiah's "call narrative," the literary moment detailing how he came to be a prophet, is what's at issue in the abortion debate. It's the strongest possible defense of this being God's, not Jeremiah's, doing. Counter to the pro-life argument, Jeremiah's declaration in its biblical context is not a principle but an *apologia*, an explanation of and justification for taking his prophetic message of repentance seriously. In the Bible, it is not an argument that every fetus should be born (and grow up to become a Hebrew prophet).

The New Testament Saul-Paul stands firmly in this tradition when he makes the same defense of his authority to preach a message not everyone was inclined to accept. Educated and committed to the Judaism of his birth, Paul knew his (Hebrew) Bible inside and out. So it's no surprise that when he speaks in defense of his authority, he says, "But . . . God who had set me apart before I was born and called me through his grace, was pleased to reveal his Son to me, so that I might proclaim him among the Gentiles," appealing with the strongest precedent to the same logic as the great prophets of old.[5] (Jeremiah predates Paul by some 550 years.)

Biblical accounts avow that just as there were prophets such as Jeremiah tasked with passing God's messages on to their communities, false prophets also existed.[6] Some people claimed to speak God's words but were really motivated by a different agenda. So we find among biblical prophets' first words justification for their calling, defending their identity as true prophets. Isaiah claims to have stood in the temple's holiest place, where he saw God on a throne and after an oral cleansing heard the divine question "Whom shall I send?," to which Isaiah responded, "Here I am, send me."[7] Ezekiel tells of being in Babylonian exile and witnessing God's throne on a flying chariot, from which he heard the words "I am sending you." Ezekiel then ate the scroll of God's words, which he was to declare to the people.

Jeremiah, the prophet most beaten up by his vocation, says he didn't even have the chance to choose. Not only was he a true prophet, his opening lines declare, but he was chosen by God to be one before he was ever born. That's the literary and historical context of the lines that undergird the Christian "sanctity of life," anti-abortion position.

But what is embedded in the metaphor-laden poetry of a prophet's call narrative—in other words, an evocative justification for how Jeremiah came to be saying the things that got him into so much trouble—is what pro-lifers read literally in support of the claim that a fetus is a person known by God, a person like all others with divinely ordained purpose, and therefore should be protected at all costs. Among the problems—biblical logic, for one—is the practical fact that "all cost" is most immediately and enduringly paid by the pregnant woman, who is also, by this logic, a person known by God, with divinely ordained purpose, who should be protected at all costs. It's hard to imagine that criminalizing her, much less demanding of her all that is required to raise this child to be prepared to realize all productive possibility, would enable her to realize the potential of her divinely ordained purpose if her circumstances lead her to conclude that she cannot.

We all want the easy way, the clear and straightforward path to making a decision, to naming what is right and wrong. That's simply human. If we're honest with ourselves, most of us are happy to defer to an authority, someone with the credentials and qualifications to make the decision, call the shots. It's a lot of work to wrestle with complexity, much less to reckon with those pesky gray areas. But it's our responsibility, and is finally much more satisfying, to go through that difficult process in order to arrive at a decision or judgment that we can own with deep, personal integrity as the result of a hard-won clarity. I'm going on about this because the case of abortion is one of these issues that must be wrangled with rather than superficially adopted because of what some confident authority has told you to believe.

I think we can all agree that in a perfect world, no one would kill anyone else. There certainly are plenty of biblical texts that argue against killing. But there are *a lot* of cases in the Bible where killing is accepted as commonplace and sometimes even demanded by God. I'm not talking about God taking lives, but about human beings killing other human beings. The point is, I don't hear anyone arguing against a general sanctity of life. What's at issue is what exactly you mean by "the sanctity of life." The particular circumstances of real, individual cases matter.

This may be where the civilians-with-firearms and us-against-them in war comes into play. To preserve a greater sanctity of life, gun rights advocates and supporters of military intervention claim that it may be necessary to kill. That is, on a personal level, the argument is that to preserve the life of one's family, it may be necessary to kill someone whose intention is to brutalize and maybe kill family members. The same argument applies on the national level: we must kill them to preserve us, who are doing a better job of recognizing and upholding the sanctity of life. The person protecting her family doesn't *want* to kill the intruder any more than the United States *wants* to go to war. (I hope.)

Now, consider that very same logic in the context of abortion. No one wants an abortion. No one, especially not the woman who might seek it. No one sets out to have an abortion like a person might visit an art museum or elect on a Saturday afternoon to ride a roller-coaster at the state fair. Even under acceptable legal circumstances, the decision is an agonizing one. But the woman carrying the fetus, who would take on the role of primary caretaker and guardian arguably for the rest of her life, might think of her decision in those broader terms of the sanctity of life. Only she knows (and the knowing is always hard-won) whether bringing the fetus to term best honors the (greater) sanctity of life. There are myriad details that she must weigh in order to make that decision. The Bible offers no explicit command, one way or the other.

Finally, consider that within the Bible, God actually sanctions, even commands terminating pregnancies. And God acts as the agent of abortion. By way of a few examples, recall that God commands in a particular moment that all nonvirgin Midianite women be killed, which quite likely meant a lot of terminated pregnancies.[8] They were nonvirgins, after all. Then there's Hosea's prophecy of punishment whereby God would actively cause pregnant women to miscarry, killing otherwise healthy fetuses.[9] And in another case, God's righteousness calls for aborting Samarian women's babies in a most gruesome manner—oh, and dashing infants to death, too.[10] Here again, the Bible's oddities and surprises undermine modern readers' efforts to extrapolate for absolutist claims immediately applicable to their own (or other persons') lives. Of one thing we can be sure: the Bible demands nuance, regularly undermining one-size-fits-all prescriptive interpretations.

\*\*\*

While we're on the topic of unnerving texts such as those in which God demands abortion and sanctions infanticide, it's hard to know what exactly to do with the story of Elijah's successor, who loses his cool when he is taunted for being bald. In context, the incident follows Elisha's extraordinary selection as *the* prophet (from among many), who not only steps into the great Elijah's shoes, so to speak, but with "a double portion" of Elijah's spirit. Which makes the whole thing even weirder.

Elijah alone of all the prophets is said not to have died a normal, human death but was simply taken up into the heavens. So when Elisha, knowing that Elijah's time was just about up, asked for a double portion of his spirit, it was no small thing. Elijah said so. "You have asked a hard thing," he said, but added that if Elisha happened to see his departure, then indeed he'd get that double portion.[11]

Sure enough, Elisha witnesses the fiery chariot scoop Elijah up and away in a whirlwind to the heavens. And after tearing his own coat in a ritual act of mourning, Elisha picks up Elijah's coat, which had fallen when Elijah was borne aloft, thus giving rise to the phrase "taking up the mantle."[12] With that, we can assume that Elisha got a double dose of Elijah's extraordinary spirit even as he

became Elijah's recognized successor, to the acclaim of the fifty or
so prophets who saw the spirit and deferred to him. Elisha promptly
"healed" waters that had proved problematic (though the Bible
doesn't say how), demonstrating to all that he was Elijah's successor
in deed as well as word.

Elisha goes on to perform many wonders, none of which puts
hair back on his head. He is bald and apparently unhappy about it.
Woe to the children who tease him for it. Seriously, in the Bible, not
half a second after we read that Elisha healed a spring of water so
that "no longer shall death and bereavement come from it," which
sounds like a most amazing act to perform—and "the water has
remained wholesome to this day," no less—do we read of his turning
murderously on a bunch of children, which is exactly as bad as it
sounds.[13]

On his way up to Bethel, "little children" came out of the city and
teased Elisha, saying, "Go up, you baldhead, go up, you baldhead."
Elisha "looked behind him and saw them." In other words, he'd already passed by the loud-mouthed kids. It's not as if they blocked
his way or were otherwise threatening to him. Plus, remember that
whatever the age and size of his taunters, Elisha was a grown man
with servants. Just a little earlier, he had boasted of the "fifty strong
men" who were among his companions. Nevertheless, he uses his
great prophetic power to curse them in the name of Yahweh, where-
upon two bears emerge from the forest and mangle forty-two of the
offending children, presumably to death. Even if the children didn't
die, this seems excessive. And there's no explanation, no detail,
just that. Nonplussed, the narrator continues, "He went on from
there to Mount Carmel, and from there he returned to Samaria."
Meanwhile, we're left speechless.

This great prophet with his mandate from God, working "in the
name of Yahweh" to heal and otherwise perform good deeds, sum-
mons wild bears against little kids who tease him. Justify it as you
will, and many have tied themselves in knots trying, this is a remarkable tale. Elisha got bears to maul children who teased him,

and the narrator doesn't care. The reader is left wondering how on earth this could be. In an effort to make some kind of sense of this, and to do so in a way that would exonerate Elisha and therefore also God, some people have attempted to show that the "little children" were not so much little children as small-minded or immature adults, and that the word translated "tore" or "mauled" doesn't presume the victim's death.[14] Such efforts hardly mitigate the surreal horror of the event as narrated.

What do we do with this story? I submit that admitting its horror doesn't require condoning the action. There may be another story or ancient collective memory behind this episode that we no longer have access to. Or it may be a case of showing Elisha among the people and capable of fantastic wonders. Close reading shows differences in the Elisha and Elijah stories that can be instructive. Elijah mostly operates alone or against the political establishment, whereas Elisha is embedded in community and a counselor to kings and performs about twice as many miracles as Elijah does.[15] In this story, Elisha, with his fifty men, moves among the people and effects dramatic action merely by calling on God. Again, this doesn't excuse the assault but may help to put the episode in a literary and historical perspective.

*** 

While we're (still) on the topic of killing children, what about those Egyptian first-born sons whose deaths marked the tenth and final plague before Pharaoh released the Hebrews?[16] Surely among the dead were newborns, infants, and others too young to have committed any particular crimes of their own. Or what of Job's children, killed as part of the wager God makes with the *satan*?[17] Or the psalmist's blessing whoever would dash his enemy's babies against the rocks?[18]

What, a discerning reader of Judges might ask, is up with Jephthah and his daughter, killed for his foolishness?[19] Jephthah, who already had the spirit of Yahweh and the allegiance of the people of Gilead, makes an unnecessary and ultimately fatal vow: should he prevail against the Ammonites, he'll sacrifice whoever comes out of his house first. What did he think was going to happen? While Jephthah gets what he wanted (victory against Ammon), he loses much more. The first to come out of his house is none other than his daughter, "his one and only child." In a pique, Jephthah turns his regret on her: "You have brought me low; you have become my calamity." Yet in the face of this, his daughter, the innocent party to be killed for his foolish vow, is the dignified and principled one: Do to me what you promised, she says. After all, God made good on God's end of the deal. She asks only for a couple of months to mourn the end of her life, "to lament her virginity" with a group of girlfriends. Awful.

***

Making some kind of sense of such a story requires reading to the end of the book of Judges—with apologies, since the end is so full of pornographic violence as to be virtually unreadable. But there it is, in the Bible. The book concludes with a gruesome story of rape and dismemberment, and it's told with a nonchalance that's downright chilling.[20] The only bright spot is how the narrator indicts the action as taking place because of a general breakdown of leadership in Israel, when "there was no king in Israel" and "every man [gender-specific, *ish*] did what was right in his own eyes," implicitly judging the men's behavior wrong.

The story goes that a man, a certain Levite, stops off at a town in the north, "in the remote hill country of Ephraim," with his concubine, "a woman from Bethlehem" in the south. The woman runs from the man back to her father's house; he chases her, seeking "to speak to her heart" and so win her back. After a few days of fraternity between the woman's father and the Levite son-in-law, when her father is unable in his daughter's interest to delay the leaving further, the Levite departs with her.

But that night they end up in the public square of Gibeah with no offer of lodgings. Things look grim until an old man comes along. The Levite talks the old man into an invitation, including referring to the concubine as "your" (the old man's) maidservant. All is well inside the old man's house until men pound on the door demanding that the old man send the Levite out "that we may know him," which under the circumstances (hostile) suggests rape. The old man refuses to turn over the Levite but offers an alternative. "Look here," he says, "my daughter the virgin and his concubine." And so it goes. The old man gives his blessing: "Ravish them, and do to them the good in your eyes."

If this sounds familiar, you're right. Lot does the same concerning his daughters in Sodom: men from the town clamor to rape male visitors; their host offers girls and women instead. The men protect themselves by sacrificing women, subjecting them to brutality. In Lot's case, the women are spared. In Judges, they are not. Not the concubine, anyway. (The daughter disappears from the story.)

The Levite pushes his concubine outside to the lascivious gang. "They raped her and tortured her all night until the morning," the narrator says, and then "they let her go." She finds her way back to the house and falls at its doorway, lying there until daybreak. The Levite, preparing to leave, all but stumbles over her body. He commands her, "Arise and let us be going," but she doesn't answer. He puts her on the donkey and leaves. Is she dead? The text doesn't say.

The next we hear of her, the man is back at his house, where he promptly "took the knife and seized his concubine. He cut her limb by limb into twelve pieces and sent her throughout all the territory of Israel."[21] In a pile-up of awfulness, outrageous violence against the Benjaminites follows—no woman, child, or beast survives, but six hundred men escape to the wilderness.[22] With no women, but an imperative that a tribe not be extinguished, four hundred virgins are taken from another town to marry off to the all-male tribe. But they are not enough for the Benjaminite men, so another two hundred virgins are abducted from a religious festival.

What are we to make of a story like this? The Bible presents some ideas of its own. For one thing, this is not the final word in Judges. The very end rings with judgment that such behavior is wrong. Indeed the book's overall structure makes women's experience parallel the moral rectitude of the community. The plight of women highlights the book's pattern of devolution within Israelite society, from responsible and effective in the early chapters to outright social breakdown and chaos at the end. In the first chapter not only is a woman, Achsah, named, but she asks for and gains property of her own; a few chapters later, we read that another woman, Deborah, is the leader of all Israel and leads a successful military operation correcting abuses against the people. But reading on, we get Jephtah's daughter and, by the end, this nameless victim of terrible abuse, and finally mass rape.

Given this pattern, we should expect to read at the end of Judges exactly what we do read: a story in which, from the editors' point of view, things are badly wrong. In other words, these awful stories at the end of Judges are presented in the context of the whole book not as a model but as the opposite, as an indictment of aberrant behavior unacceptable for God's people. That's what the editors seem to think, anyway. And indeed, they conclude with "Every man did was right in his own eyes." Hear the echo of the old man's "Do to [his daughter and the concubine] what is good in your own eyes."

Consider also how this story came to sit next to very different stories, intriguingly also about women. In the Hebrew Bible, the book following Judges is Samuel, which begins with Hannah, a pious woman who is barren but much loved by a doting husband. There's a sweetness to the story in which Hannah's prayer to conceive is answered, eliciting a lovely poem of praise, which the Gospel of Luke elaborates on, with Mary as the subject ("The Magnificat").[23] Hannah bears Samuel, who serves God faithfully from youth, becoming one of Israel's greatest prophets, the first to anoint Israelite kings. In the Greek ordering of Hebrew Bible books, an arrangement reflected in the Christian Old Testament, the horrific Judges story is followed immediately by the book of Ruth, an entirely woman-centered story whose heroine is a model of loyalty, intelligence, and decorum. Ruth, the story concludes, is ancestress of the royal line favored by God: David's. In other words, both the Jewish and the Christian canonical ordering of biblical texts offer readers relief from the barrage of attacks against women that concludes the book of Judges with stories of admirable women treated with kindness and dignity.

***

Readers accustomed to hearing religious prohibitions against drinking and dancing may be surprised to find that the Bible refers to dancing as a perfectly acceptable social act, that wine shows up over and over again in both testaments, and that both wine and dancing are even seen as appropriate for worship.[24] Does the Bible promote immorality, then? I'll leave that judgment up to you. And I don't mean that dismissively. It's crucial that we recognize when our wishful thinking, when our notions of what the Bible *ought* to say complicate our reading and wrestling with what's actually there. No one seems to be above this impulse.

Pope Francis has started a heated debate about the wording of the Lord's Prayer. At issue is how the Bible doesn't always say what believers want it to say—in this case, undermining the morality of none other than God. The pope's concern is with the plea in the Lord's Prayer that God "not lead us into temptation." He argues that God would never do such a thing, so we shouldn't pray like that. His suggestion to revise the Lord's Prayer as traditionally recited by Christians the world over is, I'm sorry to say, wrong. Not theologically (a judgment I'll leave up to the faithful), but literally. I'm sorry because his version is nicer, and I like it better. But whether we like it or not, on this the Bible is clear. And the biblical witness is all we've got. In both versions, Jesus's prayer asks God not to lead us into temptation or trial.[25] It does not ask God to help us from being so led, as the pope proposes. The original Greek of the texts that we have and from which our translations come uses a verb that within its context cannot mean anything other than "lead us not."

But there are elements of the prayer, often overlooked, that might grant us some insight. The Lord's Prayer, which appears in the Gospels of Matthew and Luke, is repeated and reiterated in churches across the world every week.[26] Usually introduced as how Jesus "taught us to pray," we engage with it exactly as you'd expect: as an individual's prayer to God, "the Father." The trouble is with the language of the prayer. There's no "me," "my," or "I" in it. Instead, it's all "us" and "our." We Americans are accustomed in our modern times with our modern Christianity to prioritize the individual, specifically the individual's relationship to God. But when the one prayer that Jesus "taught us to pray" gets into the part where one asks for daily bread, forgiveness, avoiding temptation, and rescue from evil (that's the sum of it), it's all collective. It directs us to ask for *our* bread, forgiveness of *our* sins, and to spare *us* "the time of trial." Luke adds another item, again collective: to rescue *us* from the evil one.

It's not only the people praying included in the "us," but everyone. What's more, Jesus's statement immediately preceding the prayer, that God "knows what you need before you ask," suggests that the prayer's "us" isn't so much beseeching God (who already knows what we need) for sustenance as it serves to remind the person doing the praying that he or she is not the only one with a need for bread.[27] The needs of the individual are not separate from the needs of others.

Jesus introduces the proper context for prayer as not merely individual but private, which might seem on the surface to make its undeniably collective nature incongruous. In truth, that Jesus specified a private context for the prayer further strengthens the collective nature of its contents. What I mean to say is that Jesus doesn't merely overlook the individual and use plural language such as people might if they're praying in unison with others (as in the context of a modern church). By introducing it as a private act, he clarifies that individuals should pray for collective benefit.[28]

And so the prayer becomes not a simple "Can I have?" request to God, but an earnest plea that we would be part of a world in which all are fed, each seeks to be good, where we are assured that human error or offense won't generate catastrophic retaliation, and that we in the collective wouldn't be susceptible to evil.

Yes, we don't have an original Bible, and some ancient manuscripts differ from the biblical. Yes, Jesus didn't write anything that we have and may have meant something else. And yes, Jesus probably spoke in Aramaic, so the biblical versions may themselves be translations. But they are what we have. They are what has endured in the canonical text that gives us the Lord's Prayer. And they say, "Lead us not."

The problem is not how to edit but how to understand the prayer as it is. The truth is, as we've explored throughout this book, the Bible is full of such conundrums, texts that defy our expectations. Remember Isaiah 45:7, where God says "I created good and evil," and how God tells the *satan* to afflict Job (in the severest ways short of death) simply to win a wager to make the point that Job is extremely righteous.[29] Or consider that it is God who hardens the Egyptian pharaoh's heart to prevent him from liberating the Hebrews until after God had performed wonders and produced plagues.[30] Or remember how King David was incited by God to action, for which God then punished not only David but the whole nation.[31]

These Hebrew Bible/Old Testament texts are just as much part of the Christian Bible as the New Testament. And the New Testament has some startling texts of its own. Think about how Jesus said to the rich young man that to follow him, he needed to sell all he had and give it to the poor. Not figuratively, not metaphorically, but literally. Or how in Christ there is neither male nor female, but women shouldn't be allowed to speak in church.[32] The Bible is a messy, messy book with all sorts of unsettling and sometimes flatly contradictory information. The problem isn't so much figuring out what we want the Bible to say as figuring out how to deal with what it does say, especially when that's surprising, bewildering, contradictory, or just plain outlandish to us.

In the case of the Lord's Prayer, present discussions have overlooked a critical point: its collective nature, the "us" parts of it. Yet there is a long tradition within biblical texts of collective guilt or sin and collective forgiveness and reconciliation. "Comfort, comfort my people, says your God. Speak tenderly to Jerusalem and cry to her that she has served her term, that her penalty is paid, that she has received from the LORD's hand double for all her sins," the prophet Isaiah proclaims.[33] Individual complicity or innocence is irrelevant here. It's the people, the group as a whole that God deems had erred, did time, and is restored.

The Bible's rich complexity demands engagement of heart and mind, not a literal application of select texts. The Lord's Prayer that we've inherited reflects that; it is an earnest plea that even in our desire to be and do as God wills, we not end up actually doing wrong, damaging or otherwise undermining the very health and wholeness the world so needs. Rigorous learning and study informed by compassion and selfless desire should inform us. Head and heart.

But if we do go ahead with the pope's Lord's Prayer revision to reflect what we believe about God (never mind the explicit biblical language), I submit another proposed change, equally minor and equally based on what we believe about God. I propose that it be the "Our Mother" for a while. I'm not joking. Think about it. The Bible begins with a declaration of God as equally male and female.[34] And don't believers all agree that God is above, beyond, or otherwise not bound by constraints, least of all gender? The Bible comes from patriarchal circumstances that informed ways of talking and even thinking about God, hence the whole He-Him-Father language. But today mothers are just as much heads of households and families as fathers. So I'm suggesting that if we can't come up with a neutral word ("Our Parent" sounds awfully sterile), then why not use the alternative gender, at least for the next two thousand years? Just to even things out. Our Mother, who art in heaven. It has a nice ring.

# Chapter 11

# The Perennial Bestseller

Thousands of years ago, before refrigeration or antibiotics or flush toilets or public education, when the earth's people were far, far fewer and travel was slow, if it happened at all, when communities were as different from each other as the rainforests of South America from the high plains of central Asia, when gods were everywhere and into everything, the texts that would become today's Bible were born, texts that would speak and even sing, millennia later, to youth in a neon-lit internet café in South Korea, to great-grandparents in rural Appalachia, and to businessmen in smoggy Mexico City. That the Bible, which took shape in so different a world from today's should continue to have resonance and meaning for people now is nothing short of astonishing.

Besides its use in predictable settings such as synagogues and churches, the Bible also shows up in fits and starts in nonreligious, secular settings. Sometimes its users aren't even aware of the biblical basis of their references, much less of those references' biblical contexts. From characters and poems to sayings and storylines, the Bible permeates our culture. Yet despite its familiarity, surprising peculiarities lie within. Take these famous phrases and sayings, for example (twelve of them, for good measure).

We'll start with an easy one: **"forbidden fruit."** If you guessed Genesis, specifically the Garden of Eden creation story in Genesis chapters 2–3, good for you. This phrase, referring to a temptation that's ultimately bad, stays close to its biblical context as the product of a tree that God requested *adam* avoid. But wait, what tree was that, again?

When God forbids *adam* to eat from it, God calls it "the tree of the knowledge of good and evil." When Eve (who either hadn't yet existed or who hadn't yet been differentiated from Adam, however you understand *adam*, when God gave that warning) reiterates the prohibition in her conversation with the snake, she identifies it as the "fruit of the tree in the middle of the garden" and reasons it to be "desirable as a source of wisdom." After they eat the forbidden fruit, God notes another tree's fruit that *adam* (singular, no mention of Eve) shouldn't have: "the tree of life" and so lest *adam* "eat and live forever," banishes *adam* (singular, no mention of Eve) from the Garden.[1]

Simple on the surface, the story is full of nuance and complexity. Even the "forbidden fruit" raises questions. Among them: isn't wisdom, or at least the distinction between what's good and what's bad something every parent strives to instill in children? And given the way the story ends, shouldn't we understand "forbidden fruit" also to be the rejection of death? After all, fruit from the tree of life likewise became forbidden.

By the way, nowhere in the story is either tree identified as an apple tree.

***

If you guessed that **"an eye for an eye"** appears in Exodus, you're right.[2] If you guessed Leviticus, right again.[3] If you guessed Deuteronomy, yup, it's there, too.[4] Matthew? Indeed.[5] How about in Hezekiah? Nope. There's no such book.

"An eye for an eye" gets quadruple play in the Bible. It appears three times in the Hebrew Bible and once in the New Testament. In the contexts of Exodus, Leviticus, and Deuteronomy, it appears as part of a law code. We find this law also in the ancient (ca. 1754 BCE) Babylonian law code of a king named Hammurabi.

Exactly how such law codes operated in the ancient world remains a matter of some debate. There is much to suggest that many laws were meant more as instruction (which is also a more etymologically accurate translation of *torah* than "law") than as line items to be applied in a strictly literal manner. Whatever the case, this *lex talionis* (law of retaliation) had the effect of *limiting* violence—a fact often lost on modern users. That is, it specified that in the case of assault, the victim was not to respond with an even greater assault. Rather than a call for gruesome violence, the code demanded equal justice—reparation, yes, but only as much as exactly corresponded to the crime.

In the New Testament, "an eye for an eye" appears in the context of Jesus's teaching out of what was scripture in his time. He referred to this set of texts, commonly accepted as authoritative, as the Torah and the Prophets and began this particular set of teachings by reminding his audience that his goal was not to "abolish the law [*torah*] or the prophets . . . but to fulfill it."[6] He rather sternly admonishes them to abide by the terms of that Hebrew Bible, and then goes on to explicate specific laws for his particular audience. In that context, Jesus refashions "an eye for an eye" into the admonition to "turn the other cheek," which may have its place, but in this case arguably denies justice to the one who lost an eye.[7]

***

The biblical **"scapegoat"** really was a goat. Poor thing. In the book of Leviticus are instructions for an annual practice originating with the priest Aaron. Aaron gathered up all of the community's sins and laid them on a goat, who was then cast out into the wilderness.[8] An odd practice to us, in the biblical narrative we read that thus were the people relieved of the burden of their sins. The biblical scapegoat was, then, an individual innocent who nevertheless bore away the people's sins. In this sense, the scapegoat prefigures Jesus, centuries before Jesus ever was.

The goat, says Leviticus, was "for *azazel*," a term that appears nowhere else in the Bible. Some translators simply render that term "a scapegoat," assuming from its context the abstract idea of removal of sins. Others transliterate and capitalize "Azazel," following a tradition represented in the Dead Sea Scrolls and other ancient literature (1 and 2 Enoch, e.g.) that personifies the word as a shady character named Azazel. There, Azazel is among the hybrid human-divine pre-Flood troublemakers (corrupting human beings with weapons and ornamentation, among other things). It's possible that the same traditions associated with Azazel in this other literature informed the final form of Leviticus, but we don't know for sure.

\*\*\*

**"How the mighty have fallen"** has to do with the deaths of Saul and Jonathan. It forms part of David's lament, a cry declaring the dead's greatness. That Saul and David were at war with each other adds surprise and a striking poignancy.[9] Further jarring to our modern ears, we read that the messenger who told David that Saul and Jonathan had died explained that he was coming from the battlefield and happened on a fatally wounded Saul leaning on his spear while (David's) enemy forces closed in. The messenger reports that Saul had begged the messenger to kill him. The man did, and brought the kingly trappings along with news back to David. Given such a situation, the reader might be as shocked as the messenger when David calls for the messenger's death. The narrator portrays David's love for Saul and for Jonathan, too, as so great that he was utterly broken-hearted over their deaths.

In truth, the love that David and Jonathan shared is its own biblical strangeness. Stories of their relationship portray a particularly intimate fondness and care for one another. Their souls are said to have been bound together.[10] They even made a personally binding contract, a covenant, between the two of them.[11] David declares his affection for his friend so "greatly beloved" as to rank it "wonderful, surpassing the love of women," giving rise over centuries of scholarship and interpretation to speculation as to the extent and nature of their love.[12]

***

**"A drop in the bucket."** Who knew this started with the Bible? It appears in the Hebrew Bible book of Isaiah, at the beginning of the section scholars identify with an anonymous prophet of the Isaiah-ish tradition. "Deutero-" or "Second" Isaiah preached at the beginning of a new era—the end of exile, the beginning of renewed liberty (538 BCE)—in contrast to First Isaiah, who lived and worked around 700 BCE. It is the nations—small and great—that the prophet reckons no more than "a drop in the bucket" compared to the breadth and might of God.[13]

This prophet faced the great challenge of convincing the Israelites, who had been in exile in Babylon for a good fifty years or more, to take up the conquering liberator's (Cyrus of Persia's) invitation to leave Babylonia and return to Judah and there to rebuild the temple in Jerusalem. This turned out to be a hard sell.

For one thing, many Israelites knew only Babylonia as home, having been born and grown to adulthood there. For another, it wasn't necessarily so bad there on a day-to-day level, while back in Judah the land had been decimated and was devastatingly poor. What's more, whatever property the exiles may have left behind when they were taken away would surely have been seized and repurposed in the ensuing decades by those who had remained. Finally, and most crucial to the biblical writers and editors, many exiles believed their Jerusalem-temple-centered God to have been defeated by the Babylonian high god Marduk. So this Deutero-Isaiah had to work hard to convince his audience that their God was alive and well and, what's more, sovereign not only over Judah but over the whole world, even the whole universe. This God took a special interest in them, Deutero-Isaiah declared, and would facilitate their return home.

***

That forcefully optimistic tone is at odds with the world-weary tenor of Ecclesiastes (Hebrew Qoheleth), where we find both **"There is nothing new under the sun"** and **"Eat, drink, and be merry."**[14] The former launches the whole book, a kind of meditation on purpose in the face of the ultimate futility of it all. The speaker concludes that given such circumstances, the best thing a person can do may be simply to eat, drink, and take whatever enjoyment one can. Or not. Qoheleth also confesses that he tried merriment and revelry and found them to be useless.[15] So, once again, the Bible pulls the rug out from under its own feet, and we are left, thrown back on our own faculties, to make sense of things.

***

**"The writing's on the wall"** means much the same today as it does in its biblical context: that a particular future is inevitable. If you know the inherent strangeness that the scribe of the biblical graffiti was a disembodied hand and the script Aramaic, double points for you. Trick question: Who was Belshazzar?

The story appears in the book of Daniel. Its setting is a Babylonian palace banquet, a great feast at which sacred vessels from the Jerusalem temple are used for drunken revelry. In the midst of the party, a disembodied hand writes, out of thin air, "Mene mane tekel upharsin," which sort of kills the buzz. The narrator says that the Babylonian king Belshazzar was terrified and called for a translation. No one could make sense of it until the queen suggested calling from among the Jewish exiles the eminently qualified Daniel. Belshazzar did so. Daniel arrived. And out of words that refer to units of measurement by weight that *sound* like the words "to number," "to weight," and "to divide," Daniel interpreted a dire prophecy: "God has numbered your kingdom and brought it to an end. You have been weighed in the balance and found wanting. And your kingdom has been divided and given to the Medes and the Persians."[16] This would indeed come to pass, and thus endeth the Babylonian exile.

The book is a bit confusing, though, or better: confused. For one thing, Belshazzar was never king, of Babylonia or anywhere else, though he did act in his absent father's stead. And his father was not Nebuchadnezzar but Nabonidus, a controversial king who claimed never to have wanted the throne, though his son Belshazzar apparently craved it. Cyrus of Persia put an end to all that when he defeated Nabonidus's Babylonia in 539 BCE and released the conquered from their exile there. But that's another story.

***

Fast-forward to the New Testament, and we find **"the blind leading the blind."** The context is one of those episodes in which Jesus challenges received traditional laws. What may be particularly surprising to modern readers is Jesus's explicit critique of a literal application of oral laws intended to clarify and protect biblical texts. Of those who wish slavishly to apply the received traditions as literal laws, he calls them hypocrites trading God's word for human tradition and tells his disciples to ignore them: "They are blind guides of the blind. And if one blind person guides another, both will fall into a pit."[17]

***

This is not to say that Jesus advocated callous disregard for the injured or disabled. On the contrary. After all, most people have heard of the **"Good Samaritan."** The parable appears in Luke's Gospel, and its message of helping others lives on.[18] As a matter of fact, there are laws on our own twenty-first-century American books actually called "good Samaritan laws" to protect a person who steps in in the case of an emergency to lend help but may be subject to a lawsuit later, if things don't go so well.[19] Most of us know that a good Samaritan is a person who simply happens to be around when something goes bad and lends help without any expectation of reward. This is in keeping with the biblical parable.

But there's more to the biblical context. It wasn't just a guy who happened by, but one of the Samaritans—a subset of Israelites at odds with Jesus's Jewish audience. In other words, a sworn enemy of the victim. And it wasn't just that he offered aid and made a personal sacrifice to help the wounded but that he did so after upstanding members of the injured person's own group had passed by and failed to help. Think of a set of people you feel at odds with. Now picture yourself injured and helpless. People who can help happen along, members of your own social set. They ignore your need and leave you to suffer. It is only someone from the people you dislike who gives you what you need, even at her own expense and trouble. That's the nuance in the story of the Good Samaritan.[20]

*** *** ***

You could say that each individual in that story we expect to offer help saw the injured man but walked on and **"washed his hands of the matter."** Any time we express our done-with-it attitude with this gesture, we're channeling none other than Pontius Pilate, the Roman governor of Judea and in Jerusalem at the time of Jesus's execution. In Matthew's recounting of Jesus's trial, where this phrase occurs, Pilate makes an effort to both follow the laws of the time (prosecute sedition) and appease inflamed Jews offended by Jesus's teachings and what people were saying about him (that he was the Messiah).

Failing in the latter, Pilate makes a show of washing his hands while telling the angry crowd, "I am innocent of this man's blood; see to it yourselves."[21] What follows has given rise to all sorts of anti-Semitic ugliness. Matthew reports that the people responded, "His blood be on us and on our children." Jews have been called Christ-killers ever since. But that's wrongheaded for all sorts of reasons, not least that in the very next verse it is Pilate who flogs Jesus and Pilate who turns him over to be crucified, and the "soldiers of the governor" take Jesus away. What's more, as noted earlier, it's of course the Romans who crucify Jesus, crucifixion being a state-sponsored event.

But back to the crowd's fateful exclamation (only in Matthew, by the way). Remember "how the mighty have fallen"? It was a crime to kill "the LORD's anointed." That's why David killed the messenger who had done Saul in. At issue with Jesus was whether or not he was "the LORD's anointed," aka the Messiah. The crowd said no, and they'd take their chances in having Jesus killed. As for the biblical reference to their children, what we've got here is literal, first-generation children, not Jews for all time.

***

**"In the twinkling of an eye"** has such a delightful ring it's no wonder it has had such staying power. Like the other phrases examined in this chapter, it too is a translation. And like so many evocative, poetic, and otherwise pleasing turns of biblical phrase, we might assume we owe it to the King James team. Yet a good 250 years before King James's tome (1611), John Wycliffe's Bible translated from the Latin "in the twynklying of an iye." It appears in Shakespeare's *The Merchant of Venice* (1596). And indeed the "original" Greek bears this out with a word meaning "wink" or "twinkle" behind exactly that in the English.

The phrase appears in 1 Corinthians 15:52, in the context of Paul's imagining a great transformation of the dead "at the last trumpet," when "the dead will be raised imperishable." This has given rise to competing claims about what happens to Christians after death, from an immediate transformation to join the ranks of immortal angels or after a waiting period during which the dead remain, well, dead, until the cosmic second coming of Jesus, wherein all the Christian dead will be raised to immortality.

\*\*\*

This tiny sample represents a mere fraction of biblical phrases and imagery that have found their way into modern discourse, making familiar what nevertheless contains surprising peculiarities. Individual characters and stories also show up in reimaginings that are sometimes quite rich and provocative. It isn't always necessary to know their biblical origins to appreciate modern usage, but the value of knowing about the Bible, regardless of what one believes, is at the least delicious fodder for cocktail party conversation, at best a safeguard against the kinds of misuse that cause discord and outright damage.

## Chapter 12

# Ten Commandments for Reading the Bible

I've had some trouble nailing down the best title for this chapter. A real stickler has been finding the best word to describe the kind of interaction with the Bible that these "commandments" address. "Reading" is the most obvious, since reading is usually the starting point for whatever action a person takes in light of the Bible. You'd think. Truth is, a lot of people who seek to apply the Bible or claim to be informed by the Bible in their thinking and behavior don't actually read it, especially not in full. (Some people even think simply holding it demonstrates a laudable piety.) Yet you've seen from earlier chapters how the meaning or potential interpretation of any given biblical text might alter in light of other texts—all of which are still "the Bible."

So I considered "Using" instead. Indeed, when you get right down to the gist of the following individual commandments, it has less to do with how people read than with how they apply what they (think they've) read. Note, for example, the difference between reading (say, slowly; or in the Bible's original language with notes from erudite scholars over the millennia on said text) and applying, aka "using" the text (say, by determining that women should be forbidden pain killers during childbirth based on a particular way of reading Genesis 3:16; it's happened).[1] What I detail in these commandments has as much to do with use as with reading. So I thought maybe "Using" or more narrowly "Applying" might be the best choice.

But hang on. Some of the charges I detail primarily conform neither to reading nor to applying but are more a philosophy of treatment—an "approach," if you will. So I thought maybe "Dealing with" would be better. Each commandment arguably has its roots in the matter of approach to or dealing with the Bible.

Anyway, you see the problem. A collage of these words would do the trick, but what a trick that would be. So, like a translator's dilemma, we're stuck with the choice. And that brings me back to the most obvious: "Reading" it is.

*** 

Before I get to the commandments, here are a few, more general do's and don'ts.

Summarizing the Bible has become a popular way to teach biblical literacy. Ironically, as I hope you appreciate, such retellings may be the most problematic way to approach biblical texts. Treating the Bible as a continuous narrative that one can understand in a long Cliff's Notes–like way is fundamentally flawed. Knowing about the Bible's historical and literary contexts, its contradictions and messy theologies puts the lie to these often well-meaning efforts to introduce the Bible or its individual books. I suspect that it's the Bible's enduring influence in secular as well as religious spheres that has led to a proliferation of such retellings.

Many "introduction to the Bible" texts try to do this recap and retelling. You can now see the immediate problems: Whose Bible? In what order do the books appear, and by what titles? Did or did not Joshua and company rid the land of its inhabitants to settle as people of God, and what's that God's name, anyway? In which way did God create the world—by speaking from some remote disembodied locale or by planting and shaping and walking around? On and on we go, from Genesis through Chronicles (or is it Revelation?).

Surely, the best treatments of biblical texts short of the Bible itself recognize and maybe even draw attention to the Bible's fundamental oddness(es), honor its sometimes clunky and contradictory nature, celebrate the diversity of its literature and perspectives on God, and generally reject any effort to flatten with pedantic and patronizing simplification.

Having said a bit about pitfalls modern readers face and infelicitous ways we might read the Bible, how *should* one approach it?

To start, maybe don't presume to know "what the Bible says" unless you've committed to reading the whole thing through with scholarly input along the way. That is, don't make a brief text, a nugget read here or there, the be-all and end-all of what you think the Bible says. Even more important, supplement such reading with learning *about* the Bible—its languages, cultures, diversity of literature, history of development. At the least, take advantage of other resources to hand. But be careful, some are more worthy of authority than others.

An easy first step is to invest in a study Bible. There are some excellent study Bibles available—and some not-so-excellent ones, too. Study Bibles have, in addition to (a translation of) the biblical text, marginal notes by a team of qualified individuals that elucidate or explain things along the way. They may detail a historical reference; explain the range of meanings in Hebrew or Greek behind a given translation; provide comparison to other ancient versions; or point readers to other texts, either similar or in contradiction to the one at hand. Many include separate essays, timelines, maps, and other helpful matter that aren't part of the Bible per se. In total, this material can be a superb crash course, a kind of Bible 101, undertaken in the comfort of one's own home.

Not all study Bibles serve the purpose of giving readers the tools to understand texts for themselves. To that end, steer clear of editions that tell you what to believe—what God is and wants, for example—or tell you what a text says in order to tell you how to live.[2] In choosing a study Bible, make note of the identity and credentials of its contributors. People who have earned academic degrees studying the history and literature of the biblical world from institutions committed to information for the information's sake (and not first to promote a particular religious perspective) usually provide the most well-founded, most objective material.

Another useful exercise in reading any given part of the Bible is to have in front of you several different translations of that text. The internet has made this especially easy, since several websites make it possible to look up a particular set of verses and see many translations of it side by side. Some even show the text in its original (-ish—remember the problem with using "original"), broken down into a literal translation with details about each word's vocabulary and grammar, what translators call a "crib," "pony," or "trot." This may not tell anything about the text's background or literary context, but it helps readers see for themselves how the text might be read differently from any single translation.

Having such resources to hand, learning *about* the Bible besides what's in it, can rattle dearly held assumptions and get you in trouble over the Thanksgiving dinner table, but I'm confident that they'll enrich your reading and even your faith, adding depth and nuance to this multifaceted ancient book whose power endures still today.

***

One final qualification: I realize that the "Ten Commandments" part of this title suggests a high level of arrogance on my part. So let me say straight off that I have no illusions of being a modern Moses, with whom I have little in common except perhaps a bad sense of direction, much less of being God.

It's just that I've had the opportunity to learn about the Bible not only personally but also professionally. And let me tell you, there are more things to learn about it than I possibly could in this lifetime. What I've learned, plus the recognition that one cannot learn it all, as well as my observations about the ways people handle the biblical texts have led me to develop these ten commandments for reading the Bible. They're not biblical, of course, and they are open to debate.

And now, on to the commandments.

No, wait. As with nearly everything biblical, yet another caveat is in order. Although each of these commandments ostensibly reflects one of the biblical Ten Commandments, you've seen that there are at least two different versions of the biblical commandments. And different faith groups count them differently. Here, I simply picked one way of numbering and provide only the bare biblical commandment by way of comparison with each of my rules for reading. Curious readers may want to check out the Bible's extrapolations for themselves.

Okay, *now* on to the commandments.

## 1. Thou shalt not make the Bible God (// Thou shalt have no other gods before me)

You may be thinking, "Enough said." Yet people claim that the Bible has saved them, that the Bible elicits wonder and awe, that the Bible is finally beyond human understanding. Since all of these are attributes also applied to God, you can see how someone might confuse the two and even elevate the Bible above an ultimately mysterious, radically free, and "other" God.

What's more, in Genesis we read about the world created through speech, "God said, 'let there be' . . ." And the Gospel of John picks this up with "In the beginning was the Word and the Word was with God and the Word was God." In other words, some biblical texts themselves would seem to blur the distinction between God and the Bible.

Jews and Christians believe that we learn about God through the Bible and listen to God within it. But by allowing that God is also *other than* the Bible, believers allow for the possibility of surprise. They acknowledge that God transcends even this rich and living collection of texts. Recognizing that God is other than the Bible allows for the possibility of experiencing God in other relationships, too—with a religious community, with family and friends, with the earth and its nonhuman inhabitants, and in the simple space and time of our ordinary days.

## 2. Thou shalt not worship the object itself (// Thou shalt not make for thyself an idol)

Bibles come to us today as pages bound between two covers. For a long time, these texts came in the form of scrolls, yet even in that form, the collection was already considered sacred. It was "Bible." In other words, what constitutes the Bible isn't its form as an object, a codex, which is the fancy name for "book" as we know it—but what's inside.

In that way, one's approach to the Bible is more appropriately like that of a believer to an icon, not to be confused with an idol. Icons are objects or images that allow the worshiper a means to contemplate and maybe even access, or be accessed by, what is radically other, holy, and divine. Icons, which serve as a means to worship God, are different from idols, which are objects mistakenly worshiped *as* gods.

The most famous Christian icons may be those from the Greek Orthodox tradition. The idea is that contemplating an icon is not so much focusing on the thing itself but a way to connect with what lies behind it. Contemplating an icon can be like opening a window to the divine, a bridge of understanding, even communication between the profane and the sacred. In other words, Mary is not the figure in brilliant blue against a golden background within a sturdy frame, but Mary might make herself accessible to the viewer *through* the image.

Similarly, while the Bible as a material object is not itself God (see commandment #1), it can be a portal for connecting with God, a mechanism for communication and understanding. Simply appreciating the belief that God so wants a relationship with people that there *is* a Bible makes for powerful theology. The danger lies in confusing the means with the real thing—in making the icon into an idol.

## 3. Thou shalt not presume that any given translation is the text itself (// Thou shalt not take the name of the LORD in vain)

The biblical commandment warns that while knowing God's name does not put us in possession of God's very self, abuse of it constitutes a violence against God.

God's personal moniker, a four-letter word in Hebrew that shows up in most English translations as LORD or Jehovah, is presented in the Bible as a special means whereby God makes Godself present and intimately accessible to the people of God.

Remember, the Bible's original languages are Hebrew, Greek, and Aramaic, though we don't actually have an original Bible. Not only do most of us read the Bible in translation, but there are sometimes several possible "originals." Consequently, any given translation is itself an act of interpretation. We do well to adopt humility in proposing what exactly any given text means.

We get an explanation of YHWH (alternatively transliterated JHVH) in Exodus, where God "gives" and explains to Moses the divine name—"I am who I am"—a play on the verb "to be." Like this connotation of the divine name, translation is a living thing.

As long as languages are used, they are said to be "living," and like any living thing, they change. So no matter how good a translation may be, it is never perfect for all time. Just because we have a Bible that we can read, we ought not presume that in our favorite translation of the text, we have the final word on what the Bible says, much less what it means.

## 4. Mind the gap(s) (// Remember the Sabbath day and keep it holy)

The Sabbath in ancient biblical tradition is set-apart time, a gap in the ordinary, mundane, predictable, or expected, when holiness shines through. "Mind the gap." When I was in England some years ago, I was struck by this warning, posted and regularly announced in the train station. It told passengers to notice and be careful—there's a gap between the platform and the train. Commandment #4 is both warning and invitation. Mind the gap.

In the case of the Bible, that gap is any space in the logic of a text where it leaps past what we'd expect (hang on, where did Cain get his wife?), leaves out information we'd really like to know (the precise nature of Mary Magdalene's relationship to Jesus), or sets its eye where we're not looking (erotic sex in the Song of Songs rather than, say, the identity of the lovers). But what can feel like hiccups or missteps in the Bible remind us that we're not in charge. We need to check our expectations and prepare to be surprised. They're "the crack" Leonard Cohen sings about, "that's how the light gets in." By acknowledging and respecting the Bible's fractures, disagreements, and silences, you allow not only for what is ineffable and unknown but also for yourself to be in relationship to it.

The biblical Sabbath is a hiccup in ordinary time, a gap or crack in habits of the day-to-day that opens up for God. To observe the Sabbath is to break from what is conventionally human: our control over making a living and making sense of the world. It makes space for what defies human expression, respects the silence of simply being, and recalls our limits in remembering that it is God, not we, who creates and sustains. So, too, the Bible's upending our habits of reading and religious assumptions can be the gap that makes space for what's even more wonderful (or scary) than we thought.

The Bible doesn't read like a modern book. It jumps around, disagrees with itself, skips over things we think it should include, and is utterly unapologetic about it all. When we stop trying to make it entirely sensible and consistent and instead relax and accept the Bible for what it is, we discover that precisely what it is not (seamless, consistent, univocal) offers an invitation to engage it—arguing, contemplating, imagining, and listening.

If this interrogating and even differing with what you might read in the Bible worries you, take comfort: not only does the Bible itself model disagreement, argument, and various points of view, but the Bible predates our individual efforts and will outlast them.

## 5. Honor the knowledge and wisdom of your predecessors (// Honor thy father and mother)

Your elders are not always right, but they've been around the block, learned some things along the way, and so have a bit of wisdom to offer. In the case of the Bible, really smart, skilled, and talented people have been studying it—its literary art, historical context, theological principles—for hundreds and hundreds of years. Don't accept their conclusions without applying your own brain, but don't ignore or dismiss them outright either. And don't ever presume you're an island of wisdom needing no background information in formulating ideas about any given text.

There is an attitude prevalent among certain Christians that the Holy Spirit will guide your reading, so whatever you may glean from a biblical text is actually God interpreting and dictating it directly for you. This is a dangerous abdicating of one's God-given intellectual capacity and replacing it with lazy ignorance. I'm reminded of the story of a monk and the garden he restored on monastery grounds. One day, a superior came to visit the monastery. Impressed with the order and beauty of the grounds, he said to the gardener-monk, "It's a wonder what you and the Good Lord have done here," to which the monk replied, "You should have seen what it looked like when the Good Lord was taking care of it by himself."

Use your own brain by learning from experts, and with all that scholarship in hand think for yourself. Then question your thinking, do some more research, and think again.

## 6. Thou shalt not use the Bible for character assassination (// Thou shalt not kill)

Like the biblical commandment, you'd hope there's no need for such a rule. But people kill, and people routinely apply biblical texts to dismiss and demean other people, their way of life, their perspectives, and their beliefs as wrongheaded, and even call for the people and religions themselves to be eliminated. What's more, both commandments (mine and the biblical) would seem to have biblical justification for breaking them.

This biblical commandment gets a lot of attention not least because it's embedded in texts that prescribe capital punishment and part of a collection that doesn't just condone but commands the killing of other people. Hebrew has many words for ending a life, as does English, and a pretty good equivalent here is "murder," which leaves open the possibility that other kinds of killing may be okay in some circumstances. (I'm not necessarily agreeing, just saying.)

Yes, the Bible is full of material that can be weaponized against other people, but don't let your interpretation of a text dehumanize either yourself or anyone else.

## 7. Thou shalt not forsake wisdom to embrace careless interpretations (// Thou shalt not commit adultery)

Don't abandon the integrity of your own humanity—your basic sense of right and wrong, inclination toward compassion, and desire to make the world beautiful and good—in order to adopt the sensibility of texts that promote intolerance, cruelty, or inequity.

Don't be seduced by the superficial, easy, or simplistic.

There are biblical passages in both the Old and New Testaments that are frankly unacceptable at face value, for example, demonizing others simply for being "other," amputating the hand of a sinner, forbidding persons to speak because of their gender. Among several options for dealing with such problematic texts—acknowledging them without adopting them, for example—is this: consider such texts to be a kind of moral exercise. Maybe their value lies precisely in their pushing us to reject them. They press us to use head and heart to articulate what's wrong about such texts, to stand up and say, "No. And here's why."

I understand that one could argue this is a slippery slope. Where does it end, the dismissal of particular texts and acceptance of others? My answer: that's exactly my point. Application of some biblical interpretation or other without rigorous information-gathering and soul-searching is a dangerous and hurtful cop-out.

We must wrestle with the rightness or wrongness of any given directive with humility, seek every bit of information we can get hold of, employ empathy, and apply the complicated business of love so championed throughout the Bible to reject any belief, idea, or action that hints of the kind of narrow-minded piety that demeans others or compromises their health and well-being.

## 8. Thou shalt not take biblical texts out of context (// Thou shalt not steal)

Although many biblical texts, ancient and foreign as they are, make sense even in today's world, they were not written first and only for us today. Knowing something about their ancient contexts appropriately nuances our reading of them. For example, recall that one text in the Old Testament forbids divorce; another commands it. In the case of the first, divorcing their Jewish wives in a patriarchal context left the women destitute, so prohibiting divorce was an act of social justice. In the case of the second, the postexilic community couldn't risk diluting its identity with foreign wives, so they were to be divorced. Without knowing the historical context, a reader could assume, depending on which text she reads, that God does not—or, wait, does—want her to get divorced when a modern circumstance may be nothing like either one of the biblical.

Or consider those texts in which Jesus seems to reprimand his audience for insufficient faith. Jesus's saying "If you have faith . . . even if you say to this mountain, 'Be lifted up and thrown into the sea,' it will happen." Well, don't despair if Mount Denali (or the mulberry tree, as Luke would have it) remains resolutely in place despite your herculean faith.[3] Maybe Jesus's audience didn't exactly include you, or maybe it's a metaphor, maybe the text worked differently within its greater literary context than we expect. Maybe there's something else going on entirely.

## 9. Thou shalt not presume to issue divine judgment of others (// Thou shalt not bear false witness against your neighbor)

One's judgment of others—of how they are and should be—based on one's particular interpretation of any given biblical text, may turn out to be wrong. Remember, determining an "original" text may be impossible, and translation is itself interpretation. So even apart from common courtesy, know that one's sense of an absolute meaning for any given text as it leads to judging another person or a whole group of people may be misplaced, even flat-out wrong. Responsibility for oneself is quite enough for any person.

## 10. Thou shalt not desire a different Bible than the one you have, no matter how exasperating it can be sometimes (// Thou shalt not covet your neighbor's wife or anything that belongs to your neighbor)

Everyone has a Bible within the Bible—some favorite texts and some never acknowledged. Remember those peacenik quotes from Isaiah and Micah? I for one am glad to see how popular they are. It chokes me up a bit to see outside the UN building in New York City that powerful bronze statue, *Let Us Beat Swords into Plowshares*, a gift from the Soviet Union back when there was such a thing and we suffered mutual suspicion and fear. And I confess I'd just as soon never see a statue of Joel's contrary quote—beating plowshares into swords. But those texts do share real estate within the collection we call the Bible. Maybe you share my familiar affinity for "The LORD is my shepherd" but not so much "It is a fearful thing to fall into the hands of the living God."[4] We seldom hear people reciting the genealogies of Genesis with the same passion as gems from Proverbs or the Sermon on the Mount, and details pertaining to how exactly the ancient Hebrews were to build the Tabernacle rarely make it onto cross-stitch.

To take the Bible seriously doesn't mean we can't have favorite sections, texts that speak to us in some way or another. But it also means accounting for and acknowledging (not necessarily endorsing) texts that make us uncomfortable or that we simply don't like. Rather, take the whole thing—your whole Bible, whatever that is—and see the other rules again, from the top.

\*\*\*

When I was a beginning student of the Bible, I kept stumbling on an abbreviation that puzzled me. In the notes citing chapter-verse passages, I'd find "cf." followed by more chapter-verse citations. But launching into an academic study of the Bible was such a drinking-from-a-firehose experience that I didn't investigate the "cf." conundrum for some time, figuring it would become clear soon enough. It didn't. Finally I looked it up.

Turns out "cf." is an abbreviation for the Latin word *confer*, which means "compare." Suddenly a whole lot more than those two little letters made sense to me. While a given verse or passage or book may seem to have an immediately clear meaning or message, that conclusion benefits from nuance, even correction when considered in light of comparable or contradictory texts within the Bible. That fact brought home for me the multivalent nature of these texts and the demand that we engage them with all of our faculties.

Among the most admirable, most lovable qualities of the Bible is its diversity. The Bible says not one thing but many. And the ways in which it disagrees with itself are instructive. Those contradictions give pause. They make us create space to consider thoughtfully how we might read beyond the literal, maybe revise received traditions and interpretations in light of new knowledge and experience.

Martin Luther's central argument was that a person's Christian faith (and so life) should be informed entirely by the Bible. All debates about God's nature and being, all declarations of what's right and what's wrong, all instructions for how to go about one's life and work should begin and end with the biblical texts. *Sola scriptura*, "by Scripture alone." That in Luther's world people's access to the Bible was mediated by a class of priests—Roman Catholic ascetic men—he found unacceptable in the highest degree. Rather, he advocated giving the people a Bible they could read for themselves and getting out of their way.

This is heady stuff, the democratization of the Word of God. As a kid born and raised in the Lutheran Church, I ate it up. I'm grateful for this prioritizing of text, and I'm grateful too for the spirit of investigation, inquiry, and debate that marked my early experience.

But ironically, the more I studied, the more I could see, too, where the priests were coming from: that some background knowledge is crucial to making sense of the ancient and archaic and still foreign texts. It can be dangerous to proceed without such knowledge. I sympathize with Luther's opponents in this. Though I finally take Luther's side, I do so with the caveat that "the Bible alone" requires bringing in, studying, and taking seriously other sources, too. Paradox of paradoxes.

What I'm trying to say is that if you depend only on the Bible for developing a theologically sound manner of living, then you must approach the text in the most generous and open-minded way. Think for yourself with the best information available. And don't be afraid to disagree with what you read, even when it's in the Bible. So sure, *sola scriptura*, if indeed that presumes intellectual rigor and the courage to stand up to tradition, to the very text itself, with a selfless and wide-ranging sense of love and justice.

That—to me, anyway—is biblical. It is, finally, something to love.

# NOTES

## Introduction: An Arranged Marriage

1. Normally, when referring to the texts of the (Protestant) Christian Old Testament, I use the term "Hebrew Bible," following the norm in biblical scholarship. It's not a perfect system, but it recognizes not only that for some people (Jews), there is no other testament but also that for all Bible-believers (Christians and Jews), it is a vibrant part of the whole, not superseded by the New Testament. Because this particular case—the misleading reduction of God to angry versus loving—reflects the assumption that "the Bible" is composed of those two major parts, I use here the language (Old and New Testaments) of the people who espouse this theology.

2. See Ex 12:37, then add women and children.

## Chapter 1

1. The nomenclature here is a bit tricky. When talking about the people responsible for giving us the earliest biblical material, we might use "Hebrews," "Israelites," or "Jews." Most scholars think that the religion of Judaism we would recognize today began to take shape during the sixth century BCE Babylonian exile. It was then, too, that some of the texts that would become the Hebrew Bible began to be collected and edited as authoritative scripture (and more were written). That process of canonization continued for centuries before the Hebrew Bible was finalized. So, when talking about canonization, "Jews" quite accurately identifies the agents. However, when talking about the earlier stages of

generating and passing along what would become some of those texts, we might talk about those people as "Israelites" or "Hebrews."

2. The Jewish Hebrew Bible ends with Chronicles, specifically a mandate to return to Jerusalem; the Christian Old Testament ends with Malachi, meaning "my messenger," which ends with a sense of expectation—anticipation of the prophet Elijah's return.

3. I find it ironic that Luther was so hell-bent on the Jewish version. Luther, who wrote such hateful anti-Semitic affirmations as *On the Jews and Their Lies*.

4. For a long time, well into the twentieth century, it was generally accepted that the Hebrew Bible took the shape it has today in the first century, specifically on an unseasonably cool afternoon in the summer of 90 CE in the charming academic village of Jamnia, where a breeze off the Mediterranean stirred the meeting notes of Jewish scholars assembled there for a vote on what's in and what's out of the Bible, before tracking east to Jerusalem. Okay, not quite *that* specific. But until recently, people assumed precise circumstances for the Bible's development, thinking that the contents of the Hebrew Bible were decided in one moment in one place, by Jewish scholars assembled in Jamnia (alternatively Jabeh) some time around the year 90 CE. Unfortunately, as with nearly anything simple and precise, the Bible proves defiant. Scholars now recognize that that story, which may have *some* historical veracity, doesn't tell the whole story of canonization, which was likely a bit more organic. Texts that had continued resonance or relevance for the community over time simply gained priority, for example. One of the criteria for books to be included in the Jewish Hebrew Bible was that they come from before the time of Ezra, when the age of prophecy was understood to have ended.

5. See 2 Sam 7:4–17.

6. Ezek 1:28.

7. Isa 45:1; 2 Chr 36:22–23.

8. Mk 5:1–20; Mt 8:28–34; Lk 8:26–39. Matthew changed the location from Gerasa to Gadara, which is nevertheless still a good ten kilometers from the Sea of Galilee.

9. Jona Lenderling, "Legio X Fretensis," Livius, modified May 7, 2020, http://www.livius.org/articles/legion/legio-x-fretensis/.

10. Jack Fellman, "Hebrew: Eliezer Ben-Yehuda and the Revival of Hebrew," Jewish Virtual Library, accessed October 4, 2017, http://www.jewishvirtuallibrary.org/eliezer-ben-yehuda-and-the-revival-of-hebrew.

11. John Dryden, "Preface Concerning Ovid's Epistles," Bartleby, accessed October 4, 2017, http://www.bartleby.com/204/207.html.

12. For more on the topic, see Martien Halvorson-Taylor, *Song of Songs, International Exegetical Commentary on the Old Testament* (Stuttgart: Kohlhammer, forthcoming).

13. For an engaging account of how one biblical scholar reckons with the Bible's problems to find them ultimately enriching to Christian faith, see Peter Enns, *For the Bible Tells Me So . . . : Why Defending Scripture Has Made Us Unable to Read It* (HarperOne, 2014).

## Chapter 2

1. For the record, there's also a little bit of Aramaic in the Hebrew Bible, mostly in the book of Daniel.

2. Still in the mid-second century, we find Justin Martyr quoting from them without distinction as "the Memoirs of the Apostles."

3. Irenaeus, *Against Heresies*, 3.7.11.

4. Papias makes such a connection around 120–140 CE. And Tertullian explicitly claims the gospel for Mark (*Against Marcion*, 4.5).

5. For a more detailed treatment, see Bart D. Ehrman, *Forged: Writing in the Name of God—Why the Bible's Authors Are Not Who We Think They Are* (HarperOne, 2011), 220–236.

6. Gal 1:15.

7. Jer 1:4–5; Isa 49:1.

8. See Arthur J. Dewey et al., *The Authentic Letters of Paul: A New Reading of Paul's Rhetoric and Meaning* (Polebridge, 2010).

## Chapter 3

1. Ex 20:7; Lev 19:12; Deut 5:11.

2. Jer 7:9.

3. Another alternative within Hebrew grammar, one that English doesn't have, is an ending that indicates the noun is dual. It's often used of paired body parts, for blessedly obvious reasons.

4. Gen 21:33.

5. Deut 32:8.

6. There are two Hagar-leaving stories in Genesis: in chapter 16 and again in chapter 21. This is from chapter 16.

7. Gen 16:13.

8. Ps 82:1–8.

9. Gen 1:27–28a.

10. The Documentary Hypothesis posits four main, literary "strands" woven into the first five books: the Yahwist or Jahwist (J) strand, which prefers the divine name Yahweh; the Elohist (E) strand, which prefers Elohim; the Deuteronomist (D), basically the book of Deuteronomy; and the Priestly (P) strand, which combined and edited received texts as well as making original contributions (such as Genesis chapter 1).

11. Ex 3:18.

12. Phil 2:6, 9–11.

13. 2 Sam 7:12–16.

14. Jn 14:28, cf. Jn 10:30. For a nice discussion on this point, see Mark Roncace, *Raw Revelation: The Bible They Never Tell You About* (CreateSpace, 2012), especially his "Doctrine" chapter (121–162).

15. Lk 1:32, 35.

16. Gen 18:1–19:22.

17. E.g., see the *Prayer of Joseph* in which Jacob declares himself to be an angel and "the first born of every living thing." Translation of J. Z. Smith in James H. Charlesworth, ed., *The Old Testament Pseudepigrapha*, vol. 1, *Apocalyptic Literature and Testaments* (Doubleday, 1983), cited in Bart D. Ehrman, *How Jesus Became God: The Exaltation of a Jewish Preacher from Galilee* (HarperOne, 2014), 58.

18. Sir 45:1–5.

19. See, e.g., Gen 16.

20. *Sacrifices of Cain and Abel* 9–10; Ex 4:16; *Questions on Exodus* 3.29, cited in Ehrman, *How Jesus Became God*, 81, 82.

21. Deut 32:11.

22. Jn 14:16, 25.

23. Lk 1:35; Mk 1:10; Mt 3:16; Lk 3:22.

24. Lk 1:15, 2:25–32.

25. Acts 2:1–4.

26. Christians, believing Jesus to be somehow also God, read this retrospectively as Jesus asking to be spared the ordeal of crucifixion (Mt 26:39; Mk 14:36; Lk 22:42).

27. Lev 19:18; Mk 12:31; 1 Jn 4:8.

28. Hos 11:1–9.

29. Mt 5:29, 18:9; Mk 9:47; Mt 12:46–50; Lk 14:26; Mt 21:12–13; Mk 11:15–17; Lk 19:45–46; Jn 2:13–16.

30. Isa 45:6–7.

31. 1 Sam 16:14; Ezek 20:25–26; 1 Kings 22; Lk 14:26.

## Chapter 4

1. "Meet under the Ayers Clock November 20," *Indiana Landmarks News*, October 26, 2016, https://www.indianalandmarks.org/2016/10/save-ayres-clock-indianapolis/.

2. Alice Wood, "Of Wings and Wheels," PhD dissertation, University of Edinburgh, 2007.

3. Akkadian is the language of ancient Assyria and Babylonia, places with considerable influence on the ancient Israelites.

4. 1 Sam 4:4.

5. Num 21:6–9.

6. Num 21:9.

7. 2 Kings 18:4.

8. The Ophites and Naassenes.

9. Mt 10:16.

10. Gen 2:23.

11. Job 5:12, 15:5.

12. This contributes to the argument that the original *adam* in Eden was not specifically a man but a genderless or androgynous human being that somehow included within itself both the man and the woman. Astute readers will note how this interprets Genesis 1:26–27.

13. Gen 3:22. In this statement, like God's use of the plural in Genesis 1:26, we hear hints of a popular ancient image of God as presiding over a divine council.

14. Gen 3:1.

15. This quote was attributed to Pope John Paul II. But his personal secretary Archbishop Stanislaw Dziwicz denies that he ever said that. Frank Bruni, "Vatican Raises Doubts about Pope's View of 'Passion' Film," *New York Times*, January 19, 2004, https://www.nytimes.com/2004/01/19/international/middleeast/vatican-raises-doubts-about-popes-view-of-passion.html.

16. 1 Cor 15:22.

17. Num 22:22; 1 Kings 11:14, 23.

18. A paraphrase of Isa 14:12–20.

19. 1 Chr 21:1; Mt 4:1–11; Lk 10:18.

20. Hebrew grammar explicitly identifies the donkey as female throughout the story.

21. Another especially remarkable thing about this story isn't evident from the story at all. You have to look outside the Bible to appreciate it. In 1967, just across the Jordanian border from Israel, archaeologists landed on quite a find: a substantial inscription, damaged but not beyond repair, written on the walls of an ancient building. It is not only among the first Aramaic inscriptions, but among the first examples of "words in red"—not Jesus's in this case, but for emphasis nonetheless. Its author(s) used both black and red ink. In that text, likely contemporaneous with the biblical Numbers 22 (ninth–eighth centuries BCE), we also meet Bal'am, son of Be'or (not insurmountable differences). This Bal'am, like our biblical Balaam, is a prophet, but there the similarities end. Sort of. The Jordanian inscription shows a prophet, upset by the content of his special knowledge of the gods, *elohin*, and refers to the doings of deities Bal'am calls Shaddayin. Yes, like the Hebrew *shaddai*.

22. Kyle Buchanan, "Let's Talk about *Noah*'s Crazy Giant Rock Monsters," *New York*, March 30, 2014, https://www.vulture.com/2014/03/noah-giant-rock-monsters.html.

23. Jude 14.

24. Gen 5:24.

25. Gen 5:4.

26. Ex 12:37.

27. Ex 12:37–38.

28. 1 Cor 10:4. Paul reveals familiarity with what appears to have been a longstanding Jewish interpretation of the rock as mobile as reflected in such texts as Pseudo-Philo's Book of Biblical Antiquities, the Tosephta Sukka, and Targum Onqelos to Num 21:16–20 cited by Peter Enns, "The Moveable Well in 1 Cor 10:4: An Extrabiblical Tradition in an Apostolic Text," *Bulletin for Biblical Research* 6 (1996): 23–38.

29. Jon 1:17.

30. Isa 27:1; Pss 74:13–23, 104:26; Job 3:8, 40:15–41:26.

31. Job 40:15–24.

32. Ex 25:22.

33. Josh 6:4–15; 1 Sam 4:3–22, 6:5.

34. 2 Sam 6:8.

35. Deut 32:17; Ps 106:37.

36. Mk 16:9; Lk 8:2.

37. Mk 5:1–20.

38. Mt 8:28–34.

39. Lk 8:26–39.

40. Acts 19:13–17.

41. E.g., Num 22:22.

42. Dan 8:15, 9:20–23.

43. Dan 10:13–21.

44. Lk 1:5–19, 26–38.

45. The image of Gabriel blowing a horn on Judgment Day likely evolved from references to God's trumpet or a trumpet sounding (1 Thess 4:16; Rev 8–11; 1 Cor 15:52) that became linked to the rare named angel. Such association first shows up in writings of John Wycliff (1300s) and really took off after mention in John Milton's *Paradise Lost* (1667).

46. Mt 1:20; Lk 2:15; Mk 1:13.

47. Mt 28:1–8.

48. Lk 24:4–7.

## Chapter 5

1. Gen 6:9.

2. E.g., Mic 6:8.

3. Gen 5:32. Even if the phrase "in his generation" is a qualification, still, called "blameless" and all, the guy was judged to be pretty darn good.

4. See, e.g., Ps 78:51; 1 Chr 4:40.

5. This promise first appears in Genesis 12:1–3.

6. The story appears in Genesis 12:10–20.

7. Scholars suppose that these two stories, in Genesis 12 and in Genesis 20, come from two different literary sources: the Yahwist and Elohist, respectively.

8. For a more detailed analysis of Hagar's story, see Phyllis Trible, *Texts of Terror: Literary-Feminist Readings of Biblical Narratives* (Fortress, 1984), 8–35.

9. Gen 16:1.

10. Gen 16:2.

11. Gen 16:6.

12. Gen 16:9.

13. Gen 21:9–10.

14. Gen 21:13.

15. Gen 25:19–34.

16. Gen 31:32.

17. Gen 37:1–36.

18. Gen 38:26.

19. Gen 1:1–16. The others are Rahab, the prostitute from Jericho; Bathsheba, "the wife of Uriah," object of David's damning infidelity; and of course the mother of Jesus, Mary, who conceived exactly how, again?

20. Ex 2:11–12.

21. Ex 2:14.

22. Ex 32:21.

23. Ex 32:22.

24. 1 Sam 26:1–27:12.

25. 2 Sam 7:1–17.

26. 1 Kings 9:4–9.

27. Compare 1 Chr 20:1–2 and 2 Sam 11:1–2.

28. Compare 1 Chr 18:7–8 and 2 Sam 8:10–11. See also 1 Chr 16:1–43.

29. 1 Kings 9:4–9.

30. 1 Sam 16:14.

31. 1 Sam 9:1–2; compare 1 Sam 10:20–22.

32. Mic 6:8; Hos 14:5; Am 5:24.

33. Jon 3:4.

34. Mk 15:40, 16:8.

35. Mt 1:16–2:21.

36. Lk 1:34, 38, 2:19, 48, 51.

37. Lk 8:19–21, 11:27–28.

38. Lk 8:19–21.

39. Lk 23:49, 55.

40. Lk 23:10; Acts 1:14.

41. Jn 2:4.

42. Jn 19:26–27.

43. Mt 16:18–19.

44. Mt 8:14; 1 Cor 9:5.

45. Mt 16:23; Mk 8:33.

46. Jn 19:26–27; Lk 22:49–51.

47. Lk 22:31–34; Mt 26:69–75; Mk 14:66–72; Lk 22:56–66.

48. Gal 2:11–14.

49. The Bible doesn't make clear the chronology of these meetings, the council of Jerusalem, as it appears in Acts, and the incident at Antioch, as Paul tells it in Galatians (Acts 15; Gal 2).

50. Isa 45:7.

51. Isa 6:10.

52. Gen 18:20–32.

53. Ex 32:9–14.

54. Job 1:1–2:6.

## Chapter 6

1. Gen 11:10–11, 13–14.

2. Gen 25:7, 47:28.

3. Jack Wellman, "How and Why Did People in the Bible Live So Long?," *What Christians Want to Know*, accessed November 7, 2017, https://www.whatchristianswanttoknow.com/how-and-why-did-people-in-the-bible-live-so-long/.

4. Eugene H. Merrill, "The Lifespans of the EB-MB Patriarchs: A Hermeneutical and Historical Conundrum," *Southwestern Journal of Theology* 57, no. 2 (Spring 2015): 267–280.

5. David J. Zucker, "The Ages of the Patriarchs/Matriarchs: A Preliminary Study," *Jewish Bible Quarterly* 43, no. 1 (January–March 2015): 49–53.

6. Nahum Sarna, *Understanding Genesis* (Schocken, 1970), 84.

7. For a brief description and translation of one version (G), see Editors, "The Sumerian King List," Livius, 2006, modified August 21, 2016, http://www.livius.org/sources/content/anet/266-the-sumerian-king-list/.

8. Gerhard von Rad, *Genesis: A Commentary* (S.C.M., 1961), 66–71.

9. "The genealogy sets in motion and puts into the length and breadth of human history the power of the blessing which God bestowed on his people." Claus Westermann, *Genesis 1–11: A Continental Commentary*, trans. John J. Scullian (Augsburg: 1984), 354.

10. Num 21:8–9.

11. Num 21:5–9.

12. See A. Kirk Grayson, "Nineveh," in *The Anchor Bible Dictionary*, vol. 4, 1118, cited in Steven L. McKenzie, *How to Read the Bible: History, Prophecy, Literature—Why Modern Readers Need to Know the Difference, and What It Means for Faith Today* (Oxford Scholarship Online, 2005).

13. G. Hort, "The Plagues of Egypt," *Zeitschrift für die alttestamentliche Wissenschaft* 69 (1957): 84–103; 70 (1958): 48–59.

14. Ziony Zevit, "Three Ways to Look at the Ten Plagues," *Bible Review* 6, no. 3 (June 1990): 16–23, 42; Fred Blumenthal, "The Ten Plagues: Debunking Egyptian Polytheism," *Jewish Bible Quarterly* 40, no. 4 (2010): 255–258.

15. Josh 10:12–13; David Sedley, "'Joshua Stopped the Sun' 3,224 Years Ago Today, Scientists Say," *Times of Israel*, October 30, 2017,

https://www.timesofisrael.com/3224-years-later-scientists-see-first-ever-recorded-eclipse-in-joshuas-battle/.

16. Mt 2:1–18.

17. Mk 15:33, 38; Lk 23:44–45; Mt 27:45, 51–54.

18. Jennifer Viegas, "Quake Reveals Day of Jesus' Crucifixion, Researchers Believe," Science on NBC News, May 24, 2012, http://www.nbcnews.com/id/47555983/ns/technology_and_science-science/t/quake-reveals-day-jesus-crucifixion-researchers-believe/#.WgH51YXydFA.

19. Though both parties—the magi and Herod—were wealthy and powerful, here's a sum of their differences. The (foreign) magi were wise, humble, and generous; the (national) Herod was narrow-minded, arrogant, and greedy. One intended to honor; the other intended to kill. Kristin Swenson, *God of Earth: Discovering a Radically Ecological Christianity* (Westminster John Knox, 2017), 40–43.

20. David E. Garland, *Reading Matthew: A Literary and Theological Commentary on the First Gospel* (Smyth & Helwys, 1999), 264; Géza Vermes, *The Passion* (Penguin, 2005), 108–109. The Day of Yahweh appears in Hebrew Bible texts as a time of reckoning, marking an end of the corrupt present and ushering in a corrected, even righteous future. See also Isa 2:12; Am 5:18; Joel 2:31. Zephaniah 1:8 calls it the "day of Yahweh's sacrifice," which likely informed the New Testament's description of Jesus's crucifixion with Old Testament "Day of Yahweh" characteristics (darkness, for example).

21. Eschatology is definitively end-of-the-world material.

## Chapter 7

1. Lev 19:14, 33–34, 5–8.

2. Mt 7:12; Lk 6:31.

3. Shabbat 31a of the Talmud.

4. Gen 32:22–32.

5. 1 Kings 12:6–17.

6. Prov 10:2, 20:17, 13:24.

7. Prov 11:8.

8. Prov. 4:2, 9:4–5.

9. Mt 3:1; Mk 1:2; Lk 3:4; Jn 1:23.

10. As this is no small topic, there are some good books on sex in the Good Book for further study, if you're so inclined. Among them, Jennifer Wright Knust, *Unprotected Texts: The Bible's Surprising Contradictions about Sex and Desire* (HarperOne, 2011); Michael Coogan, *God and Sex: What the Bible Really Says* (Twelve, 2010).

11. E.g., Mk 10:6–7; Mt 19:3–12.

12. See Knust, *Unprotected Texts*, 50–53, 70–71; Wayne A. Meeks, "The Image of the Androgyne: Some Uses of a Symbol in Earliest Christianity," *History of Religions* 13, no. 3 (1974): 165–208.

13. 1 Tim 3:2, 12; Titus 1:6.

14. See 1 Cor chapter 7.

15. E.g., 1 Cor 6:9, 18.

16. *Onania* (1712), purportedly by John Marten, "launched the masturbation panic in eighteenth century Europe" (Angus McLaren, *Impotence: A Cultural History* [University of Chicago Press, 2008], 77).

17. Rom 5:12–21. He repeats the logic in 1 Cor 15:21–22.

18. See, for example, Knust, *Unprotected Texts*; Coogan, *God and Sex*.

19. Ps 139:13–16.

20. Jer 1:5.

21. This law is often mistaken as a cruel and gruesome justice. But it served the purpose of limiting retaliation commensurate with the crime rather than, say, killing a whole city for a single person's murder. I discuss this in more detail in *Bible Babel: Making Sense of the Most Talked About Book of All Time* (Harper Perennial, 2011).

22. For a fuller treatment of this topic, see Bart D. Ehrman, *Jesus before the Gospels: How the Earliest Christians Remembered, Changed, and Invented Their Stories of the Savior* (HarperOne, 2016), 151–156.

23. Mk 15:2–15.

24. Mt 27:11–26.

25. Lk 23:1–25.

26. Jn 18:28–19:16.

27. Mk 10:17–22; Mt 19:16–22; Lk 18:18–25.

28. Mt 5:22, 29, 23:13–15.

29. Jas 2:24; Rom 3:28.

## Chapter 8

1. Ex 4:24–26.

2. Ex 4:24, Jewish Publication Society of America translation.

3. Ex 34:29, 30, 35.

4. Among others, as recently as Ruth Mellinkoff, *The Horned Moses in Medieval Life and Thought* (University of California Press, 1970), 77, who calls it a mistranslation.

5. See Mellinkoff, *The Horned Moses*, 77; Bena Elisha Medjuck, "Exodus 34:29–35: Moses' 'Horns' in Early Bible Translation and Interpretation," MA thesis, McGill University, 1998.

6. From a lecture delivered on February 5, 2009, Thomas Römer, *The Horns of Moses: Setting the Bible in Its Historical Context*, trans. Liz Libbrecht (Open Edition Books, 2013).

7. Römer, *The Horns of Moses*, 6.

8. Ruth 4:7.

9. Deut 25:5–10.

10. Gen 13:12.

11. Gen 19:17.

12. Mk 16:8. The earliest Greek copies, over one hundred, lack any further ending. None of Clement of Alexandria, Origen, Eusebius, or Jerome attest to knowing a longer ending. Bruce Metzger, *A Textual Commentary on the Greek New Testament*, 2nd edition (Hendrickson, 2005).

13. The first additional ending, in what is a longer verse 8, readers will observe as a bit clumsy, not jibing with the rest of the Gospel's style nor with its sensibilities about Jesus. The second additional ending, verses 9–20, is also a bit out of sync with Mark's style, but it reflects other Gospels as well as the apocalyptic ideas circulating at the time and follows the earlier narrative with a happier ending: Mary told the mourning disciples her happy news.

14. Ps 118:25, 26; Mt 21:9.

15. Zech 9:9; Mt 21:5.

16. Another contender for Mary Magdalene's hometown is Magadan.

17. For information about the origins of the excavation and the general scope of its discoveries thus far, see reports by its director, including Marcela Zapata-Meza, "Magdala 2016: Excavation the Hometown of Mary Magdalene," *Bible History Daily*, July 8, 2016, https://www.biblicalarchaeology.org/daily/archaeology-today/magdala-2016-excavating-the-hometown-of-mary-magdalene/. For general information about the "Magdala Stone," see Ariel Sabar, "Unearthing the World of Jesus," *Smithsonian Magazine*, January 2016, http://www.smithsonianmag.com/history/unearthing-world-jesus-180957515/.

18. See Josephus, *Antiquities of the Jews, Book XVIII.*

19. Sabar, "Unearthing the World of Jesus."

20. Mk 16:9 (from the longer ending of Mark, probably later than the rest of the Gospel); Lk 8:2.

21. Lk 8:1–3.

22. Lk 23:49.

23. "Saints and Feasts: Mary Magdalene, the Holy Myrrh-bearer and Equal to the Apostles," *Greek Orthodox Archdiocese of America*, accessed June 15, 2020, https://www.goarch.org/chapel/saints.

24. Mt 27:61, 28:1; Mk 15:27, 16:1; Lk 23:55; Jn 19:39–42.

25. Lk 24: 1–10.

26. Mt 28:9.

27. Mk 16:9; Jn 20:16.

28. See 1 Cor 15.

29. Jn 11:2.

30. See also Steven L. McKenzie, *How to Read the Bible: History, Prophecy, Literature—Why Modern Readers Need to Know the Difference and What It Means for Faith Today* (Oxford University Press, 2005), especially "Not the End of the World as We Know It" (119–146).

31. Rev 13:16–17.

32. Rev 7:3.

## Chapter 9

1. With stunning economy, the text in Genesis 2:4b suggests in its opening line that a person's entire purpose is helping (with the aid of water) fields to grow.

2. For one example, see Ken Ham and Stacia McKeever, "The Seven C's of Creation," Answers in Genesis, May 20, 2004, https://answersingenesis.org/bible-history/seven-cs-of-history/.

3. Gen 6:19–21, 7:2–3, 8–9, 14–16, and (arguably) 8:19.

4. Daniel Simons, "Selective Attention Test," YouTube, March 10, 2010, https://www.youtube.com/watch?v=vJG698U2Mvo.

5. Gen 6:19; 7:2, Jewish Publication Society of America (JPS) version.

6. Deut 12:15, JPS version.

7. Ex 20:21.

8. 1 Sam 14:31–35.

9. See, e.g., Acts 15:1–29. By contrast, 1 Cor 10:23–33.

10. Ex 21:2–11; Dt 15:12–18; Lev 25:39–43.

11. Lev 15:24.

12. Lev 20:18.

13. Ex 12:8–9, 46; Deut 16:7–8.

14. See, e.g., Josh 15:63, 16:10, 17:11–13.

15. According to the biblical account, Joshua lived around 1200 BCE.

16. See, e.g., Amihai Mazar, *Anchor Bible Reference Library: Archaeology of the Land of the Bible, 10,000–586 B.C.E.*, 1st edition (Lutterworth, 1990). There are more such site-specific nonconformities (Ai, e.g., which shows no evidence of the kind of defeat narrated in the Bible).

17. See, e.g., Josh 11:16–23.

18. From the notes in the JPS Study Bible (1751).

19. Isa 2:4; Mic 4:3.

20. Mic 4:4.

21. Joel 3:10.

22. See, e.g., Deut 22:19, 29.

23. Mt 5:31–32; Mk 10:2–12; Lk 16:18.

24. Ezra 9:2.

25. Ezr 9:1–11:44.

26. Jer 25:11–12, 29:10–14.

27. Dan 9:20–25.

28. Mt 27:37; Mk 15:26; Lk 23:38; Jn 19:19–22.

29. Mt 27:3–10; Acts 1:18–19.

30. Mal 3:10; Jn 10:10.

31. Jer 20:14–18.

32. Mt 7:7; Lk 11:9.

## Chapter 10

1. It has a lot to say, however, throughout both the Hebrew Bible and the New Testament, to condemn adultery.

2. Only in the prophetic book of Hosea do we find criticism of Jacob, and only for his deceitfulness. There we read that Jacob would "be punished according to his ways," which include, in that text, his fetal wrestling with Esau and adult wrestling with God (Hos 12:4–5).

3. Deut 30:15–20. It bears repeating: this has nothing to do with abortion.

4. Jer 1:5, JPS.

5. Gal 1:15–16.

6. See, e.g., 1 Kings 22:1–40.

7. Isa 6:1–8.

8. Num 31:15–18.

9. Hos 9:14.

10. Hos 13:16.

11. 2 Kings 2:10–13.

12. 1 Kings 19:19 gives readers a preview of this when Elijah throws his cloak over Elisha's shoulders, after which Elisha follows him.

13. 2 Kings 2:19–25.

14. For example, Elizabeth Mitchell, "Elisha, Little Children, and the Bears," Answers in Genesis, June 3, 2016, https://answersingenesis.org/bible-questions/elisha-little-children-and-the-bears/.

15. See 2 Kings 9:9.

16. Ex 12:29.

17. Job 1:6–19.

18. Ps 137:9.

19. See Judges chapter 11.

20. See Judges chapter 19.

21. Like the oxen Saul sends in pieces, her dismembered body is a call to war (1 Sam 11:7).

22. Judg 21:16, 20:48.

23. 1 Sam 2:1–10; cf. Lk 1:46–55.

24. See, e.g., the prophet Miriam's song and dance in Exodus 15:20–21 or the Prodigal Son's return in Luke 15:23–25. See, e.g., the vine as a God-given plant issuing wine that gladdens the heart (Ps 104:15–16) or Jesus's making more wine when the wedding at Cana ran out (Jn 2:1–11). For more on the topic, see Daniel Sack, *Whitebread Protestants* (Palgrave, 2001), 11–31.

25. Mt 6:9–13; Lk 11:2–4.

26. Mt 6:9–13; Lk 11:2–4. According to the reigning source theory, that the prayer doesn't appear in Mark or John indicates that it was probably original to Q (from the German *Quelle*, meaning "source"), a lost document common to Matthew and Luke.

27. See Tod Lindberg, *The Political Teachings of Jesus* (HarperCollins, 2007), 76–79.

28. And that benefit is that all may have what they need, that we would seek mutual forgiveness, that we all might avoid what is damaging, and that we might be spared apocalyptic horror. Luke adds the request that we might (together) be rescued from what is evil.

29. Job 2:1–6.

30. Ex 9:12.

31. 2 Sam 24:1–25.

32. Gal 3:28; 1 Cor 14:34.

33. Isa 40:2.

34. Gen 1:27.

## Chapter 11

1. Gen 3:22–24.

2. Ex 21:23–24.

3. Lev 24:19–20.

4. Deut 19:21.

5. Mt 5:38.

6. Mt 5:17.

7. Incidentally, this is also the context for "going the extra mile."

8. Lev 16:8.

9. 2 Sam 1:19, 27.

10. 1 Sam 18:2.

11. 1 Sam 18:3.

12. 2 Sam 1:26. See, e.g., the thirteenth-century biblical illustration *La Somme le Roy* (British Museum); Tom M. Horner, *Jonathan Loved David: Homosexuality in Biblical Times* (Westminster John Knox, 1978).

13. Isa 40:15.

14. Eccl 1:9; Eccl 2:24, 8:15, King James Version.

15. Eccl 2:1.

16. Dan 5:25:–28.

17. Mt 15:14.

18. Lk 10:25–37.

19. See, e.g., Virginia's Good Samaritan Law, Va. Code §8.01-225.

20. For more on this parable and on other parables with nuances that might surprise modern readers, see Amy-Jill Levine, *Short Stories by Jesus: The Enigmatic Parables of a Controversial Rabbi* (HarperOne, 2014).

21. Mt 27:24.

## Chapter 12

1. J. Cohen, "Doctor James Young Simpson, Rabbi Abraham De Sola and Genesis Chapter 3, verse 16," *Obstetrics and Gynecology* 88, no. 5 (November 1996): 895–898, https://www.general-anaesthesia.com/rabbi-genesis.html.

2. Those are fine, if you're looking for particular pastoral direction.

3. Mt 21:21; Mk 11:23; Lk 17:6.

4. Ps 23:1; Heb 10:31 (Hebrew Bible and New Testament, respectively).

# INDEX

*For the benefit of digital users, indexed terms that span two pages (e.g., 52–53) may, on occasion, appear on only one of those pages.*